ABITUR 2001

Prüfungsaufgaben mit Lösungen

Englisch

Leistungskurs
schriftliches und mündliches Abitur
Gymnasium
Baden-Württemberg
1986–2000

STARK

Die Jahrgänge ab 1997 wurden nach den Regeln der neuen Rechtschreibung abgefasst.

ISBN: 3-89449-035-7

© 1986 by Stark Verlagsgesellschaft mbH · D-85318 Freising · Postfach 1852 · Tel. (0 81 61) 1790
16. neu bearbeitete Auflage 2000
Nachdruck verboten!

Inhalt

Hinweise
Stichwortverzeichnis

Übungsaufgaben zum Sternchenthema 'Pygmalion' and 'Educating Rita'

Aufgabe 1	C 1
Aufgabe 2	C 8
Aufgabe 3	C 17

Mündliches Abitur

Textbeispiel 1: Future of Hong Kong Settled	Mü-1
Textbeispiel 2: Suggestions on Reading Shakespeare	Mü-4
Textbeispiel 3: City People Enrich Country Life	Mü-7
Textbeispiel 4: Dole Attacks Sex and Violence Diet from Hollywood	Mü-10

Übungsaufgaben zum Sternchenthema Paul Auster 'Moon Palace'

Aufgabe 1: Moon Palace: Central Park	D 1
Aufgabe 2: Moon Palace: The Relationship with Thomas Effing	D 7
Aufgabe 3: Moon Palace: The Meeting with Orlando	D 13

Leistungskurs Englisch – Textaufgaben Landeskunde

1. Europe's Modern Monarchs – The British Monarchy 1
2. Religions in America 7
3. New Arrivals: Dream and Reality 13
   – Immigration into the US/Melting Pot
4. Britain: A Smouldering Anger 19
   – Immigration into Britain/Minorities/Commonwealth
5. The Disintegrating Commonwealth 25
6. Parents scupper plans for grammar schools – Education 31
7. Values that can be bought – Education 37
8. Britain: Facing up to Violence – Minorities/Youth 43
9. War and Peace in Northern Ireland 49
10. Defusing the 'Jobs Bomb' 54
11. International Relations 59

Fortsetzung nächste Seite

Leistungskurs Englisch – Abituraufgaben

Abiturprüfung 1986	Political Interpretations of 'Lord of the Flies'	86-1
Abiturprüfung 1987	The British attitude towards Northern Ireland	87-1
Abiturprüfung 1988	'Gregor' by Kinkead-Weekes	88-1
Abiturprüfung 1989	Death of a Salesman – a tragedy about modern life	89-1
Abiturprüfung 1990	Immigrants in the U.S.A.	90-1
Abiturprüfung 1991	Death of a Salesman – culture related reactions	91-1
Abiturprüfung 1992	Suppressed emotions in 'Brave New World'	92-1
Abiturprüfung 1993	The role of religion in modern America	93-1
Abiturprüfung 1994	BNW – The Controller	94-1
Abiturprüfung 1995	The Great Gatsby – Automobiles	95-1
Abiturprüfung 1996	America and the World	96-1
Abiturprüfung 1997	The Great Gatsby – The valley of ashes	97-1
Abiturprüfung 1998	Pygmalion – Higgins and Eliza	98-1
Abiturprüfung 1999	U.S.A.– race relations	99-1
Abiturprüfung 2000	Pygmalion – critics' reactions	2000-1

Jeweils zu Beginn des neuen Schuljahres erscheinen die neuen Ausgaben der Abiturprüfungsaufgaben mit Lösungen.

Autoren:

Abituraufgaben 1994–2000 und Beispiele zum Mündlichen Abitur: Joachim Haas
Abituraufgaben 1986–1993 und Textaufgaben zur Landeskunde: Hansjörg Hauf †
Sternchenthema 'Moon Palace': Hilmar Kammerer
Sternchenthema „Pygmalion", „Educating Rita": Joachim Haas

Hinweise

Die schriftliche Abiturprüfung

Die vorliegenden **Textaufgaben** orientieren sich in Textlänge und Aufgabenapparat an den Aufgabenbeispielen, mit kleinen Abweichungen (bei den Aufgaben Nr. 5 Landeskunde ist der Text etwas kürzer, bei Nr. 7 Landeskunde gibt es 13 statt 10 Punkte im Bereich Language und bei Nr. 11 Landeskunde 14 statt 10 Punkte im Bereich Comprehension).

Zwei Themen sind zwei Mal vertreten (Commonwealth und Education), um eine selbstständige Lösung nach einer stärker gelenkten, gemeinsamen Erarbeitung zu ermöglichen.

Die **Übersetzungen** gehören jeweils auch zum Themenbereich der Textaufgabe, damit ein inhaltlicher Zusammenhang zwischen Textaufgabe und Übersetzung besteht. Es ist jedoch möglich, die Textaufgaben und Übersetzungen beliebig zu kombinieren.

Für die Bearbeitung der Textaufgabe sind **210 Minuten** vorgesehen, für die Übersetzung **90 Minuten**.

Bei der Erledigung der Aufgaben ist zu beachten, dass nur beim Aufgabenteil II (Comprehension) und III (Comment) die Verwendung eines einsprachigen Wörterbuches zulässig ist; nicht jedoch bei dem sprachlich-grammatischen Teil und der Übersetzung.

Die **Lösungen** können nur als Anregungen und Möglichkeiten gesehen werden. Die gestellten Aufgaben ermöglichen auch ganz andere richtige Antworten – dies gilt besonders für den Bereich Comprehension und Comment.

Teilweise sind die Aufgaben und Lösungen auch als konzentrierte Wiederholung bzw. Zusammenfassung landeskundlicher Themen zu verwenden.

Die mündliche Abiturprüfung

Auswahl der Prüfungstexte

Als Prüfungstext dient ein authentischer Text (200–250 Wörter) höheren Schwierigkeitsgrads, der mehrere längere und in ihrer Konstruktion schwierige Sätze enthalten muss.

Durch die Prüfungstexte soll der Lehrplan für die vier Kurshalbjahre weitgehend abgedeckt sein. Zum literarischen Schwerpunktthema kann höchstens ein Text dem Fachausschussvorsitzenden zur Auswahl vorgelegt werden.

Jedem Prüfungstext sind eine, höchstens zwei Leitfragen beigegeben. Sachliche Anmerkungen und Wortangaben sind möglich und auf ein Mindestmaß zu begrenzen.

Vorbereitung

In der Vorbereitung (20 Minuten) befasst sich der Schüler unter Aufsicht mit dem Text, von dem die mündliche Prüfung ausgeht. Während der Vorbereitung darf sich der Schüler Aufzeichnungen machen; er darf diese jedoch in der Prüfung nicht ablesen. Die Benutzung eines Wörterbuches oder anderer Hilfsmittel während der Vorbereitungszeit ist nicht gestattet.

Prüfung

Die Prüfung wird in der Fremdsprache abgehalten. Sie umfasst Lesen, Fragen zum Text und das weiterführende Gespräch. Dauer der Prüfung: etwa 20 Minuten.

Lesen: Die Prüfung beginnt mit dem Lesen des vorbereiteten Textes oder eines Teils davon. Sinnentstellendes Lesen oder Aussprachefehler können den Ausgangspunkt für Einstiegsfragen bilden. Hauptkriterien für die Bewertung der Leseleistung sind korrekte Aussprache und sinnentsprechende Intonation. Fehler, die die Verständigung erschweren, sind in besonderem Maße zu berücksichtigen.

Fragen zum Text: Bei Schülern mit der Fremdsprache als Leistungskurs können neben den Fragen zur Überprüfung des inhaltlichen Verständnisses auch solche zu formalen und sprachlich-stilistischen Aspekten des Textes gestellt werden. Dies gilt insbesondere dann, wenn sich im Laufe der Prüfung herausstellt, dass der Text nicht voll verstanden wurde. Von einer zusammenhängenden Herübersetzung eines längeren Abschnitts des Textes ist abzusehen.

Weiterführendes Gespräch: Das Gespräch in der Fremdsprache stellt, sowohl was den zeitlichen Umfang als auch was seine Bedeutung für die Gesamtbeurteilung angeht, den eigentlichen Kern der mündlichen Prüfung dar. Dieses Gespräch, in dessen Verlauf dem Schüler Gelegenheit zur zusammenhängenden Äußerung zu geben ist, geht vom vorgelegten Text aus. Dabei ist zu prüfen, ob sich der Schüler vom Wortlaut der Vorlage lösen kann und inwieweit er zu spontaner selbstständiger Formulierung fähig ist. Bei der Bewertung der Leistung des Schülers kommt der sprachlichen Richtigkeit des Gesagten eine hohe Bedeutung zu.

Praktische Ratschläge

- Treten Sie locker und selbstsicher auf.
- Reden Sie deutlich und in ganzen Sätzen und schauen Sie die Prüfer beim Sprechen an.
- Machen Sie sich übersichtliche Notizen, formulieren Sie diese nicht aus.
- Lesen Sie Ihre Notizen nicht ab, sondern tragen Sie Ihre Gedanken in freier Rede vor.
- Antworten Sie ausführlich, und versuchen Sie den Prüfungsverlauf selber zu lenken, so können Sie verhindern, dass Sie durch viele Zusatzfragen aus dem Konzept geraten.
- Sagen Sie offen, wenn Sie etwas nicht wissen, dadurch können Sie verhindern, dass der Prüfer lange „bohrt" und so die kostbare Prüfungszeit verstreicht.

Stichwortverzeichnis

Points of Interest

Britain and Europe
- Eurosceptics 96-3, 99-5/6

Brave New World
- Art and Love 94-1
- BNW – paradise or nightmare? 93-3
- characterize John 92-4
- Huxley's utopia come true? 92-4
- Shakespeare 94-1
- The Controller 94-1

Death of a Salesman
- American Dream 90-3
- Biff and Happy's character 91-3
- Willy's role as a father 89-3
- The Requiem scene 91-3
- time-shifts (examples, functions) 89-3

Educating Rita/Pygmalion
- a romance 98-6
- character constellation C 21; 98-5
- characterization C 3, C 13, C 21
- class C 13
- comparison Frank/Higgins 00-6/7
- critical reception 00-1/2
- Educating Rita – success as a play 00-7
- education C 13
- Eliza opposes Higgins 98-6
- Eliza's change 98-6
- equality C 4
- film versions C 21
- Frank and Rita, their relationship C 21
- Higgins's attitude towards Eliza 98-4; 00-1/2
- language and class C 3, C 21; 98-7
- male attitude towards women C 13
- meaning of names C 21
- motivations as students 99-6
- relationships to the teachers 99-6
- Rita and Eliza – a comparison C 4; 98-6/7
- Shaw's epilogue 00-5
- setting C 3
- relationships to the teachers 99-6

- Rita and Eliza – a comparison 98-6/7
- Shaw's epilogue 00-5

Education
- day school/boarding school 39
- general education 33
- Public Schools 33
- specialization 33

The Great Gatsby
- author's intentions 95-5
- automobiles 95-5
- characterization 95-5
- comparison Carraway/Gatsby 95-5
- criticism of the Buchanans 95-5
- Gatsby and Tom Buchanan 96-3
- the novel's relevance 95-6
- symbolic meaning 97-3; 97-4

Lord of the Flies
- Jack and Ralph 86-3
- the last scene 88-3
- a pessimistic story 86-3
- Piggy 88-3
- symbols 86-3

Minorities in Britain
- immigration restrictions 21
- prejudices 21
- social and political problems 87-3
- violence 45

Moon Palace
- American core values D 3
- American landscapes D 9
- art D 15
- the art of hunger D 1/2
- black power D 13
- cave experiences D 7
- Central Park D 1
- characterization D 3; D 9
- coincidences D 8; D 15
- Effing's character D 9
- Effing's mental attitude D 15

- Effing's narrative reliability D 7
- Julian Barber – Thomas Effing D 8
- Marco's philosophy of life D 3
- Marco's state of mind D 3
- mobility D 9
- New York D 13
- quest for identity D 9
- softball D 1
- the West D 7

Northern Ireland
- possible solutions 51
- religious conflict 87-3
- terrorism and bloodshed 51

Religion
- free exercise of religion 9
- young people and cults 9
- the "electronic church" 93-3

United Kingdom
- capital punishment 45
- Common Market 26; 92-4
- Commonwealth 21; 26
- constitutional monarchy 3
- Empire to Commonwealth 26
- functions of the British Monarch 3
- new aspects of the Empire 00-4
- social and political problems 87-3

USA and the 20th century 00-7

USA – Immigration, Minorities
- American Dream 90-3, 98-7/8, 99-5
- Americans the "Chosen People" 90-3, 99-5
- civil rights movement 87-3
- land of the free and the brave 99-5
- melting pot 15; 91-3
- reasons for emigration 15, 99-5

US – European Relations
- American leadership 95-6, 95-7
- European doubts 95-6, 95-7, 99-5/6
- Germany Americanized 61
- international relations 96-1
- interventionism/isolationism 96-1
- post Cold War era 95-6, 95-7
- preservation of peace 61
- USA envy of the world 97-4
- USA leader of the West 61

US-Supreme Court
- landmark decisions 93-3

Work – Unemployment
- jobs 56
- labour markets 98-4/8
- social and political problems 87-3
- we live to work 56
- we work to live 56

Grammar and Style

abstract nouns D 3; D 15; 98-3; 00-5
active/passive D 14; D 15; 2; 44; 55; 86-2; 87-3; 90-3; 92-3; 96-2; 97-3, 99-4
adjective/adverb 91-2; 96-2
adjectives, comparison of 26
American English 2; 20
antonyms 8; 14
climax 89-2
colloquial English C 3; C 12; 96-2
conditional clause 26; 55; C 12; 87-3; 98-3
continuous form, use of 14; 88-2
definite article, use of 32; 38; 50; 88-2; 91-3; 94-2
do, use of 8; 38, C 8
elliptic structure 97-3
emphasis 98-3
figure of speech, metaphor 20; 50; 90-3; 93-3
gerunds C 21
-ing form, explanation of D 2; 50; 55; 89-2; 90-3; 92-3; 93-2; 95-4
inversion 55; 60; 87-2; 90-2

irregular plural 86-2
metaphors 99-4
modal auxiliary 93-2; 93-3
participles 94-3
passive voice 00-5
question tag 97-3
relative clause 32; 38; 44; 8-3; 91-2; 95-4
relative pronoun, can it be left out? 9; 14; 44; 89-3
reported speech C 3; D 14; 98-3
stylistic devices C 21; D 2; D 15; 89-2; 90-3; 91-2; 97-3
– imagery 00-5
– understatement 00-5
subordinate clause D 14
substitutes 98-3, 99-4
tenses, use of (present perfect, past tense) 2; 8; 14; 20; 26; 32; 38; 44; 60; 88-2; 89-2
various 2; 50; 55; 60; ; C 3; C 12; C 13; C 21; 86-2; 92-3; 97-3; 00-5
verbs 94-2; 97-3
word order 95-4

> **Leistungskurs Englisch (Baden-Württemberg): Textaufgaben**
> **Literarisches Sternchenthema: Educating Rita and Pygmalion – Aufgabe 1**

Text A

... The telephone rings and startles him slightly. He manages a gulp at the whisky before he picks up the receiver and although his speech is not slurred, we should recognize the voice of a man who shifts a lot of booze.

FRANK: Yes? ... Of course I'm still here. ... Because I've got this Open University woman coming, haven't I? ... Tch. ... Of course I told you. ... But darling, you shouldn't have prepared dinner should you? Because I said, I distinctly remember saying that I would be late. ... Yes. Yes, I probably shall go to the pub afterwards, I shall need to go to the pub afterwards, I shall need to wash away the memory of some silly woman's attempts to get into the mind of Henry James or whoever it is we're supposed to study on this course. ... Oh God, why did I take this on? ... Yes. ... Yes I suppose I did take it on to pay for the drink. ... Oh, for God's sake, what is it? Yes, well – erm – leave it in the oven. ... Look if you're trying to induce some feeling of guilt in me over the prospect of a burnt dinner you should have prepared something other than lamb and ratatouille. Because, darling, I like my lamb done to the point of abuse and even I know that ratatouille cannot be burned. Darling, you could incinerate ratatouille and still it wouldn't burn. What do you mean am I determined to go to the pub? I don't need determination to get me into a pub ...

There is a knock at the door (...)

The door swings open revealing RITA

RITA: *(from the doorway)* I'm comin' in, aren't I? It's that stupid bleedin' handle on the door. You wanna get it fixed! *(She comes into the room)*

FRANK: *(staring, slightly confused)* Erm – yes, I suppose I always mean to ...

RITA: *(going to the chair by the desk and dumping her bag)* Well that's no good always meanin' to, is it? Y' should get on with it; one of these days you'll be shoutin' 'Come in' an' it'll go on forever because the poor sod on the other side won't be able to get in. An' you won't be able to get out.

FRANK stares at RITA who stands by the desk

FRANK: You are?

RITA: What am I?

FRANK: Pardon?

RITA: What?

FRANK: *(looking for the admission papers)* Now you are?

RITA: I'm a what?

FRANK: *looks up and then returns to the papers as RITA goes to hang her coat on the door hooks*

RITA: *(noticing the picture)* That's a nice picture, isn't it? *(She goes up to it)*

FRANK: Erm – yes, I suppose it is – nice ...

RITA: *(studying the picture)* It's very erotic.

FRANK: *(looking up)* Actually I don't think I've looked at it for about ten years, but yes, I suppose it is. *[Act I, Scene I]*

Text B

THE FLOWER GIRL: *[disappointed, but thinking three half pence better than nothing]* Thank you sir.
THE BYSTANDER: *[to the girl]* You be careful: give him a flower for it. Theres a bloke here behind taking down every blessed word youre saying. *[All turn to the man who is taking notes]*.
THE FLOWER GIRL: *[springing up terrified]* I aint done nothing wrong by speaking to the gentleman. Ive a right to sell flowers if I keep off the kerb. *[Hysterically]* I'm a respectable girl: so help me, I never spoke to him except to ask him to buy a flower off me.
General hubbub, mostly sympathetic to the flower girl, but deprecating her excessive sensibility. Cries of Dont start hollerin. Who's hurting you? Nobody's going to touch you. Whats the good of fussing? Steady on. Easy easy, etc., *come from the elderly staid spectators, who pat her comfortingly. Less patient ones bid her shut her head, or ask her roughly what is wrong with her. A remoter group, not knowing what the matter is, crowd in and increase the noise with question and answer:* Whats the row? What-she do? Where is he? A tec taking her down. What! him? Yes: him over there: Took money off the gentleman, etc.
THE FLOWER GIRL: *[breaking through them to the gentleman, crying wildly]* Oh, sir, dont let him charge me. You dunno what it means to me. Theyll take away my character and drive me on the streets for speaking to gentlemen. They –
THE NOTE TAKER: *[coming forward on her right, the rest crowding after him]* There! there! there! there! who's hurting you, you silly girl? What do you take me for?
THE BYSTANDER: It's aw rawt: e's a genleman: look at his bə-oots. *[Explaining to the note taker]* She thought you was a copper's nark, sir.
THE NOTETAKERR: *[with quick interest]* Whats a copper's nark?
THE BYSTANDER: *[inapt at definition]* It's a – well, it's a copper's nark, as you might say. What else would you call it? A sort of informer.
THE FLOWER GIRL: *[still hysterical]* I take my Bible oath I never said a word –
THE NOTE TAKER: *[overbearing but good-humored]* Oh, shut up, shut up. Do I look like a policeman?
THE FLOWER GIRL: *[far from reassured]* Then what did you take down my words for? How do I know whether you took me down right? You just shew me what youve wrote about me. *[The note taker opens his book and holds it steadily under her nose, though the pressure of the mob trying to read it over his shoulders would upset a weaker man]*. Whats that? That aint proper writing. I cant read that.
THE NOTETAKER: I can. *[Reads, reproducing her pronunciation exactly]* "Cheer ap, Keptin; n' baw ya flahr orf a pore gel."
THE FLOWER GIRL: *[much distressed]* It's because I called him Captain. I meant no harm. *[To the gentleman]* Oh, sir, dont let him lay a charge agen me for a word like that. You –
THE GENTLEMAN: Charge! I make no charge. *[To the note taker]* Really, sir, if you are a detective, you need not begin protecting me against molestation by young women until I ask you. Anybody could see that the girl meant no harm.
THE BYSTANDERS GENERALLY: *[demonstrating against police espionage]* Course they could. What business is it of yours? You mind your own affairs. He wants promotion, he does. Taking down people's words! Girl never said a word to him. What harm if she did? Nice thing a girl cant shelter from the rain without being insulted, etc., etc., etc. *[She is conducted by the more sympathetic demonstrators back to her plinth, where she resumes her seat and struggles with her emotion]*. (from Act I)

I. Language

1. Text A

Answer questions dealing with the underlined words/phrases or structures within the given context. Follow the instructions added to each item.

a) ll. 4/5: "... Because I've got this Open University woman coming, haven't I? Of course I told you. ..."
Imagine Frank's girlfriend is talking to a friend about this conversation. Write down what she would say using reported speech. (2 VP)

b) l. 8: "I shall need to <u>wash away</u> ..."
Give a suitable synonym. (1 VP)

c) ll. 10/11: "... Yes, I suppose <u>I did take it on</u> to pay ..."
First find a suitable substitute (keeping to the structure) and then explain what is peculiar about this form. (2 VP)

d) Rita frequently speaks a very rude form of colloquial English. Find two examples in the text illustrating this. (1 VP)

2. Text B

a) l. 42: "..., you need not begin protecting me against <u>molestation</u> ..."
Explain in a complete sentence. (2 VP)

b) l. 31: reassured
l. 36: reproducing
l. 42: protecting
l. 47: insulted
Find the corresponding nouns (not the -ing form). (2 VP)

II. Comprehension

Answer questions 1–4 below using complete sentences only. Keep to the information in the given text unless you are explicitly asked to go beyond it. Put any quotation from the text in brackets, with line numbers added.

1. Compare the main characters' first encounters here in these scenes. What is different? What is similar?
(80–100 words) (4 VP)

2. Already in both scenes some important character traits of the four protagonists are revealed. Which ones? Where can they be seen again in later events?
(100–120 words) (4 VP)

3. What role does the setting play in these scenes? Give other examples which illustrate the significance of the setting – mainly in *Pygmalion* and to a lesser extent in *Educating Rita*.
(180–200 words) (5 VP)

4. What role does language play in these two extracts?
(60–80 words) (2 VP)

III. Comment/Composition

Choose *one* of the following topics (200–300 words). (10 VP)

1. Compare Rita and Eliza.
2. Discuss the problem of equality in *Pygmalion* and *Educating Rita*.

Lösungsvorschlag

I. Language

1. **Text A**

   a) He told me that he'd got this Open University woman coming and that he had of course told me ....

   b) to get rid of / to rid myself of / to do away with

   c) I did accept it.
   Usually, you would take the simple past form of "to take" – I took it on. But here Frank wants to put emphasis on the fact that he needs the money and that is why he accepted this particular job offer.

   d) The most striking example can be found in lines 20/21 when Rita enters Frank's office. First of all it is very rude just to blow in like that, not bothering to say hello and then she says "stupid bleedin' handle" which is very close to swearing. Another good example would be in line 25 when she speaks about some anonymous person and calls him "poor sod".

2. **Text B**

   a) You talk about *molestation* or *being molested* when a person (male or female) attacks or harms another often weaker person (or a child) in any physical or psychological way.

   b) reassurance / reproduction / protection / insult

II. Comprehension

1. The first encounters of the main protagonists are of paramount importance in both plays. The way they are introduced and the dramatic situations they are already subjected to set the tone for the remainder of the action and have a very striking effect on the audience's attitude and expectations. Both authors have obviously opted for their beginnings to be fast, funny and full of noise (*Pygmalion*) or verbal wit (*Educating Rita*). These ingredients are apparently used in order to indicate straightaway on the opening pages what kind of relationships will develop later on and to wet the reader's/ viewer's appetite.

2. If we take each character separately it is rather striking that both Rita and Eliza seem to be the more active people whereas Frank and Higgins tend to be more reluctant to show any form of spontaneous reaction. They are the educated, rather wealthy and classy people as opposed to Rita and Eliza who very obviously lack both education and upbringing. This apparent and emphasized lack of refinement is compensated by their unrelenting, sparkling energy which will be later on channelled into a well of enthusiastic imagination that is constantly counterpointed by either Frank's mounting self-pity in *Educating Rita* or Higgins' exaggerated snobbishness in *Pygmalion*.

3. Despite its limited size and the enormous cost of extravagant stage sets, the setting of a play has always played an important role in theatre. This also applies to the two plays we are talking about here although most of the action in both plays is set in a normal study or drawing-room. In the opening scenes of *Pygmalion* this restriction is already abandoned and Shaw takes the audience/reader out into the streets of an old

England the modern theatre-goer is hardly familiar with. It has often been said that this first scene does not really belong to the rest of it, but if we have a closer look, we must conclude that quite to the contrary of this statement, this first scene is an integral part of the play and enables the reader/viewer to establish the flower-girl in her natural surroundings. We get to know Eliza while doing her job under very unpleasant conditions and are made to understand that her present life is one of hardship, misery and despair. The setting helps us to get a deeper understanding of her motives later on to want to get out of the slums and become a respectable girl. A simple description of her former lifestyle would not have left the same impression on us. The same can be said about the study/office in scene I in *Educating Rita* where the confined space of Frank's small and untidy work-space symbolizes the narrowness of the protagonists' existence from which they both want to get away but are seemingly incapable of doing.

4. Both plays obviously deal with language and its significance with regard to social influence and acceptability. It is not surprising that both authors try to stress the importance of language from the very beginning. Whereas Shaw goes as far as to use the Cockney dialect even in writing, Russell emphasizes Rita's origin by highlighting her readiness to use quite a rude language that gives her some sort of freshness which more or less enthralls Frank. Higgins, on the other hand, is rather driven by a pure professional interest since he is a well-known professor of phonetics.

III. Comment/Composition

1. *Compare Rita and Eliza.*

To a certain extent one might argue that the two female protagonists in Shaw's and Russell's plays cannot be compared since they have been given a completely different socio-historical background and are mostly driven by somewhat rather differing incentives. Still, at the end of the day, they can be given a very common denominator and their approach to class distinctions, their very fresh and naive attitude towards authority and their generally positive outlook on life makes them two characters worth being compared.

What they both do have in common is very obvious but at the same time makes all the difference: they are both working-class and female. But being female and working-class at the beginning and at the end of the 20th century is a different matter and contributes largely to the elements that stand for the differences between Eliza and Rita. Rita is not rich but with her own salary and her husband's wages she and Denny can afford a little house, have some sort of social life and are aware of the fact that although they will never be able to live in luxury, neither will their future be financially insecure. Eliza, on the other hand, does not really know how to make ends meet and her being born into the working-classes equals being poor, rejected and having no future. When she meets Higgins, she knows that she will have to grasp this peculiar but promising chance of getting away from the miserable conditions in which she is living. By improving her speech and her manners, she hopes to be instantly capable of applying for a better job that although unlikely to give her access to some higher class, will at least probably open her some doors to a more comfortable job.

Rita, however, is not driven by this idea of financial security. Quite the contrary. She is prepared to give up the security of her marriage and family-life in favour of a very interesting but possibly fruitless career in literature. It must be conceded that Rita, too, wants to learn to speak properly, to be accepted by her peers (at university) and she gets a thrill out of long discussions about novels and plays in the same way Eliza seems to enjoy her appearances in better society after having gone through Higgins' school.

2. *Discuss the problem of equality in* Pygmalion *and* Educating Rita.

One of the many themes both plays touch on is society's attitude towards women on the one hand and the relationship between men and women on the other. Here again, things have changed from Eliza's Edwardian England as depicted by Shaw to Rita's modern day northern England as presented by Russell. The society that made Eliza was still very much a patriarchal one with strict rules and codes of behaviour especially for women. Although Rita was born into a modern world that should have already been influenced by the wind of feminist thoughts, her being firmly rooted in the working-class of a northern English city (such as Liverpool) has certainly prevented her from being swept away by this wind. So both our heroines are faced with a deep-seated dilemma: on the one hand, Eliza, who has to live with a widespread prejudice against women she cannot do anything about and is inherent in a society that still regards women as second-class citizens; on the other hand, Rita, whose life in modern England is not much different (at least in the north), because the ideas of a patriarchal society have survived most attempts at reform.

Thus the situation Rita is caught up in is not really different from the one Eliza tries to get away from. Her only advantage seems to be that this artificial inequality in modern England is not supported by the law and she has actually got the chance of leaving her "cage", even if such a departure might reveal itself to be quite a painful one. Eliza cannot rid herself of the chains Edwardian England has put on her. At best she can try to cope with her situation by making herself presentable to be able to find an appropriate husband who would be willing to accept her aspirations.

> **Leistungskurs Englisch (Baden-Württemberg): Textaufgaben**
> **Literarisches Sternchenthema: Educating Rita and Pygmalion – Aufgabe 2**

Text A

The lights come up on FRANK who is sitting in the armchair listening to the radio
RITA enters, goes straight to the desk and slings her bag on the back of her chair
She sits in the chair and unpacks the note-pad and pencil-case from her bag. She opens the pad and takes out the pencil-sharpener and pencils and arranges them as before.
5 *FRANK gets up, switches off the radio, goes to the swivel chair and sits*

FRANK: Now I don't mind; two empty seats at the dinner table means more of the vino for me. But Julia – Julia is the stage-manager type. If we're having eight people to dinner she expects to see eight. She likes order – probably why she took me on – it gives her a lot of practice –
10 RITA: *starts sharpening her pencils*
FRANK: – and having to cope with six instead of eight was extremely hard on Julia. I'm not saying that I needed any sort of apology; you don't turn up that's up to you, but ...
RITA: I did apologize.
FRANK: 'Sorry couldn't come', scribbled on the back of your essay and thrust through the
15 letter box? Rita, that's hardly an apology.
RITA: What does the word 'sorry' mean if it's not an apology? When I told Denny we were goin' to yours he went mad. We had a big fight about it.
FRANK: I'm sorry. I didn't realize. But look, couldn't you have explained? Couldn't you have said that was the reason?
20 RITA: No. Cos that wasn't the reason. I told Denny if he wasn't gonna go I'd go on me own. An' I tried to. All day Saturday, all day in the shop I was thinkin' what to wear. I got back, an' I tried on five different dresses. They all looked bleedin' awful. An' all the time I'm trying to think of things I can say, what I can talk about. An' I can't remember anythin'. It's all jumbled up in me head. I can't remember if it's Wilde
25 who's witty an Shaw who was Shavian or who the hell wrote *Howards End*.
FRANK: Ogh God!
RITA: Then I got the wrong bus to your house. It took me ages to find it. Then I walked up your drive, an' I saw y' all through the window, y' were sippin' drinks an' talkin' an' laughin'. An' I couldn't come in.
30 FRANK: Of course you could.
RITA: I couldn't. I'd bought the wrong sort of wine. When I was in the off licence I knew I was buyin' the wrong stuff. But I didn't know which was the right wine.
FRANK: Rita for Christ's sake; I wanted *you* to come along. You weren't expected to dress up or buy wine.
35 RITA: *(holding all the pencils and pens in her hands and playing with them)* If you go out to dinner don't you dress up? Don't you take wine?
FRANK: Yes, but ...
RITA: Well?
FRANK: Well, what?
40 RITA: Well you wouldn't take sweet sparkling wine, would y'?
FRANK: Does it matter what I do? It wouldn't have mattered if you'd walked in with a bottle of Spanish plonk.
RITA: It was Spanish.
FRANK: Why couldn't you relax? *(He gets up and goes behind Rita's chair, then leans on*
45 *the back of it)* It wasn't a fancy dress party. You could have come as yourself. Don't

you realize how people would have seen you if you'd just – just breezed in? Mm? They would have seen someone who's funny, delightful, charming ...

RITA: (*angrily*) But I don't wanna be charming and delightful: funny. What's funny? I don't wanna be funny. I wanna talk seriously with the rest of you, I don't wanna spend the night takin' the piss, comin' on with the funnies because that's the only way I can get into the conversation. I didn't want to come to your house just to play the court jester.

FRANK: You weren't being asked to play that role. I just – just wanted you to be yourself.

RITA: But I don't want to be myself. Me? What's me? Some stupid woman who gives us all a laugh because she thinks she can learn, because she thinks that one day she'll be like the rest of them, talking seriously, confidently, with knowledge, livin' a civilized life. Well, she can't be like that really but bring her in because she's good for a laugh!

FRANK: If you believe that that's why you were invited, to be laughed at, then you can get out, now. (*He goes to his desk and grabs the pile of essays, taking them to the window desk. He stands with his back to* RITA *and starts pushing the essays into his briefcase*) You were invited because I wished to have your company and if you can't believe that then I suggest you stop visiting me and start visiting an analyst who can cope with paranoia.

RITA: I'm all right with you, here in this room; but when I saw those people you were with I couldn't come in. I would have seized up. Because I'm a freak. I can't talk to the people I live with any more. An' I can't talk to the likes of them on Saturday, or them out there, because I can't learn the language. I'm a half-caste. I went back to the pub where Denny was, an' me mother, an' our Sandra, an' her mates. I'd decided I wasn't comin' here again.

FRANK *turns to face her*

RITA: I went into the pub an' they were singing', all of them singin' some song they'd learnt from the juke-box. An' I stood in that pub an' thought, just what the frig am I trying to do' Why don't I just pack it in an' stay with them, an' join in the singin'?

FRANK: And why don't you?

RITA: (*angrily*) You think I can, don't you? Just because you pass a pub doorway an' hear the singin' you think we're all O.K., that we're all survivin', with the spirit intact. Well I did join in with the singin'; I didn't ask any questions, I just went along with it. But when I looked round em mother had stopped singin'; an' she was cryin', but no one could get it out of her why she was cryin'. Everyone just said she was pissed an' we should get her home. So we did, an' on the way I asked her why. I said, 'Why are y' cryin', Mother?' She said, 'Because – because we could sing better songs than those.' Ten minutes later, Denny had her laughing and singing again, pretending she hadn't said it. But she had. And that's why I came back. And that's why I'm staying.

Black-out

RITA: *goes out.* (Act I, Scene VII)

Text B

MRS PEARCE: [*returning*] This is the young woman, sir.
The flower girl enters in state. She has a hat with three ostrich feathers, orange, sky-blue, and red. She has a nearly clean apron, and the shoddy coat has been tidied a little. The pathos of this deplorable figure, with its innocent vanity and consequential air, touches Pickering, who has already straightened himself in the presence of Mrs Pearce. But as to Higgins, the only distinction he makes between men and women is that when he is neither bullying nor exclaiming to the heavens against some feather-weight cross, he coaxes women as a child coaxes its nurse when it wants to get anything out of her.
HIGGINS: [*brusquely, recognizing her with unconcealed disappointment, and at once, babylike, making an intolerable grievance of it*] Why, this is the girl I jotted down last night. She's no use: I've got all the records I want of the Lisson Grove lingo; and I'm not going to waste another cylinder on it. [*To the girl*] Be off with you: I don't want you.
THE FLOWER GIRL: Dont you be so saucy. You aint heard what I come for yet. [*To Mrs Pearce, who is waiting at the door for further instructions*] Did you tell him I come in a taxi?
MRS PEARCE: Nonsense, girl! what do you think a gentleman like Mr Higgins cares what you came in?
THE FLOWER GIRL: Oh, we are proud! He aint above giving lessons, not him: I heard him say so. Well, I aint come here to ask for any compliment; and if my money's not good enough I can go elsewhere.
HIGGINS: Good enough for what?
THE FLOWER GIRL: Good enough for yə-oo. Now you know, dont you? I'm come to have lessons, I am. And to pay for em tə-oo: make no mistake.
HIGGINS: [*stupent*] Well!!! [*Recovering his breath with a gasp*] What do you expect me to say to you?
THE FLOWER GIRL: Well, if you was a gentleman, you might ask me to sit down, I think. Dont I tell you I'm bringing you business?
HIGGINS: Pickering: shall we ask this baggage to sit down, or shall we throw her out of the window?
THE FLOWER GIRL: [*running away in terror to the piano, where she turns at bay*] Ah-ah-oh-ow-ow-ow-oo! [*Wounded and whimpering*] I wont be called a baggage when Ive offered to pay like any lady.
Motionless, the two men stare at her from the other side of the room, amazed.
PICKERING: [*gently*] But what is it you want?
THE FLOWER GIRL: I want to be a lady in a flower shop stead of selling at the corner of Tottenham Court Road. But they wont take me unless I can talk more genteel. He said he could teach me. Well, here I am ready to pay him – not asking any favor – and he treats me zif I was dirt.
MRS PEARCE: How can you be such a foolish ignorant girl as to think you could afford to pay Mr Higgins?
THE FLOWER GIRL: Why shouldnt I? I know what lessons cost as well as you do; and I'm ready to pay.
HIGGINS: How much?
THE FLOWER GIRL: [*coming back to him, triumphant*] Now youre talking! I thought youd come off it when you saw a chance of getting back a bit of what you chucked at me last night. [*Confidentially*] Youd had a drop in, hadnt you?
HIGGINS: [*peremptorily*] Sit down.
THE FLOWER GIRL: Ah-ah-ah-ow-ow-oo! [*She stands, half rebellious, half bewildered*].

PICKERING: [*very courteous*] Wont you sit down? [*He places the stray chair near the hearthrug between himself and Higgins*].
THE FLOWER GIRL: [*coyly*] Dont mind if I do. [*She sits down. Pickering returns to the hearthrug*].
HIGGINS: Whats your name?
THE FLOWER GIRL: Liza Doolittle.
HIGGINS: [*declaiming gravely*]
    Eliza, Elizabeth, Betsy and Bess,
    They went to the woods to get a bird's nes':
PICKERING: They found a nest with four eggs in it:
HIGGINS: They took one apiece, and left three in it.
They laugh heartily at their own fun.
LIZA: Oh dont be silly.
MRS PEARCE: [*placing herself behind Eliza's chair*] You mustnt speak to the gentleman like that.
LIZA: Well, why wont he speak sensible to me?
HIGGINS: Come back to business. How much do you propose to pay me for the lessons?
LIZA: Oh, I know whats right. A lady friend of mine gets French lessons for eighteen-pence an hour from a real French gentleman. Well, you wouldnt have the face to ask me the same for teaching me my own language as you would for French; so I wont give more than a shilling. Take or leave it.
HIGGINS: [*walking up and down the room, rattling his key and his cash in his pockets*] You know, Pickering, if you consider a shilling, not as a simple shilling, but as a percentage of this girl's income, it works out as fully equivalent to sixty or seventy guineas from a millionaire.
PICKERING: How so?
HIGGINS: Figure it out. A millionaire has about £150 a day. She earns about half-a-crown.
LIZA: [*haughtily*] Who told you I only –
Higgins [*continuing*] She offers me two-fifths of her day's income for a lesson. Two fifths of a millionaire's income for a day would be somewhere about £60. It's handsome. By George, it's enormous! it's the biggest offer I ever had.
LIZA: [*rising, terrified*] Sixty pounds! What are you talking about? I never offered you sixty pounds. Where would I get –
HIGGINS: Hold your tongue.
LIZA: [*weeping*] But I aint got sixty pounds. Oh –
MRS PEARCE: Dont cry, you silly girl. Sit down. Nobody is going to touch your money.
HIGGINS: Somebody is going to touch you, with a broomstick, if you dont stop snivelling. Sit down.
LIZA: [*obeying slowly*] Ah-ah-ah-ow-oo-o! One would think you was my father.
HIGGINS: If I decide to teach you, I'll be worse than two fathers to you. Here [*he offers her his silk handkerchief*]!
LIZA: Whats this for?
HIGGINS: To wipe your eyes. To wipe any part of your face that feels moist. Remember: thats your handkerchief; and thats your sleeve. Dont mistake the one for the other if you wish to become a lady in a shop.
Liza, utterly bewildered, stares helplessly at him.
MRS PEARCE: It's no use talking to her like that, Mr Higgins: she doesnt understand you. Besides, youre quite wrong: she doesnt do it that way at all [*she takes the handkerchief*].
LIZA: [*snatching it*] Here! You give me that handkerchief. He gev it to me, not to you.
PICKERING: [*laughing*] He did. I think it must be regarded as her property, Mrs Pearce.
MRS PEARCE: [*resigning herself*] Serve you right, Mr Higgins.

PICKERING: Higgins: I'm interested. What about the ambassador's garden party? I'll say
105   youre the greatest teacher alive if you make that good. I'll bet you all the expenses of
         the experiment you cant do it. And I'll pay for the lessons.
LIZA: Oh, you are real good. Thank you, Captain.
HIGGINS: [*tempted, looking at her*] It's almost irresistible. She's so deliciously low – so
         horribly dirty –
110 LIZA: [*protesting extremely*] Ah-ah-ah-ah-ow-ow-oo-oo!!! I aint dirty: I washed my face
         and hands afore I come, I did.
PICKERING: Youre certainly not going to turn her head with flattery, Higgins.
MRS PEARCE: [*uneasy*] Oh, dont say that, sir: theres more ways than one of turning a
         girl's head; and nobody can do it better than Mr Higgins, though he may not always
115   mean it. I do hope, sir, you wont encourage him to do anything foolish.
HIGGINS: [*becoming excited as the idea grows on him*] What is life but a series of
         inspired follies? The difficulty is to find them to do. Never lose a chance: it doesnt
         come every day. I shall make a duchess of this draggletailed guttersnipe.
LIZA: [*strongly deprecating this view of her*] Ah-ah-ah-ow-ow-oo!
120 HIGGINS: [*carried away*] Yes: in six months – in three if she has a good ear and a quick
         tongue – I'll take her anywhere and pass her off as anything. We'll start today: now!
         this moment! Take her away and clean her, Mrs Pearce. Monkey Brand, if it wont
         come off any other way. Is there a good fire in the kitchen? [from Act II]

I. Language

Answer questions dealing with the underlined words/phrases or structures within the given context. Follow the instructions added to each item.

1. **Text A**

   a) l. 24:   "... It's all jumbled up in me head."
                   Find a suitable substitute.   (1 VP)

   b) l. 31:   "off licence"
                   Explain using (a) complete sentence(s).   (2 VP)

   c) ll. 41/42:   "... It wouldn't have mattered if you'd walked in with a bottle."
                   Rewrite the sentence starting: It won't matter ...   (1 VP)

   d) l. 8:   expects
      l. 22:   different
      l. 56:   confidently
      l. 62:   suggest
                   Find the corresponding abstract nouns (not the -ing form).   (2 VP)

2. **Text B**

   a) ll. 24/25:   "Good enough for yə-oo. Now you know, don't you? I'm come to have lessons, I am. And to pay for em tə-oo: make no mistake."
                   Rewrite the passage avoiding all wrong and/or colloquial forms.   (2 VP)

b) ll. 69/70: "Well, you wouldn't <u>have the face</u> to ask me for teaching ..."
Explain in a complete sentence or find a suitable synonym. (1 VP)

c) l. 80: "She offers me two-fifths of her day's <u>income</u> for a lesson."
Find an appropriate substitute. (1 VP)

II. Comprehension

Answer questions 1–3 below using complete sentences only. Keep to the information in the text unless you are explicitly asked to go beyond it. Put any quotation from the text in brackets, with line numbers added.

1. Explain why Frank is cross with Rita in this scene. Refer to the events immediately preceding this scene.
(120–150 words) (4 VP)

2. Why do these extracts represent central points in the female protagonists' development?
(180–230 words) (6 VP)

3. Characterize the male protagonists' attitude towards the two women in both extracts.
(100–130 words) (5 VP)

III. Comment/Composition

Choose *one* of the following topics: (200–300 words) (10 VP)

1. How has Rita's being involved with the Open University classes affected her social life? Discuss the problem of class in *Educating Rita* when answering the question.

2. Why is education so important to Eliza? Why does she want to learn to speak properly? Is her attitude in any way different from what Rita tries to achieve?

Lösungsvorschlag

I. Language

1. Text A

a) mixed up / upside down / confused

b) It won't matter if you walk in with a bottle.

c) It is a shop that is allowed to sell all sorts of alcoholic beverages and tobacco even in the evening.

d) expectation / difference / confidence / suggestion

2. Text B

a) Good enough for you. Now you know, don't you? I've come to have lessons, I have. And to pay for them too: make no mistake.

b) Here it is meant that the other person wouldn't have the courage to ask.
to dare to

c) salary / pay / wages

II. Comprehension

1. Frank had finally plucked up all his courage and invited Rita to one of his dinner parties. Rita was naturally flattered about the fact that a university professor was taking some interest in a working-class girl. Indeed, she was looking forward to the event and even her husband's reluctance to accompany her and the ensuing row did not make her change her mind. After she had finally decided to go on her own and even solved the problem of "being properly dressed", she set off only to find out that she did not have the self-esteem and stamina to sit through a whole evening with people who were – according to her limited perspective – far beyond her reach. While she was staring through Frank's window, she told herself that this was just not her sphere. Frank was not cross or angry about her not turning up, but rather about the way she was putting herself down, the way she was belittling herself.

2. For both central female characters these two scenes represent some sort of a turning-point in their development. Rita was still weighed down by her own failure after not going to Frank's party but realized when she finally joined the rest of her family in the pub that that was not the life she wanted to lead either. The decisive factor here is certainly not her own lack of courage but the misery and lack of perspective revealed to her during their Saturday night out at the pub. She is harshly confronted by the one-way system the British working-class is apparently operating along. Her mother's temporary break-down resulting in the words, "Because – because we could sing better songs than those." (ll. 81/82) give her the certainty that she does not want to get stuck like her mother and she decides to go for it 'while the going is good'.
The same could be said about Eliza but the circumstances which made her go and see Higgins are quite different and rather motivated by the sheer dreariness and poverty of her existence in the London slums. After having met Higgins (the then so-called notetaker), she is baffled by the possibilities offered to her provided, however, she can improve her manners and speech. Just like Rita, the encounter with "high society"

has left a striking impression on her. She decides on the spur of the moment to go to the professor's house in order to get some lessons that might turn her into a lady. On arriving at his house, she has already changed the course of her life.

3. The male characters' attitude towards the two women in this scene is largely influenced by the quality of their relationship. Whereas Frank has already taken a liking to Rita and especially enjoys her freshness and untainted charm, Higgins is not particularly interested in the flower-girl. By that point he had already satisfied his professional need and just looked at her as a disturbance. It thus takes Eliza a lot of strength to make him change his mind and then again it is rather his fondness for playing games that makes him finally want to dare to start on this rather strange adventure of turning a flower-girl into a lady. It is this attitude of using human beings as toys to play with at will that characterizes Higgins' behaviour when he deals with women. Unlike Frank – who shows elements of tenderness, understanding and concern – Higgins must, at least up to this part of the play, be seen as a snobbish male chauvinist.

III. Comment/Composition

1. *How has Rita's being involved with the Open University classes affected her social life? Discuss the problem of class in* Educating Rita *when answering the question.*

   We can only guess at what Rita was like before she decided to join one of the Open University classes. From what we learn through her conversations with Frank and her remarks about her husband she must have been quite fond of the man who proposed to her and who now wants her to have a baby. It seems to have been the normal love relationship most teenagers sooner or later go through and which eventually ends in marriage. Again, we can only infer that Rita was not forced into this marriage and that at one stage in their life together as a young couple she must have been happy and shared her husband's ideas of what life ought to be like. This safe and rather uneventful life came to a grinding halt when Rita felt that she could not take it any longer and tried to bring some fresh air into her dreary existence. In doing so she not only changed her own life, but also turned her husband's life upside down. Her husband being the man he is, cannot give in to Rita's new aspirations because he not only disapproves of literature anyway but his background and working-class upbringing will not allow him to let his wife lead an independent life. The class that has shaped him, his ideas and concepts of life and society has also taught him that a wife's place is next to her husband. Had he given in only a little bit, he might have been able to at least give their relationship a second chance. As a consequence, class and social background have a two-fold effect on two of the main protagonists in this fascinating play: the one feels at home and enjoys the few respites it offers, the other cannot breathe any more because of its shallowness and its lack of insight into the things she is interested in.

2. *Why is education so important to Eliza? Why does she want to learn to speak properly? Is her attitude in any way different from what Rita tries to achieve?*

   Before she met Higgins Eliza never thought about education as a means of escaping from her lowly situation. She was born into the poor class of Edwardian England and was very much left to her own devices. Her father has his own affairs to look after and she is mostly busy making ends meet and earning enough in order to avoid starvation. She never had the chance to get any form of education and had it not been for the professor, she would never have even vaguely thought of phonetics as her way out of hardship and misery. Not having been favoured with any sort of upbringing or schooling does not mean, however, that she is stupid as well. Once she has realized what might be possible, if only she puts her mind to it, she can easily fool most people into thinking that she is of middle-class origin (or even more) and that she belongs to a set of people who create certain types of modern speech.

This is actually the ironic touch Shaw adds to his "comedy of ideas": a practically illiterate young flower-girl whose English is barely understandable is turned into a trend-setter for London's young rich. Thus she not only manages to make herself pass as somebody of importance, but is also able to use her newly-gained assets in order to ridicule those people she used to be despised by. The language that prevented her in earlier times from being accepted or even taken seriously is now her own most efficient weapon.

This is where Rita and Eliza differ most strikingly. The more Rita learns, the more she becomes aware of her intellectual potential and the more she adds to her personal development. She basically absorbs knowledge in order to come to terms with her new life as an independent and self-sufficient woman. Eliza, however, seems to use this new talent in order to embark on a personal tour of revenge, especially against her teacher whose constant disrespect and snobbishness finally bring out the worst in her behaviour.

This can also be seen as her way of expressing her love for him. Shaw does not give in to the demands of his audience. Although it is by the end quite obvious that there is some sort of a love-hate relationship, there has never been a serious indication that Higgins and Eliza might end up as a happy couple. The same sort of relationship may be detected in *Educating Rita*, the difference being that it is there, underneath the surface from the beginning but is not necessarily expected to materialize at the end. Rita is much too occupied with her own search for a new identity and is not yet ready for a new relationship.

Leistungskurs Englisch (Baden-Württemberg): Textaufgaben
Literarisches Sternchenthema: Educating Rita and Pygmalion – Aufgabe 3

Text A

The lights come up on FRANK *sitting in a chair by the window desk with a mug in his hand and a bottle of whisky on the desk in front of him listening to the radio. There is a knock at the door*
FRANK: Come in.
5   RITA: *enters and goes to the swivel chair behind Frank's desk*
FRANK: (*Getting up and switching off the radio*) What the – what the hell are you doing here? I'm not seeing you till next week.
RITA: Are you sober? Are you?
FRANK: If you mean am I still this side of reasonable comprehension, then yes.
10 RITA: (*going and standing next to him*) Because I want you to hear this when you're sober. (*She produces his poems*) These are brilliant. Frank, you've got to start writing again. (*She goes to the swivel chair and sits*) This is brilliant. They're witty. They're profound. Full of style.
FRANK: (*going to the small table and putting down his mug*) Ah ... tell me again, and
15 again ...
RITA: They are, Frank. It isn't only me who thinks so. Me an' Trish sat up last night and read them. She agrees with me. Why did you stop writing? Why did you stop when you can produce work like this? We stayed up most of the night, just talking about it. At first we just saw it as contemporary poetry in its own right, you know, as some-
20 thin' particular to this century but look, Frank, what makes it more – more ... What did Trish say – ? More resonant than – purely contemporary poetry in that you can see in it a direct line through to nineteenth-century traditions of – of like wit an' classical allusion.
FRANK: (*going to the chair* U* *of the desk and standing by the side of it*) Er – that's erm –
25 that's marvellous, Rita. How fortunate I didn't let you see it earlier. Just think if I'd let you see it when you first came here.
RITA: I know ... I wouldn't have understood it, Frank.
FRANK: You would have thrown it across the room and dismissed it as a heap of shit, wouldn't you?
30 RITA: (*laughing*) I know ... But I couldn't have understood it then, Frank, because I wouldn't have been able to recognize and understand the allusions.
FRANK: Oh I've done a fine job on you, haven't I.
RITA: It's true, Frank. I can see now.
FRANK: You know, Rita, I think – I think that like you I shall change my name; from
35 now on I shall insist upon being known as Mary, Mary Shelley – do you understand that allusion, Rita?
RITA: What?
FRANK: She wrote a little Gothic number called *Frankenstein*.
RITA: So?
40 FRANK: This – (*picking up his poetry and moving round to* RITA) – this clever, pyrotechnical pile of self-conscious allusion is worthless, talentless, shit and could be recognized as such by anyone with a shred of common sense. It's the sort of thing that gives publishing a bad name. Wit? You'll find more wit in the telephone book, and, probably, more insight. Its one advantage over the telephone directory is that it's
45 easier to rip. (*He rips the poems up and throws the pieces on to the desk*) It is pretentious, characterless and without style.

RITA: It's not.
FRANK: Oh, I don't expect you to believe me, Rita; you recognize the hall mark of literature now, don't you? (*In a final gesture he throws a handful of the ripped pieces into the air and then goes to the chair DR* and sits*) Why don't you just go away? I don't think I can bear it any longer.
RITA: Can't bear what, Frank?
FRANK: You, my dear – you ...
RITA: I'll tell you what you can't bear, Mr Self-Pitying Piss Artist; what you can't bear is that I am educated now. What's up, Frank, don't y' like me now that the little girl's grown up, now that y' can no longer bounce me on daddy's knee an' watch me stare back in wide-eyed wonder at everything he has to say? I'm educated, I've got what you have an' y' don't like it because you'd rather see me as the peasant I once was; you're like the rest of them – you like to keep your natives thick, because that way they still look charming and delightful. I don't need you. (*She gets up and picking up her bag moves away from the desk in the direction of the door*) I've got a room full of books. I know what clothes to wear, what wine to buy, what plays to see, what papers and books to read. I can do without you.
FRANK: Is that all you wanted. Have you come all this way for so very, very little?
RITA: Oh it's little to you, isn't it? It's little to you who squanders every opportunity and mocks and takes for granted.
FRANK: Found a culture have you, Rita? Found a better song to sing have you? No – you've found a different song, that's all – and on your lips it's shrill and hollow and tuneless. Oh, Rita, Rita.
RITA: Rita? (*She laughs*) Rita? Nobody calls me Rita but you. I dropped that pretentious crap as soon as I saw it for what it was. You stupid ... Nobody calls me Rita.
FRANK: What is it now then? Virginia?
RITA: *exits*
FRANK: Or Charlotte? Or Jane? Or Emily?
Black out [Act 2, Scene V]

(* stage directions: U = up; DR = down right)

Text B

PICKERING: [*coaxing*] Do stay with us, Eliza. [*He follows Doolittle*).
Eliza *goes out on the balcony to avoid being alone with Higgins. He rises and joins her there. She immediately comes back into the room and makes for the door; but he goes along the balcony quickly and gets his back to the door before she reaches it.*
5 HIGGINS: Well, Eliza, youve had a bit of your own back, as you call it. Have you had enough? and are you going to be reasonable? Or do you want any more?
LIZA: You want me back only to pick up your slippers and put up with your tempers and fetch and carry for you.
HIGGINS: I havnt said I wanted you back at all.
10 LIZA: Oh, indeed. Then what are we talking about?
HIGGINS: About you, not about me. If you come back I shall treat you just as I have always treated you. I cant change my nature; and I dont intend to change my manners. My manners are exactly the same as Colonel Pickering's.
LIZA: Thats not true. He treats a flower girl as if she was a duchess.
15 HIGGINS: And I treat a duchess as if she was a flower girl.
LIZA: I see. [*She turns away composedly, and sits on the ottoman, facing the window*]. The same to everybody.
HIGGINS: Just so.
LIZA: Like father.
20 HIGGINS: [*grinning, a little taken down*] Without accepting the comparison at all points, Eliza, it's quite true that your father is not a snob, and that he will be quite at home in any station of life to which his eccentric destiny may call him. [*Seriously*] The great secret, Eliza, is not having bad manners or good manners or any other particular sort of manners, but having the same manner for all human souls: in short, behaving as if
25 you were in Heaven, where there are no third-class carriages, and one soul is as good as another.
LIZA: Amen. You are a born preacher.
HIGGINS: [*irritated*] The question is not whether I treat you rudely, but whether you ever heard me treat anyone else better.
30 LIZA: [*with sudden sincerity*] I dont care how you treat me. I dont mind your swearing at me. I shouldn't mind a black eye: Ive had one before this. But [*standing up and facing him*] I wont be passed over.
HIGGINS: Then get out of my way; for I wont stop for you. You talk about me as if I were a motor bus.
35 LIZA: So you are a motor bus: all bounce and go, and no consideration for anyone. But I can do without you: dont think I cant.
HIGGINS: I know you can. I told you you could.
LIZA: [*wounded, getting away from him to the other side of the ottoman with her face to the hearth*] I know you did, you brute. You wanted to get rid of me.
40 HIGGINS: Liar.
LIZA: Thank you. [*She sits down with dignity*].
HIGGINS: You never asked yourself, I suppose, whether *I* could do without you.
LIZA: [*earnestly*] Dont you try to get round me. Youll have to do without me.
HIGGINS: [*arrogant*] I can do without anybody. I have my own soul: my own spark of
45 divine fire. But [*with sudden humility*] I shall miss you, Eliza. [*He sits down near her on the ottoman*]. I have learnt something from your idiotic notions: I confess that humbly and gratefully. And I have grown accustomed to your voice and appearance. I like them, rather.
LIZA: Well, you have both of them on your gramophone and in your book of photo-
50 graphs. When you feel lonely without me, you can turn the machine on. It's got no feelings to hurt.

HIGGINS: I cant turn your soul on. Leave me those feelings; and you can take away the voice and the face. They are not you.

LIZA: Oh, you *are* a devil. You can twist the heart in a girl as easy as some could twist her arms to hurt her. Mrs Pearce warned me. Time and again she has wanted to leave you; and you always got round her at the last minute. And you dont care a bit for her. And you dont care a bit for me.

HIGGINS: I care for life, for humanity; and you are a part of it that has come my way and been built into my house. What more can you or anyone ask?

LIZA: I wont care for anybody that doesnt care for me.

HIGGINS: Commercial principles, Eliza. Like [*reproducing her Covent Garden pronunciation with professional exactness*] s'yollin voylets [*selling violets*], isnt it?

LIZA: Dont sneer at me. It's mean to sneer at me.

HIGGINS: I have never sneered in my life. Sneering doesnt become either the human face or the human soul. I am expressing my righteous contempt for commercialism. I dont and wont trade in affection. You call me a brute because you couldnt buy a claim on me by fetching my slippers and finding my spectacles. You were a fool: I think a woman fetching a man's slippers is a disgusting sight: did I ever fetch your slippers? I think a good deal more of you for throwing them in my face. No use slaving for me and then saying you want to be cared for: who cares for a slave? If you come back, come back for the sake of good fellowship; for youll get nothing else. Youve had a thousand times as much out of me as I have out of you; and if you dare to set up your little dog's tricks of fetching and carrying slippers against my creation of a Duchess Eliza, I'll slam the door in your silly face.

LIZA: What did you do it for if you didnt care for me?

HIGGINS: [*heartily*] Why, because it was my job.

LIZA:. You never thought of the trouble it would make for me.

HIGGINS:. Would the world ever have been made if its maker had been afraid of making trouble? Making life means making trouble. Theres only one way of escaping trouble; and thats killing things. Cowards, you notice, are always shrieking to have troublesome people killed.

LIZA:. I'm no preacher: I dont notice things like that. I notice that you dont notice me.

HIGGINS: [*jumping up and walking about intolerantly*] Eliza: youre an idiot. I waste the treasures of my Miltonic mind by spreading them before you. Once for all, understand that I go my way and do my work without caring twopence what happens to either of us. I am not intimidated, like your father and your stepmother. So you can come back or go to the devil: which you please.

LIZA: What am I to come back for? [from Act V]

I. Language

Answer questions dealing with the underlined words/phrases or structures within the given context. Follow the instructions added to each item.

1. **Text A**

   a) l. 32   "<u>Oh I've done a fine job on you, haven't I?</u>"
   Is Frank serious here or what does he really want to say?
   What stylistic device does he actually use? (2 VP)

   b) l. 59   "... you like to keep your natives thick ..."
   What does Rita mean? Explain in complete sentences. (2 VP)

2. **Text B**

   a) l. 7   "... and <u>put up with</u> your tempers ..."
   Find a suitable synonym. (1 VP)

   b) l. 20   comparison
   l. 35   consideration
   l. 47   appearance
   l. 74   creation
   Find the corresponding verbs. (2 VP)

   c) l. 64   "Sneering doesn't become either ..."
   Classify the *-ing* form. (1 VP)

   d) l. 71   "... <u>for the sake of</u> ..."
   Explain in a complete sentence or find a synonym. (2 VP)

II. Comprehension

Answer questions 1–4 below using complete sentences only. Keep to the information in the text unless you are explicitly asked to go beyond it. Put any quotation from the text in brackets, with line numbers added.

1. What has changed in Frank's and Rita's relationship? Refer to the text and to events immediately preceding this scene. (100–120 words) (4 VP)

2. Compare the two scenes above. Explain the development both "couples" have undergone. (160–200 words) (5 VP)

3. In this scene from *Educating Rita* various names are mentioned, a change of name is alluded to and Frank refers to Shelley's novel *Frankenstein*. What is the meaning of all this? (100–150 words) (4 VP)

4. Higgins and Frank make their counterparts in these scenes very angry. Why? You may refer to other scenes as well. (70–90 words) (2 VP)

III. Comment/Composition

Choose *one* of the following topics (200–300 words) (10 VP)

1. Language in *Educating Rita* and *Pygmalion*. Discuss.

2. Why are both plays suitable for film versions?

Lösungsvorschlag

I. Language

1. **Text A**

   a) Frank is not serious at all because he apparently thinks that he has made a complete mess of Rita's education. This is not true since she has turned into quite an eloquent person who knows a lot about literature. She is just no longer the girl he used to like so much. He blames himself for everything, is altogether unhappy about his own personal failure and hides behind a wall of sarcasm and irony. This is what he is still good at and this is how he wants to hurt Rita.

   b) Rita has realized that Frank cannot bear the fact that she has grown into an independent and well-spoken woman who does not really need her tutor's guidance any more. She is still fond of Frank and likes visiting him, but resents being treated as if she were stupid and uneducated. She thinks he wants to keep her in her place so as to be able to control her better.

2. **Text B**

   a) accept

   b) to compare/to consider/to appear/to create

   c) It is a gerund used as a subject.

   d) for the good of/for the advantage of
      because good fellowship is important to you

II. Comprehension

1. The first striking difference is that the voice of authority seems to have shifted to Rita who has obviously finished her education (academic and social) and who, despite her new life and friends has still not forgotten her old tutor. He has gone back to his old ways, trying to drown his sorrows in alcohol. Whereas it had been Frank, up to this point, who had had to encourage and motivate his student, it is now Rita who is the one who has to push, motivate and convince. Unfortunately all her efforts seem to be unsuccessful because Frank has withdrawn into his self-pity where only alcohol has a soothing effect on him.

2. Both "couples" have reached the end of their "mission". Rita has the skills she was after, Eliza can make herself pass as a real society woman. However, the end of their common efforts seems to be creating some kind of a void, a situation none of them can really be happy with (Liza: What am I to come back for? l. 88 and Rita: I don't need you l. 60). On the male side, we can notice a general withdrawal to former habits, with Frank being his old sarcastic and drunk self and Higgins being even more of a chauvinist and pompous snob than ever before. The development anybody would have expected from the clash between these classes is purely reserved to the female protagonists who have not only fully absorbed their *masters'* lessons and advice but have, very much to their *masters'/creators'* disagreement, shaped their own identities. The way this disagreement, or rather disappointment, with what has become of the two women is revealed in these respective scenes where the hurt pride and unfulfillable expectations are channelled into childish behaviour that so to speak

reverses the former relationships: the two men have to be taken by the hand to be taught a lesson in dignity and humility, whereas the two women have understood what the real qualities in life are.

3. When Rita first came to see Frank, her new tutor, in his office to start her "second career" she changed her name to Rita. One of her favourite writers was called Rita Mae Brown, hence why she thought a change of name was called for. In doing so, she wanted to get rid of her old identity, if only temporarily and escape her daily routine. Her real name Susan, at that stage in her development, stood for ignorance, working-class, hairdresser and boredom. Her new name Rita, which she eventually gets rid of once her education is done, stood for glamour, knowledge and promise. At the end of this scene, Frank calls her "Charlotte, Jane, Emily, Viginia", i.e. all names rather chosen by upper-class parents for their promising offspring. When Frank says that he ought to be known as Mary (from Mary Shelley, the creator of Frankenstein) he shows some unexpected capacity for self-critcism since he very clearly condemns himself for having created a monster (from his point of view) he can no longer control.

4. These scenes certainly represent a kind of climax in the relationship of the four protagonists. The men's behaviour is, as mentioned before, on the verge of being humiliating and very painful for their protégés. Instead of being grateful for getting some praise for his poems, Frank is looking for trouble and puts their relationship to a severe test. Rita is too clever now to fail to understand his sarcasm and this makes her angry. The same applies to Eliza who is still waiting for some sign of tenderness or fondness and getting none is too hard to bear. She can put up with being laughed at or even pushed back into the gutter, but she will never be able to swallow the ignorance and contempt as dealt out by Higgins.

III. Comment/Composition

1. *Language in* Educating Rita *and* Pygmalion. *Discuss.*

   More than in most other plays the role of language here is a very dominant one. At times, the plot or the characterization of the protagonists are even overshadowed by the weight the authors have given to this complex issue. One recognizes how language is not only used in these plays as a hallmark of social otherness and social depravity but also as a means of escape from these problems.
   When one wants to compare the two plays at this level, one has always got to bear in mind that the social backgrounds are completely different and being poor at the beginning of this century has very little to do with being poor at the end of it.
   Taking all this into account, one has to come to the conclusion that it is especially language that provides the two plays with a common ground to be compared on. Both heroines come from the working-class and speak a very restricted code. For differing reasons they intend to enlarge this code and get rid of their local dialect in order to gain access to a better – or at least different – way of life. Thus language can be seen as a means of escape from a given social background and at the same time as a ticket to, as well as of, acceptability in a higher, more respectacle social environment.
   A second point to think about is a more symbolic one which highlights language as a complex issue representing both progress and conservatism. This is clearly obvious when one has a closer look at how the four protagonists are described: on the one hand Rita and Eliza (as slang speakers), who despite their rather desperate situation, are witty, open-minded as well as full of life and energy whereas on the other hand, Frank and Higgins (the members of the intelligentsia) are stuck in their little ways,

liberal and adventurous only to a certain (comfortable) point and are unable or unwilling to free themselves from the ties of convention. This even applies to Frank whose only attempt at being different is his escape into alcohol.

2. *Why are both plays suitable for film versions?*

Turning a successful play into a film has always been a rather tricky task. The most popular contemporary medium has certain demands that theatre can only meet with difficulty. Theatre is restricted in space and time and only more daring producers tend to experiment with huge casts. This, however, has rarely prevented modern film-makers from helping themselves quite freely to the wealth of choice theatre represents. There are indeed film versions of most popular and important plays. What about the plays we have to deal with? Successful screenplays have been written for both, the classic musical version of *Pygmalion* – *My Fair Lady* – being the more widely known.

There is no question whatsoever that Shaw's play has more ingredients worth being used as film material. The opening scene in the streets of London alone provides ample room both for the presentation of a specific time in English history and pure comedy with a variety of characters ranging from plain ridiculous to a clever caricature of the typical English gentleman. This scene sets the tone for the ensuing plot and characterization thus coming up with further characters who really beg to be given life on a screen.

As opposed to this large mixture of comic characters, we have in *Rita* only two characters who always meet in one rather stuffy room. All the other events are related by the two characters and what we know about the others (Frank's girlfriend, Rita's husband, etc.) we learn from Frank and Rita or their insinuations.

It is naturally difficult to create something appealing and appetizing with these minimal ingredients and the only existing film version to date has proven that it seems to be necessary to add additional characters and supplementary scenes to enable the film to reach a wider audience. Anything else would have ended in "filmed theatre", which even at its best, is not half as good as the real thing, life on stage.

> Leistungskurs Englisch (Baden-Württemberg): Mündliches Abitur
> Textbeispiel 1: Future of Hong Kong Settled

Future of Hong Kong Settled

Two years of negotiations between Britain and China over the future of Hong Kong culminated in an agreement signed on 19 December.

Under this agreement Hong Kong reverts to Chinese sovereignty on 1 July 1997, to become a Special Administrative Region of the People's Republic of China. For the following 50 years it is to have a high degree of local autonomy to keep its separate legal system (within the confines of a new Basic Law), decide its economic, financial and trade policies, and participate, as appropriate, in international organisations and agreements.

Though 98 percent of its people are of Chinese origin and speak Chinese languages, there are important economic and social differences between Hong Kong and China. In Hong Kong GNP per head is $ 5340, in China it is $ 310. Hong Kong pursues fiercely competitive free market policies; China has a socialist system based on the commune. Hong Kong has sophisticated high-tech industries, conspicuous wealth, colourful and cosmopolitan nightlife, many different religions, connections with countries all over the world, and one of the world's highest rates of population density. Yet, apart from its excellent natural harbour, its only resources are its people and the confidence it has gained from the international financial community.

The island of Hong Kong was ceded to Britain in 1842; a few further small parcels of land followed in 1860. But 90 percent of the area of present-day Hong Kong, the New Territories, was acquired on a 99-year lease signed in 1898.

245 words   *Commonwealth Currents, February 1985 (abridged)*

Vocabulary

line 11: GNP – Gross National Product

I. Guiding question
1. What are the most striking differences between Hong Kong and China?

II. Deepening the subject: the British Empire – the Commonwealth
2. What were Britain's motives for its imperial endeavour?
3. Which were the most important colonies that Britain obtained?
4. What has become of its Empire?
5. What is the Commonwealth?

III. Questions about British politics
6. What functions does the Queen have?
7. Describe the British system of government.
8. What is the difference between Majority Vote and Proportional Representation?

IV. Transfer to American politics
9. Characterise the American system of government and compare it with the one found in Great Britain.
10. What is America's political position in the world today?

Lösungsvorschlag

I. Guiding question

1.

China	Hong Kong
– socialist system – low GNP	– competition as main policy – high GNP – highly developed industry – variety of religions – oversea connections

II. Deepening the subject

2. commercial expansionism, acquisition of new territories, wish to build an empire
3. American colonies, India, West Indies, Antipodes (Australia, New Zealand, etc.)
4. independence of colonies paralleled by Britain's economic downfall, status as a world power diminished, Commonwealth of Nations of which Britain is no more than an ordinary member, desperate effort to win back bits of its former glory (Falklands, anti-European attitude)
5. voluntary association of 53 independent states all tied together by their common colonial past

III. Questions about British politics

6. sovereign reigns, but does not rule, representative role as head of state, advisory function, little personal influence, has so-called royal prerogatives such as the possibility to dissolve Parliament
7. two Houses – House of Lords, House of Commons
   House of Commons: responsible for legislation
   House of Lords: lords and monarch must approve of a bill before it becomes an act
   Prime Minister: head of government
8. majority vote: candidate who gets most votes in a constituency is elected,
   proportional representation: seats are given to smaller competitors in proportion to sum of total of votes

IV. Transfer to American politics

9. three branches guaranteeing balance of power as opposed to British system where the judicial branch has not got policy-making possibilities in the way the American side has
10. superpower, seat in Security Council of the UNO, "policeman of the world", big economic influence

> **Leistungskurs Englisch (Baden-Württemberg): Mündliches Abitur**
> **Textbeispiel 2: Suggestions on Reading Shakespeare**

Suggestions on Reading Shakespeare

Shakespeare's plays are not difficult to read if it be remembered that they were written originally not to be read but to be played, that they contain a great deal of poetry, and finally, that because they were composed more than three hundred years ago, they have some allusions with which we are not familiar and some words which we no longer use.
5 Apart from these difficulties they may be read like modern plays for the story, the characters, and the philosophy of life which Shakespeare has packed into them. ...

To Shakespeare, a play was not a few printed pages of dialogue for the isolated reader but a vivid mimetic presentation of human conflict by impersonators on the open platform of the Elizabethan theatre for an alert audience of imaginative Londoners. ... He
10 made no attempt, moreover, to insist upon a complete physical representation of every detail of his play; on the contrary, in the burlesque of the craftsmen in *A Midsummer Night's Dream* he pokes glorious fun at the amateur Thespians who do insist that the moonshine, wall, and lion must be physically presented. The men and women who flocked to the Globe Theatre formed an audience, not a crowd of spectators; they came to
15 hear as well as to see, and Shakespeare used their ears to suggest to their imaginations much that could not be physically represented, as he does in the Prologue to *Henry V:*

> Think, when we talk of horses, that you see them
> Printing their proud hoofs i' the receiving earth.

254 words   *Outlines of Shakespeare's plays by Watt, Holzknecht, Ross [editors]*

Vocabulary

line 12: Thespians – actors

I. Guiding questions
1. What have we got to bear in mind if we want to read a Shakespeare play?
2. What specific idea of his theatre can be found in this text?

II. Questions about Shakespeare's Macbeth
3. Can you think of any scenes in *Macbeth* which are very suitable for a theatrical production?
4. In the above text a Prologue is mentioned. Is there anything similar in *Macbeth*?
5. What is the function of the three witches?
6. To what extent can Macbeth be called a tragic character?

III. Questions concerning other literary forms: the short story
7. Have you read any short stories? Which one(s)? By whom?
8. What are the main characteristics of a short story?
9. Is there anything in the one you read that is very typical of a short story?

IV. Transfer to book report
10. What else have you read in class or at home? A play? A novel?
11. Can you tell the plot in a few sentences?
12. What are the main differences between a novel and a short story/play?

Lösungsvorschläge

I. Guiding questions

1. plays are written to be performed not to be read, huge amount of poetical language has to be accounted for, historical context is different from ours, reader has to put himself in a "Shakespeare frame of mind"
2. people who want to go to a theatre have to be prepared to use their imagination in order to make up for the deficiencies of the stage, i. e. the restricted setting

II. Questions about Shakespeare's Macbeth

3. mysterious scenes involving the witches for suspense and shock, banquet scenes, soliloquies giving actors possibility to use their acting, speaking talents
4. The first scene introducing the three witches has the function of a prologue because the tone of the play is set, characters and plot introduced and the outcome is already hinted at.
5. In addition to what has been said above, the three witches influence Macbeth in his actions, comment on the action and are altogether in their symbolic function the embodiment of disorder, disease, darkness and chaos.
6. development of honest, courageous soldier to ruthless killer, driven by irresistible forces of evilness, a man eaten up by his own ambition, his wife plays on his weakness to make decisions and persuades him to continue

III. Questions concerning other literary forms

7. Name the title and the author of the short story you read and sum up the content. You may also say if you liked/didn't like the story and explain why.
8. sudden beginning, short, restricted setting, small cast of characters, uncomplicated plot, simple plot often leads to climax, different forms of endings, e. g. sudden, open, happy ending
9. List some typical short story characteristics you noted in the story and give examples (e. g. sudden beginning, open ending: How did "your" short story begin, how did it end?)

IV. Transfer to book report

10. Here you are asked to report freely about an English book you recently read.
11. To sum up briefly the story means listing the protagonists, the place, the time and the main action. Don't forget to mention how the story ends.
12. novel: fiction in prose, lenghty, character development, variety of narrators and points of view, various stylistic devices (satire, irony ...)
    short story: see above
    play: dialogues, monologues, division in acts and scenes, dual nature as text to be read and text to be performed

> Leistungskurs Englisch (Baden-Württemberg): Mündliches Abitur
> Textbeispiel 3: City People Enrich Country Life

City People Enrich Country Life

City people moving into the country face suspicion, anger and envy but they are bringing benefits and a lifeline, says the Rural Development Commission according to a report in the Daily Telegraph.

Instead of being blamed for pushing up house prices and forcing locals to leave, some are regarded as "saviours" by communities.

Hundreds of town and city escapers have brought entrepreneurial skills to set up small businesses, says a commission report. They have provided more jobs in deprived areas and have given a much-needed boost to local economies.

Villages which were losing young people forced to seek work elsewhere have seen the exodus halted.

New technology enables many companies to operate almost anywhere. Redundant old buildings of charm and character have been taken over by newcomers.

They have been given a new lease of life with their change of use without any harm to the environment, says the report.

Mr Richard Butt, RDC chief executive, said: "Sometimes these so-called incomers are met with suspicion. There is jealousy because they have money, but it is essential to keep remote areas alive."

So many businesses are flourishing in the countryside because of the finance and skills brought in.

204 words   *The Daily Telegraph, 8 February 1994, p. 6 (abridged)*

Vocabulary

line 11: redundant – [here] abandoned, not being lived in

I. Guiding questions
1. To what extent do city people enrich country life?
2. What problems do they have to face in the country?

II. Questions for further discussion: e. g. problems of big cities in Britain and America, racial discrimination, crime and violence, Megalopolis, environmental problems, London Docklands
3. What reasons do people have for moving out of the inner cities?
4. What does eventually become of the abandoned inner cities?
5. Who is very often left behind and what kind of problems do these people have to cope with?

III. Transfer to immigration: USA/GB
6. What is the situation of the Blacks today in America and in Britain?
7. What was the role of the *Civil Rights Movement*? What has it achieved in the States?
8. What waves of immigration do you know and where are the main differences in American and British Immigration policies?

Lösungsvorschläge

I. Guiding questions
1. businesses have been set up, creation of jobs, exodus of young people has been stopped, restoration of old buildings, villages have come alive again
2. looked at with suspicion, envious villagers, jealousy

II. Questions for further discussion
3. increasing violence, drugs, bad schooling, pollution, pressure of city life, minority problems
4. inner cities fall in disrepair because of lack of money, the wealthy people move away, the unwealthy are left behind
5. people who cannot afford to move away are left behind and are tied up in this never-ending vicious circle of unemployment, bad housing, crime

III. Transfer to immigration
6. improvements i. e. quota system, but still subtle forms of discrimination (also discrimination in reverse), segregation is predominant in a social sort of way, appearance of a black underclass caused by bad education, unemployment, crime
7. legislative measures through non-violent forms of protest resulting in numerous positive changes like desegregation, black upward mobility, fair job opportunities
8. European wave, Asian wave, Hispanic wave
basically similar in their efforts to curb the influx of immigrants, trying e. g. to tighten entry requirements, Americans put greater emphasis on egalitarian ideals, inalienable rights in unison with the American dream, equality, liberty and pursuit of happiness are still cherished

> Leistungskurs Englisch (Baden-Württemberg): Mündliches Abitur
> Textbeispiel 4: Dole Attacks Sex and Violence Diet from Hollywood

Dole Attacks Sex and Violence Diet from Hollywood

The directors and writers *Oliver Stone* and *Quentin Tarantino* came in for particular criticism from the Senate majority leader, who condemned their films *Natural Born Killers* and *True Romance* as "revelling in mindless violence and loveless sex."

He also denounced (...) some recording groups for "marketing evil through commerce."

5 Senator Dole urged the entertainment industry to clean up its act to "help our nation maintain the innocence of our children" and said: "The mainstreaming of deviancy must come to an end."

But he notably avoided any mention of three leading stars of often very violent films, *Sylvester Stallone, Bruce Willis and Arnold Schwarzenegger*, all of whom are Republi-
10 cans.

Senator Dole's attack, made in Los Angeles during a visit to raise money for his presidential campaign, marked an intensification of his drive to win the support of conservatives concerned about the deterioration of American morals and the coarsening of its culture.

15 "We have reached the point where our popular culture threatens to undermine our character as a nation," he said. "A line has been crossed, not just of taste but of human dignity and decency. It is crossed every time sexual violence is given a catchy tune; when teen suicide is set to an appealing beat; when Hollywood's dream factories turn out nightmares of depravity." (...)

208 words   *The Daily Telegraph, 2 June 1995*

Vocabulary

line 6: mainstreaming of deviancy   –   Gewohnheit, das Abweichende zur Norm zu erheben

line 17: to give sth. a catchy tune   –   to make sth. more acceptable and even more appealing

I. **Guiding questions**
   1. What branch of the American entertainment industry is harshly criticized here?
   2. What does this criticism basically consist of?

II. **Questions about American politics:** elections, the party system
   3. Senator Dole is a Republican. Try to sketch in the main differences between democrats and republicans.
   4. Dole is a presidential candidate. Try to outline the most important steps in an American election.

III. **Transfer to other subjects:** e. g. American society, the legal system, landmark decisions, American entertainment, art and culture, interrelationship art and politics
   5. Violence is one of the most discussed issues in modern America. What might have led to this coarsening of American society?
   6. What role, according to you, do the media in general and TV or cinema in particular play regarding the increase of violence?
   7. Apart from very violent films, Americans have recently been very much into ones featuring rather dumb people, e. g. *Forrest Gump*. Can you think of any reason that might explain this completely different approach?

Lösungsvorschlag

I. Guiding questions
1. Dole criticizes the film and recording industry.
2. He criticizes the increase of violence and debased language in the American entertainment industry in general and in the American film industry in particular. He wants to put a stop to the glorification of violence and the tendency to make acts of violence "fashionable".

II. Questions about American politics
3. democrats: supported by working class and minorities, rather reticent in international affairs, liberal in current issues like abortion, death penalty and minority problems, tend to support the poor in tax questions, favour higher spendings on social welfare
republicans: supported by wealthier middle-class, rich farmers, policy of strength and interventionism, support big business, want to cut back on social welfare scheme, less liberal in social questions
4. primaries or conventions or caucuses to elect a candidate, National Convention for nomination of presidential candidate, indirect election through electoral college

III. Transfer to other subjects
5. widening of class barriers, the haves and have-nots, minority problems, drug trafficking, unemployment and decline in education, decline of inner cities
6. TV as sole form of past-time activity, increase of violence even in children's programmes
7. violence and hero worshipping has been a predominant feature of major American box-office hits over the last two decades, violence for its own sake, senseless killings and brutal sex scenes have been important assets of any film that wanted to succeed, saturation of audience, back to normality, stars the normal "guy" can identify with

> **Leistungskurs Englisch (Baden-Württemberg): Textaufgaben**
> **Literarisches Sternchenthema: Paul Auster – Moon Palace – Aufgabe 1**

There is no question that the park did me a world of good. It gave me privacy, but more than that, it allowed me to pretend that I was not as bad off as I really was. The grass and the trees were democratic, and as I loafed in the sunshine of a late afternoon, or climbed among the rocks in the early evening to look for a place to sleep, I felt that I was
5   blending into the environment, that even to a practiced eye I could have passed for one of the picnickers or strollers around me. The streets did not allow for such delusions. Whenever I walked out among the crowds, I was quickly shamed into an awareness of myself. I felt like a speck, a vagabond, a pox of failure on the skin of mankind. Each day, I became a little dirtier than I had been the day before, a little more ragged and confused,
10 a little more different from everyone else. In the park, I did not have to carry around this burden of self-consciousness. It gave me a threshold, a boundary, a way to distinguish between the inside and the outside. If the streets forced me to see myself as others saw me, the park gave me a chance to return to my inner life, to hold on to myself purely in terms of what was happening inside me. It is possible to survive without a roof over your
15 head, I discovered, but you cannot live without establishing an equilibrium between the inner and the outer. The park did that for me. It was not quite a home, perhaps, but for want of any other shelter, it came very close.

Unexpected things kept happening to me in there, things that seem almost impossible to me as I remember them now. Once, for example, a young woman with bright red hair
20 walked up to me and put a five-dollar bill in my hand – just like that, without any explanation at all. Another time, a group of people invited me to join them on the grass for a picnic lunch. A few days after that, I spent the whole afternoon playing in a softball game. Considering my physical condition at the time, I turned in a creditable performance (two or three singles, a diving catch in the left field), and whenever my team was at
25 bat, the other players kept offering me things to eat and drink and smoke: sandwiches and pretzels, cans of beer, cigars, cigarettes. Those were happy moments for me, and they helped to carry me through some of the darker stretches when my luck seemed to have run out. Perhaps that was all I had set out to prove in the first place: that once you throw your life to the winds, you will discover things you had never known before, things that
30 cannot be learned under any circumstances. I was half-dead from hunger, but whenever something good happened to me, I did not attribute it to chance so much as to a special state of mind. If I was able to maintain the proper balance between desire and indifference, I felt that I could somehow will the universe to respond to me. How else was I to judge the extraordinary acts of generosity that I experienced in Central Park? I never
35 asked anyone for anything, I never budged from my spot, and yet strangers were continually coming up to me and giving me help. There must have been some force emanating from me into the world, I thought, some indefinable something that made people want to do this. As time went on, I began to notice that good things happened to me only when I stopped wishing for them. If that was true, then the reverse was true as well: wishing too
40 much for things would prevent them from happening. That was the logical consequence of my theory, for if I had proven to myself that I could attract the world, then it also followed that I could repel it. In other words, you got what you wanted only by not wanting it. It made no sense, but the incomprehensibility of the argument was what appealed to me. If my wants could be answered only by not thinking about them, then all
45 thoughts about my situation were necessarily counterproductive. The moment I began to embrace this idea, I found myself staggering along an impossible tightrope of conscious-

ness. For how do you not think about your hunger when you are always hungry? How do you silence your stomach when it is constantly calling out to you, begging to be filled? It is next to impossible to ignore such pleas. Time and again, I would succumb to them, and once I did, I automatically knew that I had destroyed my chances of being helped. The result was inescapable, as rigid and precise as a mathematical formula. As long as I worried about my problems, the world would turn its back on me. That left me no choice but to fend for myself, to scrounge, to make the best of it on my own. Time would pass. A day, two days, perhaps even three or four, and little by little I would purge all thoughts of rescue from my mind, would give myself up for lost. It was only then that any of the miraculous occurrences ever took place. They always struck like a bolt from the blue. I could not predict them, and once they happened, there was no way I could count on seeing another. Each miracle was therefore always the last miracle. And because it was the last, I was continually being thrown back to the beginning, continually having to start the battle all over again.

[969 words]   Paul Auster, MOON PALACE, Faber and Faber Limited
                                              London 1997, pp. 57-59

Vocabulary:
line 1:	privacy	– the state of being alone and not watched or disturbed
line 6:	stroller	– person walking in a slow and casual way
line 15:	equilibrium	– the state of being physically or mentally balanced
line 22:	softball	– a game similar to baseball, but played on a smaller field with a larger soft ball
line 35:	to budge	– to move or make sth / sb move slightly
line 49:	plea	– an urgent emotional request; an appeal
line 49:	to succumb	– to yield to sth; nachgeben, (einer Versuchung) erliegen
line 53:	to scrounge	– to take sth without asking permission
line 54:	to purge	– entfernen, aus dem Kopf schlagen

I. Language (ohne Wörterbuch zu bearbeiten): **items 1–7**

Deal with the words/phrases or structures within the given context.
Follow the instructions added to each item.

1. 02–03:   "The grass and the trees <u>were democratic</u>, and..."
            Explain the underlined phrase; you may change the sentence
            structure.   (1 VP)

2. 08:   "...a pox of failure on the skin of mankind."
   46–47:   "...along an impossible tightrope of consciousness."
   51:      "...as rigid and precise as a mathematical formula."
   56:      "...like a bolt from the blue."
            Name the stylistic devices used in these phrases.   (2 VP)

3. 16–17:   "It was not quite a home, perhaps, but <u>for want of</u> any other
            shelter, it came very close."
            Find a suitable substitute for the underlined words; keep to
            the sentence structure.   (1 VP)

4. 18:   "Unexpected things <u>kept happening</u> to me..."
   38–39:   "...only when I <u>stopped wishing</u> for them."
            Explain the -ing forms and translate the phrases.   (2 VP)

D 2

5. 48–49: "It is <u>next to</u> impossible to ignore such pleas."
   Find a suitable substitute for the underlined words; keep to
   the sentence structure. (1 VP)

6. 55–56: "<u>It was only then that</u> any of the miraculous occurrences ever
   took place."
   Explain the grammatical structure used here. Translate the
   sentence. (2 VP)

7. Find the corresponding <u>abstract nouns</u> (not the -ing forms):
   11: to distinguish
   14: to survive
   15: to discover
   32: to maintain (1 VP)

II. Questions on the text

Answer the following questions in complete sentences. Keep to the information given in the text unless you are explicitly asked to go beyond it.

1. Describe how Marco Stanley Fogg gets to live in Central Park and how his stay there comes to an end. You will have to go beyond the text.
   (100–130 words) (3 VP)

2. Which changes does Marco Stanley Fogg's state of mind undergo during his stay in Central Park?
   (120–150 words) (4 VP)

3. How does Marco Stanley Fogg feel about the acts of generosity which he benefits from while being there? How does he explain them?
   (90–120 words) (3 VP)

4. To what extent does Marco's philosophy of life change through his experiences in the park?
   (140–170 words) (5 VP)

III. Comment/Composition

Choose *one* of the following topics: (200–300 words) (10 VP)

1. *Moon Palace* – a typically American work of art?

2. *Moon Palace* – a study of different characters.
   State your opinion by means of examples from the novel.

Lösungsvorschlag

I. Language

1. The grass and the trees in Central Park did not judge people by their outward appearance or by their belonging to a certain social class; people were looked at as being equal; nature in Central Park did not make any social distinctions.

2. ll. 08 and 46/47: metaphors
   ll. 51 and 56: similes

3. ...but because I did not have/there wasn't/because of a lack of any other shelter, it came very close.

4. gerunds after verbs expressing beginning, continuation or ending
   Unerwartete Dinge passierten mir immer wieder...
   ...erst wenn ich sie mir nicht weiter wünschte/erst wenn ich aufhörte sie mir zu wünschen/sie herbeizusehnen...

5. It is almost/nearly impossible to ignore such pleas.

6. cleft sentence: The structure *it was ... that* is used here to emphasize the adverbial phrase 'only then'.
   Erst dann spielte sich (irgend)eines jener wundersamen Ereignisse je(mals) ab/ fand...je(mals) statt.

7. l. 11:   distinction
   l. 14:   survival
   l. 15:   discovery
   l. 32:   maintenance

II. Questions on the text

1. Describe how Marco Stanley Fogg gets to live in Central Park and how his stay there comes to an end. You will have to go beyond the text.

After Uncle Victor's death Marco runs short of money as he refuses to benefit from scholarships or any other financial resources at hand. He gradually reads and then sells Victor's books and all the rest of his bequest until – almost starved to death – he eventually has to give up his apartment. In search of his friend David Zimmer he happens to get acquainted with Kitty Wu and finally ends up in Central Park where he spends a couple of weeks. His physical and mental condition deteriorates rapidly and only thanks to Zimmer and Kitty, who have been looking for him for quite a considerable time, can disaster be avoided. Marco moves in with Zimmer before he takes up his job with Thomas Effing.

2. Which changes does Marco Stanley Fogg's state of mind undergo during his stay in Central Park?

At times Marco really feels at ease in Central Park because the place can provide him with a kind of private sphere. Even more it enables him to indulge in a favorable illusion about the miserable state of affairs he is actually in. Neither nature nor people strolling in the park distinguish between rich and poor, clean and dirty. People on the streets of Manhattan, however, have always made this distinction. Being stared at due to his outward appearance makes Marco become aware of and feel embarrassed about his deteriorating situation. It is in the park that Marco comes to the conclusion that a man should be conscious of his inner values rather than of the impression he makes on others and that if both sides – "the inner and the outer" – are in harmony with each other he will somehow feel sheltered.

3. How does Marco Stanley Fogg feel about the acts of generosity which he benefits from while being there? How does he explain them?

The financial support and the food he is given by complete strangers, the invitation to a softball game accompanied by snacks and drinks are happy and unexpected incidents which help Marco to overcome his most desolate moments in Central Park. Though he has never asked for anything nor made a move which might have revealed his being in need of help and sustenance, the world around him still seems to react somehow or other. Being able to exert an influence on his surroundings is quite a new and fascinating experience which he can only explain by the frame of mind he is in and which keeps the extreme wish for and the total indifference to something he is in need of in balance.

4. To what extent does Marco's philosophy of life change through his experiences in the park?

Marco puts forward the theory that a man must not wish for good things to happen because they never ever will if he does so. Thus, according to his desire or his indifference, he is either able to push back the world or to attract people who would like to and will be able to help him.

Though fascinated by the illogical nature of his argument Marco has to realize that it is almost impossible to disregard physical urges like hunger once they get too strong. Bothering about them, however, will definitely make help impossible. Therefore, in order to be redeemed from his miserable fate in Central Park he will be obliged to clear his mind of all thoughts of and hope for rescue. But Marco realizes as well that having reached this state of mind will make unexpected, miraculous things occur, events which are unique and cannot be continued or repeated or forced into existence by any act of volition.

III. Comment / Composition

1. Moon Palace – *a typically American work of art?*

Apart from the respective settings described, there are quite a number of typically American core values embedded in the novel which are represented by the attitudes and lifestyles of different characters. Marco especially shows traits of rugged individualism in his quest for personal and national identity. By being constantly on the move from one place to another, from dwelling to dwelling, and by his almost fatal 'stopover' in Central Park he symbolizes mobility as well as adventurous spirit.

Together with Kitty Wu – and partly Pavel Shum – he stands for both the history of American immigration and contemporary American history exemplified by young people trying to dispose of conventional standards in the late nineteen sixties, to cope with the impact of the Vietnam War, to define new values and to find new identities. Moreover, mobility especially from East to West, from urban areas to the vastness of the Midwest and the West and the trace of the American Frontier Spirit finding its climax in the landing on the moon, is embodied by Marco, Victor, Julian and Solomon Barber and others.

Enthusiasm for sports, especially baseball – a sportive and social event at the same time – and the importance of college education as a means of making the American Dream come true are further prevailing elements of the novel. Thus American normality and average are represented by Zimmer who, after single-mindedly finishing his college studies, becomes a lecturer and has a family with two children. Marco, on the other hand, being "unparented" and in search of his family roots for quite a long time, symbolizes the situation of broken families meanwhile rather common in America. In the end he finds his family, he temporarily gets wealthy, he owns a big Pontiac only to lose everything again and start a new life from the very beginning.

2. Moon Palace – *a study of different characters.*
   State your opinion by means of examples from the novel.

   There is quite a variety of extremely different characters depicted in the novel. Due to the narrative technique applied, most of them are described from Marco's point of view.

   Yet in the 'stories within the story', for example in Thomas Effing's report on his adventures in the West or in Solomon's *Kepler's Blood*, people are characterized vicariously by Marco.

   Getting to know just a few isolated instances of Mrs Hume's attitudes, thoughts and feelings and only a rough outline of Emily Fogg's, Dora Shamsky's or Aunt Clara's personalities, apart from Kitty Wu we do not come across any really round female characters.

   Kitty and David Zimmer are the only two major figures we might feel inclined to identify with. They seem to be sensible, reasonably ambitious, and determinedly following their professional careers. Both of them live up to American core values as regards the importance of education and a reasonable amount of property as a guarantee of a life of freedom, independence and self-sufficiency. They appear to be unselfish and helpful, understanding and indulgent to Marco's extravagances. Whereas Zimmer keeps behaving and acting in a more or less sober and down-to-earth way, Kitty can at times be humorous, even exuberant, though essentially her approach to life is defined by farsightedness and thorough consideration of things to come when in spite of her natural feelings she rationally decides to have her child aborted and later on not to let Marco come back to her.

   Marco, the protagonist, is the only character whose thoughts and feelings we may share directly by means of interior monologues and reported thoughts. Both Marco and Thomas Effing are set apart from the other persons by their extravagance. They are intelligent and eloquent, at least temporarily not interested in acquiring material values, and they have been or still are in quest of something which has never been clearly defined. Whilst Marco appears to be polite and anxious not to hurt anyone around him, Effing shows an ambivalent behavior towards his surroundings. He seems to be rude, disgusting in his manners, reckless and insulting, but at times – especially with strangers – amiable, compassionate and sympathetic.

> **Leistungskurs Englisch (Baden-Württemberg): Textaufgaben**
> **Literarisches Sternchenthema: Paul Auster – Moon Palace – Aufgabe 2**

It took us more than two weeks to get that far. Christmas had long since come and gone, and a week after that the decade had ended. Effing paid little attention to these milestones, however. His thoughts were fixed on an earlier time, and he burrowed through his story with inexhaustible care, leaving nothing out, backtracking to fill in
5 minor details, dwelling on the smallest nuances in an effort to recapture his past. After a while, I stopped wondering whether he was telling me the truth or not. His narrative had taken on a phantasmagoric quality by then, and there were times when he did not seem to be remembering the outward facts of his life so much as inventing a parable to explain its inner meanings. The hermit's cave, the saddlebags of money, the Wild West Shootout –
10 it was all so farfetched, and yet the very outrageousness of the story was probably its most convincing element. It did not seem possible that anyone could have made it up, and Effing told it so well, with such palpable sincerity, that I simply let myself go along with it, refusing to question whether these things had happened or not. I listened, I recorded what he said, I did not interrupt him. In spite of the revulsion he sometimes
15 inspired in me, I could not help thinking of him as a kindred spirit. Perhaps it started when we got to the episode about the cave. I had my own memories of living in a cave, after all, and when he described the loneliness he had felt then, it struck me that he was somehow describing the same things I had felt. My own story was just as preposterous as Effing's, but I knew that if I ever chose to tell it to him, he would have believed every
20 word I said.

As the days went by, the atmosphere in the house became more and more claustrophobic. The weather was ferocious outside – freezing rain, ice-covered streets, winds that blew right through you – and for the time being we had to suspend our afternoon walks. Effing began doubling up on the obituary sessions, withdrawing to his room for a short nap after
25 lunch and then storming out again at two-thirty or three, ready to go on talking for several more hours. I don't know where he found the energy to continue at such a pace, but other than having to pause between sentences a bit more than usual, his voice never seemed to let him down. I began to live inside that voice as though it were a room, a windowless room that grew smaller and smaller with each passing day. Effing wore the
30 black patches over his eyes almost constantly now, and there was no chance to deceive myself into thinking there was some connection between us. He was alone with the story in his head, and I was alone with the words that poured from his mouth. Those words filled every inch of the air around me, and in the end there was nothing else for me to breathe. If not for Kitty, I probably would have been smothered. After my work with
35 Effing was done, I usually managed to see her for several hours, spending as much of the night with her as possible. On more than one occasion, I did not return until early the next morning. Mrs Hume knew what I was up to, but if Effing had any idea of my comings and goings, he never said a word. The only thing that mattered was that I appear at the breakfast table every morning at eight o'clock, and I never failed to be there on
40 time.

Once he left the cave, Effing said, he traveled through the desert for several days before coming to the town of Bluff. From then on, things became easier for him. He worked his way north, slowly moving from town to town, and made it back to Salt Lake City by the end of June, where he linked up with the railroad and bought a ticket for San Francisco. It
45 was in California that he invented his new name, turning himself into Thomas Effing when he signed the hotel register on the first night. He wanted the Thomas to refer to

Moran, he said, and it wasn't until he put down the pen that he realized that Tom had also been the hermit's name, the name that had secretly belonged to him for more than a year. He took the coincidence as a good omen, as though it had strengthened his choice into
50 something inevitable. As for his surname, he said, it would not be necessary for him to provide me with a gloss. He had already told me that Effing was a pun, and unless I had misread him in some crucial way, I felt I knew where it had come from. In writing out the word *Thomas*, he had probably been reminded of the phrase *doubting Thomas*. The gerund had then given way to another: *fucking Thomas*, which for convention's sake had
55 been further modified into *f-ing*. Thus, he was Thomas Effing, the man who had fucked his life. Given his taste for cruel jokes, I imagined how pleased he must have been with himself.

[884 words]   Paul Auster, MOON PALACE, Faber and Faber Limited
London 1997, pp. 182-185

Vocabulary:

line 7: phantasmagoric – cf. phantasmagoria *n (fml)*: a changing scene of real or imagined figures, eg as seen in a dream or created as an effect in a film; German: traumhaft, traumartig
line 10: outrageousness – cf. adj. outrageous: very unusual and quite shocking
line 14: revulsion – a feeling of disgust or horror
line 18: preposterous – completely unreasonable; absurd or shocking

I. Language (ohne Wörterbuch zu bearbeiten): **items 1–10:**

Deal with the words/phrases or structures within the given context.
Follow the instructions added to each item.

1. 12: "…told it so well, with such <u>palpable sincerity</u>, that I simply let…"
Explain the underlined phrase; you may change the sentence structure. (1 VP)

2. 15: "…, <u>I could not help</u> thinking of him as a kindred spirit."
Explain the underlined phrase; you may change the sentence structure. (1 VP)

3. 23: "…and <u>for the time being</u> we had to suspend…"
Find a suitable substitute; keep to the sentence structure. (1 VP)

4. 26–27: "…to continue <u>at such a pace</u>, but other than having to pause…"
Find a suitable substitute; keep to the sentence structure. (1 VP)

5. 54–55: "…, which <u>for convention's sake</u> had been further modified into *f-ing*."
Explain the underlined phrase; you may change the sentence structure. (1 VP)

6. 17–18: "…and when he described the loneliness <u>he had felt</u> then, it struck me that he was somehow describing the same things <u>I had felt</u>."
Explain the grammatical structure of the underlined clauses. (1 VP)

7. 44–45: "<u>It was in California that</u> he invented his new name, …"
Explain the function of the underlined grammatical structure. (1 VP)

8. 47–48: "…and it wasn't until he put down the pen that he realized that Tom had also been the hermit's name, …"
   Translate the sentence above. (1 VP)

9. 53–54: "…he had probably been reminded of the phrase *doubting Thomas*. <u>The gerund had then given way to another</u>: *fucking Thomas*, which…"
   What is wrong about this statement? (1 VP)

10. 56: "<u>Given his taste for cruel jokes</u>, I imagined…"
    Explain the grammatical form of the underlined clause. (1 VP)

II. Questions on the text

Answer the following questions in complete sentences. Keep to the information given in the text unless you are explicitly asked to go beyond it.

1. Characterize Thomas Effing. Refer to the text and to other passages in the novel.
   (110–150 words) (3 VP)

2. Define the position and the function of the scene described within the context of the novel as a whole.
   (120–150 words) (5 VP)

3. How does Thomas Effing tell his story and how does it affect Marco Stanley Fogg?
   Keep to the information given in the text.
   (110–140 words) (5 VP)

4. Describe how Julian Barber turns into Thomas Effing.
   (70–100 words) (2 VP)

III. Comment / Composition

Choose *one* of the following topics: (200–300 words) (10 VP)

1. Marco Stanley Fogg's Quest for Identity.

2. American Landscapes and Mobility in *Moon Palace*.

Lösungsvorschlag

I. Language

1. Effing told his story so sincerely / with such honesty that Marco could feel / was quite sure that it was or at least could be true.

2. Marco had to think of him / was bound to think of him / could not avoid thinking of him as a kindred spirit.

3. …and for the moment / at present / until some other arrangement were made we had to suspend…

4. …to continue at that rate / so fast / so quickly, but…

5. …it had been further modified into *f-ing* because society would more easily accept it; …because it corresponded more exactly and more suitably to the language usage and code of behavior of society.

6. contact clauses: defining relative clauses in which the relative pronouns can be left off because they are in the object case.

7. cleft sentence: The structure *it was … that* is used here to emphasize the adverbial phrase 'in California'.

8. …und erst als er den Stift niederlegte, erkannte er, dass Tom auch der Name des Einsiedlers gewesen war, …

9. *doubting* and *fucking* are not gerunds, but present participles used as adjectives

10. Originally a past participle construction with a subject of its own *given* is meanwhile used as a preposition.

II. Questions on the text

1. Characterize Thomas Effing. Refer to the text and to other passages in the novel.

Thomas Effing's personality seems to be ambivalent. On the one hand he appears extremely impolite, rough, insulting to Mrs Hume and Marco, sometimes even cruel; his table manners are really bad and disgusting at home, however, perfect outside. On the other hand, he shows himself as a friendly, generous, understanding and even socially-minded person. Though physically handicapped, he is mentally strong enough to impose his will on the world around him. On account of his outspoken self-confidence he does not want to be restricted by any people, although he is dependent on them, his legs being replaced by a wheelchair, his sight by the proper and accurate use of words attributed to objects he cannot perceive. In his work he turns out to be energetic, purposeful and disciplined, and not easy to satisfy, as he expects the same qualities from others who work for and with him.

2. *Define the position and the function of the scene described within the context of the novel as a whole.*

After having been rescued from his wretched life in Central Park by Kitty and Zimmer and finishing his studies at Columbia University, Marco finds a job at Thomas Effing's. He has to read books and newspapers to the old man and take him out in his wheelchair because Thomas Effing cannot walk and pretends to be blind. In this scene Effing tells the story of his life in order to draw up his own obituary and Marco has to take down notes for a written version. Furthermore, the episode describes how Julian Barber turns into Thomas Effing and anticipates the spiritual or even family relationship between the two men and the similarity of their respective fates. Thus, the scene precedes the climax of the novel, as finally Marco finds out that Thomas Effing must have been his grandfather and that Solomon Barber is his father.

3. *How does Thomas Effing tell his story and how does it affect Marco Stanley Fogg? Keep to the information given in the text.*

While telling his story Thomas Effing completely forgets the time and the world around him. He reports his life and his adventures in Utah so thoroughly and mentions every detail as if he were trying to catch up on his earlier life and live through his past again. In Marco's view some of the incidents described are so mysterious that they seem to symbolize the deeper meaning of Effing's life. Due to a lot of details depicted Marco is so absorbed by the story that he does not ask himself whether the incidents are true or not. What he is told reminds him of his own experiences in a cave in Central Park, so that he becomes aware of some spiritual affinity with Effing without being led into recognizing any existing family bonds.

4. *Describe how Julian Barber turns into Thomas Effing.*

Having left Utah and traveled west to California Julian Barber moves into a hotel where he signs the registration form with his new name, the first name referring to his friend Thomas Moran, who – excepting other points of similarity – marks the beginning of his career as a painter. Only then does he realize that Tom had also been the name of the hermit whose identity he assumed while living in the cave. The collocation 'doubting Thomas' leads him to 'fucking Thomas' which he abbreviates to 'f-ing', thus creating a pun that sounds less obscene and rude.

III. Comment/Composition

1. *Marco Stanley Fogg's Quest for Identity.*

The quest for personal and national identity appears a characteristic trait of the majority of Americans living in a multicultural society with only some two hundred years of common history and background.
In this way, Marco, a descendant of European immigrants, whose name has deliberately been changed by bureaucratic arbitrariness, is concerned about tracing back his personal roots to their very end. Like Kitty, another, yet more recent immigrant child, he seems to be "unparented", his family being replaced by Uncle Victor, who in order not to lose his foster child, even prevents him from coming across his natural father.
Victor's theory about names contributes to Marco's building up a preliminary, provisional identity. The disfigurement of his first name at school makes him shorten his real name to M.S. i.e. the manuscript – of his own biography. He thus – according to Victor – becomes "the author of his own life".
Furthermore, Victor's old suit provides for shelter and protection, individuality and distinction at the same time, making Marco an outsider of a society which, as a matter

of fact, he does not really want to fit into. By reading Victor's bequeathed books he mentally re-enacts his uncle's chronologically ordered life. By selling them he dismantles his own past and heritage step by step until he finally ends up in Central Park, physically and spiritually exhausted, his personality reduced to nil – almost an at least accepted if not deliberately organized gradual suicide.

While taking down Thomas Effing's obituary Marco lives intensively through his grandfather's lost and regained new identity. The encounter with Solomon, who in his juvenile novel *Kepler's Blood* makes an effort to come to terms with his father's lost life and personality, leads Marco back to his very origins. After having destroyed his own offspring by agreeing to Kitty's abortion plans, he emphatically inquires into Effing's and his own past, having in mind their common experiences of life in a cave. Though his investigations fail in the end, they lead him to the West, and – with his eyes directed to the full moon coming up over the hills – he becomes aware of a new beginning of his life.

2. *American Landscapes and Mobility in* Moon Palace.

The urban landscapes of New York, and to a more limited extent of Chicago, form the main settings of *Moon Palace*.

In New York it is above all the area in and around Central Park where the most decisive parts of the action take place. Here the protagonist Marco lives, gets educated and meets those people who will have a strong impact on the landscape of his future life. Marco becomes aware of the difference between the social behavior of class-conscious people in the streets of Manhattan, and the generally speaking more democratic attitudes of those he comes across in Central Park. Though there again men's characters strongly differ from one another; some prove to be friendly, helpful and socially-minded, others egoistic, deceitful, even menacing and violent. Roughly speaking, the East represented by New York, but also by Boston and Cambridge, Massachusetts and New Hampshire stands for upbringing and education, for initiation into and life in society, whereas the West symbolizes dangers and adventures, progress and hope for economic success, change and renewal, but also the individual's quest for identity.

Moving west can be seen as a kind of general trait in *Moon Palace*. Like Thomas Moran, Julian Barber is drawn to the West and towards the Pacific, where – having overcome the conventional principles of art and having indulged in his painting to the very end of his available means – he loses his physical integrity and finally takes on his new identity as Thomas Effing. Ralph Albert Blakelock is also fascinated by the western landscape, which he depicts in harmony with its original inhabitants and with American history. To Victor and Howie Dunn the West means a possibility of earning their living as musicians whereas Marco, on the other hand, experiences that part of America, steeped in history, with the objective of coming to terms with Thomas Effing's and his own past. Still in search of his identity he at last reaches the outermost borderline of the country and looking at the moon as a possible new frontier, he feels he is given the opportunity of a fresh start.

> **Leistungskurs Englisch (Baden-Württemberg): Textaufgaben**
> **Literarisches Sternchenthema: Paul Auster – Moon Palace – Aufgabe 3**

For obvious reasons, we didn't go out that night. The next night was clear, and at eight o'clock we went down to Times Square, where we finished our work in a record-breaking twenty-five or thirty minutes. Because it was still early, and because we were closer to home than usual, Effing insisted that we return on foot. In itself, this is a trivial
5   point, and I wouldn't bother to mention it except for a curious thing that happened along the way. Just south of Columbus Circle, I saw a young black man of about my age walking parallel to us on the opposite side of the street. As far as I could tell, there was nothing unusual about him. His clothes were decent, he did nothing to suggest that he was either drunk or crazy. But there he was on a cloudless spring night, walking along
10 with an open umbrella over his head. That was incongruous enough, but then I saw that the umbrella was also broken: the protective cloth had been stripped off the armature, and with the naked spokes spread out uselessly in the air, it looked as though he was carrying some huge and improbable steel flower. I couldn't help laughing at the sight. When I described it to Effing, he let out a laugh as well. His laugh was louder than mine, and it
15 caught the attention of the man across the street. With a big smile on his face, he gestured for us to join him under the umbrella. "What do you want to be standing out in the rain for?" he said merrily. "Come on over here so you don't get wet." There was something so whimsical and openhearted about his offer that it would have been rude to turn him down. We crossed over to the other side of the street, and for the next thirty blocks we
20 walked up Broadway under the broken umbrella. It pleased me to see how naturally Effing fell in with the spirit of the joke. He played along without asking any questions, intuitively understanding that nonsense of this sort could continue only if we all pretended to believe in it. Our host's name was Orlando, and he was a gifted comedian, tiptoeing nimbly around imaginary puddles, warding off raindrops by tilting the umbrella
25 at different angles, and chattering on the whole way in a rapid-fire monologue of ridiculous associations and puns. This was imagination in its purest form: the act of bringing nonexistent things to life, of persuading others to accept a world that was not really there. Coming as it did on that particular night, it somehow seemed to match the impulse behind what Effing and I had just been doing down at Forty-second Street. A
30 lunatic spirit had taken hold of the city. Fifty-dollar bills were walking around in strangers' pockets, it was raining and yet not raining, and the cloudburst pouring through our broken umbrella did not hit us with a single drop.

We said our good-byes to Orlando at the corner of Broadway and Eighty-fourth Street, the three of us shaking hands all around and swearing to remain friends for life. As a
35 small coda to our promenade, Orlando stuck out his palm to test the weather conditions, thought for a moment, and then declared that the rain had stopped. Without further ado, he closed up the umbrella and presented it to me as a souvenir. "Here, man," he said, "I think you'd better have it. You never know when it might start raining again, and I wouldn't want you guys to get wet. That's the thing about the weather: it changes all the
40 time. If you're not ready for everything, you're not ready for anything."

"It's like money in the bank," said Effing.

"You got it, Tom," said Orlando. "Just stick it under your mattress and save it for a rainy day."

He held up a black power fist to us in farewell and then sauntered off, disappearing into
45 the crowd by the time he reached the end of the block.

It was an odd little episode, but such things happen in New York more often than you would think, especially if you are open to them. What made this encounter unusual for me was not so much its lightheartedness, but the mysterious way in which it seemed to exert an influence on subsequent events. It was almost as if our meeting with Orlando
50 had been a premonition of things to come, an augury of Effing's fate. A new set of images had been imposed on us, and we were henceforth cast under its spell. In particular, I am thinking about rainstorms and umbrellas, but more than that, I am also thinking about change – and how everything can change at any moment, suddenly and forever.

[804 words]   Paul Auster, MOON PALACE, Faber and Faber Limited,
London 1997, pp. 208-210

Vocabulary:

line 10: incongruous	–	strange because not in harmony with the surroundings; out of place; German: abwegig, ungereimt
line 18: whimsical	–	schrullig, launig
line 30: lunatic	–	wildly foolish
line 35: coda	–	the final passage of a piece of music
line 36: without ado	–	immediately; without fuss or delay
line 44: black power fist	–	fist held up as a symbol of the black power movement in favor of civil rights for black people
line 50: premonition	–	a feeling that sth is going to happen, esp sth unpleasant
line 50: augury	–	a sign of what will happen in the future; an omen

I. Language (ohne Wörterbuch zu bearbeiten): **items 1–8:**

Deal with the words/phrases or structures within the given context.
Follow the instructions added to each item.

1. 12–13: "...as though he was carrying some <u>huge and improbable</u> steel flower."
Explain the underlined phrase; you may change the sentence structure.   (1 VP)

2. 11–12: "...and <u>with the naked spokes spread out</u> uselessly in the air, it looked as though..."
Explain the grammatical structure of this phrase. Transform the underlined phrase by means of a subordinate clause.   (1 VP)

3. 16–17: "What do you want to be standing out in the rain for?" He said merrily. "Come on over here so you don't get wet."
Transform the sentences into reported speech. Start as follows: *Orlando asked ...*   (2 VP)

4. 28–29: "...it somehow seemed <u>to match</u> the impulse behind what Effing..."
Find a suitable substitute; keep to the sentence structure.   (1 VP)

5. 29–30: "A lunatic spirit had taken hold of the city."
Transform the sentence into passive voice. Start as follows: *The city ...*   (1 VP)

6. 30–31: "Fifty-dollar bills were walking around in strangers' pockets, …"
Name the stylistic device used in this clause. (1 VP)

7. 50–51: "A new set of images had been imposed on us, and we were henceforth cast under its spell."
Rewrite the sentence using active voice.
The encounter with Orlando ... (1 VP)

8. Find the corresponding abstract nouns (not the -ing forms):
   18: rude
   24: imaginary
   32: single
   48: mysterious (2 VP)

II. Questions on the text

Answer the following questions in complete sentences. Keep to the information given in the text unless you are explicitly asked to go beyond it.

1. Why does the scene described seem to Marco to be trivial and incongruous at the same time?
   (80–110 words) (3 VP)

2. Describe the effects the scene has on Marco's and Effing's behavior and mental attitude.
   (90–120 words) (5 VP)

3. Explain the importance of the scene as "a premonition of things to come". Refer to the novel as a whole.
   (150–190 words) (5 VP)

4. "Fifty-dollar bills were walking around in strangers' pockets" [ll. 30–31]. Outline the background of this statement. Go beyond the text.
   (70–100 words) (2 VP)

III. Comment / Composition

Choose *one* of the following topics: (200–300 words) (10 VP)

1. *Moon Palace* – a work of art and a work *on* art.

2. *"There are no coincidences. That word is used only by ignorant people."*
   Discuss Thomas Effing's statement. To underline your opinion refer to relevant passages in the novel.

Lösungsvorschlag

I. Language

1. The steel flower [Orlando's broken umbrella] was so enormous that you could hardly believe anything like that could exist at all.

2. absolute past participle construction instead of an adverbial clause; the subject of the clause is introduced by *with*
   ..., and as the naked spokes were spread out uselessly in the air...
   ..., and with the naked spokes which were spread out uselessly...

3. Orlando asked what we wanted to be standing out in the rain for and he added merrily that we should come on over there so we didn't get wet ; and he merrily told/asked us to come on over there so we didn't get wet.

4. ...it somehow seemed to correspond to/to fit the impulse behind what Effing...

5. The city had been taken hold of by a lunatic spirit.

6. metaphor

7. The encounter with Orlando had imposed a new set of images on us, and it henceforth cast us under its spell.

8. l. 18:   rudeness
   l. 24:   imagination
   l. 32:   singularity
   l. 48:   mystery

II. Questions on the text

1. Why does the scene described seem to Marco to be trivial and incongruous at the same time?

After having distributed some more fifty-dollar bills among complete strangers chosen at random Marco and Effing are on their way back home when they come across a quite decent and normal-looking black man of about Marco's age. There's nothing unusual about this incident apart from the fact that irrespective of a clear and cloudless sky the man is seeking shelter from the rain he pretends is falling by carrying the skeleton of an open umbrella which consists of nothing but the bare spokes without any cloth. Marco and Effing are invited to join the black man in his illusive world and they willingly do so.

2. Describe the effects the scene has on Marco's and Effing's behavior and mental attitude.

Marco really appreciates the idea of Effing's joining in Orlando's game. Both Marco and Effing know that the comedian's show does not really make sense and is even absurd, but they accept the illusion as something real and thus keep it alive. They find out that imaginary things can come into existence if man pretends that they do exist and that imagination can get so strong that even the most absurd ideas become actual facts for those who are able to accept them as being real. Walking in non-existent rain under a broken umbrella seems to Marco nonsensical and at the same time as real as spreading money among anonymous strangers in the streets of Manhattan.

3. *Explain the importance of the scene as "a premonition of things to come". Refer to the novel as a whole.*

As the weather and – according to Effing – the outcome of banking transactions are subject to abrupt and unpredictable alterations, man must have devices such as the broken umbrella ready for everything that might occur suddenly and unexpectedly. Thus this scene has a decisive impact on both Marco and Effing as an omen of things to happen and which will be followed by crucial and far-reaching changes.

Presuming to be invincible, thanks to Orlando's broken but magic umbrella, Effing forces his death to occur on the predicted day by exposing himself to heavy downpours of rain thus catching a fatal pneumonia. Following this, Marco twice happens to become reasonably prosperous and forfeits his wealth again in less than no time. He finds and then loses his grandfather as well as his father. Moreover, he gets the chance to become a father himself, but is then bereaved of his child and eventually loses Kitty too. And finally Marco finds out about the missed chances in his life because due to Victor's advance in knowledge he was hampered from ending his "unparentedness" at an earlier stage.

4. *"Fifty-dollar bills were walking around in strangers' pockets" [ll. 30–31]. Outline the background of this statement. Go beyond the text.*

Shortly before his anticipated death Thomas Effing insists on giving back the 20,000 dollars he once took from the Gresham brothers in his cave in Utah. As the three rascals had obviously robbed the money from "anonymous strangers" who for obvious reasons cannot be traced back he wants the money to be spread in fifty-dollar bills among deserving people who are unknown to him and who belong to physically or mentally handicapped or socially underprivileged groups. The distribution of the money is to be carried out following a detailed and elaborate plan in varying areas of New York.

III. Comment/Composition

1. Moon Palace – *a work of art and a work* on *art.*

   As "every man is the author of his own life" – according to Uncle Victor – he bears full responsibility for his biography whether he simply lives his life in a figurative sense, or whether he literally notes down the events as an autobiographer. *Moon Palace* is the narrator's attempt to come to terms with those fragments of his life story which he can remember and which seem important to him. Thus in his initial trials as a writer he concentrates with modest success on such topics as money, clothes, orphans, and suicide which have fundamentally defined the course of events in his life so far. Marco's biography being closely connected with the fate of other persons, his story presents itself as a patchwork of various loosely connected incidents with hardly any chronological order. Since the place of action has prevailingly been shifted to the narrator-protagonist's mind there is only a restricted reliability as for the objective truthfulness of events reported. On the other hand, the importance of words as conveyors of meaning is emphasized due to blind Thomas Effing's being dependent on their accurate, unadulterated usage. Furthermore, the works of visual art such as Blakelock's *Moonlight* and Julian Barber's paintings are exclusively presented by means of words. Marco even refuses to have his vision of these works of art disturbed by the view of the real paintings, as the description given by Effing is more detailed, direct and impressive than reality could ever be. The overwhelming power of words also becomes evident in Effing's obituary. The words and the way they are uttered by Effing seem to be so convincing that Marco – without any evidence – can't help believing in the truth, honesty and sincerity of the report.

   Apart from literature and painting it is music which plays a decisive role throughout the novel. Whereas Victor obviously appears to be a fairly gifted clarinettist with a promising career at first, Marco's efforts to play the instrument are doomed to failure from the very beginning. The clarinet in its case which Marco is almost robbed of in Central Park deteriorates in its condition but still accompanies him further on as a symbol of his connection with Uncle Victor and his family, respectively.

2. "There are no coincidences. That word is used only by ignorant people." *Discuss Thomas Effing's statement. To underline your opinion refer to relevant passages in the novel.*

   Thomas Effing is convinced of his capacity to change and shape the material world at his own will only through his thoughts. Thus by means of telekinesis and because in his opinion the whole world is made up of electricity he claims to have caused the New York black-out in 1965. Effing admires Tesla, the inventor of the alternating current, and unexpectedly happens to meet him four times in the course of half a century.

   Whether the reader agrees with Effing on his theory or not there is no denying the fact that coincidences are among the most striking structural elements of the novel. Most decisive in this respect seems to be "unparented" Marco's getting a job at Thomas Effing's, thus finding his grandfather and his father at the same time and consequently detecting the roots of his identity. Victor and Solomon come very close to meeting each other three times by chance. In retrospect their last encounter in Saint Paul explains to Marco Victor's hasty return to Chicago.

   Marco sees the movie *Around the World in Eighty Days* together with Uncle Victor in Chicago. When after eleven years and by mere accident he comes across the same film again in New York this marks the beginning of the continuous deterioration in his personal situation eventually leading to his physically and mentally almost suicidal stay in Central Park.

The most striking coincidence, however, is connected with the moon. After a meal with Kitty and Zimmer at the Moon Palace restaurant, whose neon sign has always deeply impressed him, Marco opens a fortune cookie whose motto proclaiming the moon as the future he will hit upon nine months later when he reads Tesla's autobiography after Effing's death. Marco realizes that behind all this there must be some significance regarding his own destiny, but he is unable to grasp its full meaning.

Leistungskurs Englisch (Baden-Württemberg): Textaufgaben Landeskunde
Aufgabe 1: Europe's Modern Monarchs

By all odds, the medieval institution of the monarchy should be dead in modern Europe. It violates the egalitarian principles of democracy. Its rituals and trappings are dated and often ridiculous. And its powers have been pruned almost to the vanishing point. Yet the astonishing fact is that in this final quarter of the 20th century, monarchies are flourishing in Western Europe. Today, Europe's royals are riding a crest of popularity that is unprecedented in modern history. Public opinion polls show pro-roylist sentiment running 80 percent and higher in some countries. None of the reigning monarchs faces serious political opposition. Europe's kings and queens are now exerting an influential hand in matters of state, commerce – and, of course, style. All the royal houses in Europe are seen by their people as revered symbols of stability, continuity and national unity.

And monarchs are not just for show. The current European royals are a disciplined, hard-working lot who have found effective new ways to play their roles. Queen Elizabeth II has blossomed from a willful young woman into a dignified sovereign who exerts a steadying, humanizing influence on public policy.

The royal renaissance is, in large measure, a tribute to the adaptability of Europe's sovereigns. After a post-war wave of Labor and Socialist governments tried to legislate monarchy into oblivion – or, at the very least, to curtail it dramatically – the royal houses set about mastering the delicate distinction between reigning and ruling. They took to heart the idea of 19th-century social scientist Walter Bagehot, who wrote that the king's role was "to be consulted, to encourage and to warn". Much of the authority of today's sovereign is accomplished by little more than a raised eyebrow here, a disapproving frown there. This is deliberate and necessary.

Each European sovereign receives the prime minister at a regularly scheduled audience, usually once a week. The meetings range from Denmark's cursory 15-minute report on business to England's carefully planned 90-minute review of the affairs of state. In theory, the monarch is there to listen, not to promote a point of view. Queen Elizabeth seldom hesitates to voice her concerns. Since confidentiality is the cornerstone of these meetings, many prime ministers have found the weekly chats extremely useful. "You cannot imagine," says former Prime Minister Edward Heath, "how important it is to have someone like Elizabeth in whom you can confide completely, and know that not a word will leave the room."

If anything, Europe's royals and the institution they embody are more credible now than at any other time in the last half-century. With a knighthood or a royal medal, Europe's monarchs can ennoble their citizens. With quiet diplomacy and gentle persuasion, they can influence a nation's course. With a dignified, soothing presence, they can provide a sense of continuity. "The main thing about monarchy is that it is always there," says Norway's Prince Harald. "It is a stabilizing factor, one that presidents can't give. For the king represents everyone, not just a single party." As the next generation of royalty prepares to ascend the throne, there is every indication that Western European-style monarchy will endure for a long time to come.

547 words

by Scott Sullivan, in Newsweek, November 19, 1984, abridged

Vocabulary:

line 2:	egalitarian	–	favouring the doctrine of equal rights for all citizens
line 2:	trappings	–	ornaments or decorations, expecially as a sign of public office
line 3:	to prune	–	to cut back, to reduce
line 5:	crest	–	top of a wave
line 8:	to exert	–	to bring into use
line 18:	oblivion	–	state of being quite forgotten
line 18:	to curtail	–	to restrict, to reduce
line 36:	soothing	–	calming

I. Language

1. Vocabulary (ohne Wörterbuch zu bearbeiten)
   Give synonyms or paraphrases for the following words and expressions; keep to the given context.
   a) 3–4: "Yet the <u>astonishing</u> fact is that in this <u>final</u> quarter of the 20th century, ..."
   Find a synonym; don't change the sentence. (2 VP)
   b) 7–8: "None of the reigning monarchs <u>faces serious political opposition.</u>"
   Paraphrase; you can change the sentence. (3 VP)
   c) 24: "Each European sovereign <u>receives</u> the prime minister at a regularly <u>scheduled</u> audience, ..."
   Give paraphrases; you may change the sentence. (2 VP)
   d) 29: "... many prime ministers have found the weekly <u>chats extremely useful</u>."
   Give suitable synonyms; don't change the structure of the sentence. (3 VP)

2. Grammar and Style (ohne Wörterbuch zu bearbeiten)
   a) "<u>Europe's</u> Modern Monarchs"
   Why is the possessive case used here? (1 VP)
   b) 9–10: "All the royal houses of Europe are seen by their people ..."
   Why is the passive voice used here? (1 VP)
   c) 29: "... many prime ministers have found the weekly chats extremely useful."
   Explain the use of the tense. (1 VP)
   d) Which linguistic indicators can be found in the text to show that it is written in American English? (2 VP)

II. Comprehension

Please answer the following questions in complete sentences. Keep to the (direct or indirect) information which is given in the text; use your own words as far as possible, but do not quote.

1. What is the difference between 'reigning' and 'ruling'?
   (80–100 words) (4 VP)
2. Which are the reasons for the popularity of Europe's modern monarchs?
   (70–90 words) (3 VP)
3. How do Europe's modern monarchs exercise their influence?
   (60–80 words) (3 VP)

III. Comment

Choose <u>one</u> of the following topics: (200–300 words) (10 VP)

1. Is it better to have a monarch or a president – give reasons.
2. What is a constitutional monarchy?
3. Which are the functions of the British Monarch?

IV. Translation (30 VP)

Since the Queen came to the throne in 1952 her reign has seen the British monarchy adapt to major changes in Britain's position in the world and in British society. A large proportion of the dependencies over which she reigned on her accession have become independent members of the Commonwealth, of which she is Head, and many of whose
5   members continue to recognise her as head of State. Modern communications enable the Queen and the royal family to make more overseas visits than ever before. In Britain, television has brought them much closer to the people, and meetings with ordinary men and women at home and abroad have accelerated the trend towards making the British monarchy a less aloof institution, while still evoking the national
10 memory of centuries of history. The Queen personifies both national and Commonwealth unity, and the entire royal family play a supporting role, undertaking arduous programmes. A combination of the formal and the informal is a special feature of today's monarchy, combining traditional pomp and ceremony with direct contact with people from all walks of life in their towns or at work. Both in Britain and during
15 Commonwealth tours, 'walkabouts' – mingling with the crowds – have become a popular feature.

204 words

from: The Monarchy in Britain, a Central Office of Information pamphlet, 1981

Vocabulary

line 3:	dependency	–	country governed or controlled by another
line 8:	to accelerate	–	to increase the speed of
line 9:	to evoke	–	to call up
line 12:	arduous	–	needing and using up much energy

Lösungsvorschlag

I. Language
1. Vocabulary
   a) Yet the amazing/surprising fact is that in this last quarter of the 20th century ...
   b) Hardly anybody in the legislature, the government or the political parties is earnestly/really against the reigning monarch.
   None of the reigning monarchs is confronted with real resistance/antagonism in public institutions/life.
   c) Each European sovereign grants the prime minister regularly planned/arranged audiences ...
   d) Many prime minsters have found the weekly conversation/talks/exchange of views very valuable/helpful/advantageous.
2. Grammar and Style
   a) The possessive case is chiefly used of people, countries and animals.
   If the 'of' construction were used, one would need the definite article (The Modern Monarchs of Europe) and the alliterative rhythm would be broken.
   b) 'All the royal houses of Europe' is the more important part of the sentence, and the beginning of a sentence carries a stronger stress.
   c) The present perfect 'have found' is used here as it describes something that began in the past and still goes on.
   The weekly chats were useful in the past and still are so at present.
   d) American spelling: willful (BE: wilful) line 14
                              Labor (BE: Labour) line 17
   chiefly American usage of the word: scheduled (line 24)

II. Comprehension
1. "Ruling" means the actual governing of a country, the wielding of political power. In Britain you can say that the Houses of Parliament and the Government rule the country because parliament makes the laws and the government executes and enforces them.
   "Reigning" describes the rather ceremonial role the monarch plays in the running of his country. In Britain, everything is done in the name of the monarch, but he really has no political power but to advise and warn.
2. Europe's modern monarchs are seen as symbols of stability, continuity and national unity – and that is quite an important factor in our world where many traditionally held values are becoming increasingly destabilized. This, in a large measure, is due to the monarch's flexibility in rapidly changing times.
   And I think you should not underestimate the romantic factor that goes along with having a monarch – just look at the number of magazines living on news and gossip about the royal family.
3. Europe's monarchs heed the advice of W. Bagehot and they do not attempt to get (or get back) any political power, but they are there "to be consulted, to encourage and to warn." (line 21) They talk with their prime ministers and ministers regularly and in absolute confidence, and during these audiences they can – and do – express their opinions, encourage, warn and advise. Their advice is taken seriously because normally they have reigned longer (and have seen, read, and signed countless State papers) than their prime minister has ruled.

III. Comment

1. I would rather have a monarch than a president – but only, of course, in the framework of a constitutional monarchy. Monarchs, as Norway's Prince Harald says, represent continuity and neutrality. That is something monarchs can do much better as they never depend on any party or group of parties to get elected, and presidents are only elected for a certain length of time. A president is either elected directly by the people (as in France and the US) and then he has political power and is part of the executive, making it difficult not to be partisan; or he is elected indirectly (as in the Federal Republic of Germany) and has mostly ceremonial functions and not much power. Either way a president somehow has some party affiliations and thus is not really neutral.
   A monarch inherits his position and there can be no dicussion whom he represents – he "represents everyone, not just a single party", as Prince Harald says (line 39), and can be absolutely impartial. For example, Belgium probably would have split up years ago had it not been for its king who is accepted as representing all Belgians, not just one group. Of course, if a monarch should be a weak character, some problems could arise – but a country can be governed without much active involvement on the part of the monarch.
   Another argument for a monarch is that he – normally – stays on the job for life. Thus he amasses a lot of information and experience and can help his country and its government in the informal role of an 'elder statesman' who can give advice when he is consulted.

2. The term 'constitutional monarchy' means that the monarch does not have absolute power as regards the governing of his people. The monarch is fitting into the framework of a government, a parliament and a judicial system.
   Thus the monarch has only limited political powers – in most present-day monarchies hardly any power at all – and he has to be very careful in using his discretionary powers or he might have to face a constitutional crisis or even find himself without a job in a newly created republic. In England, the current arrangement is that the monarch reigns but he does not rule; that means that everything is done in his name but he himself is not active politically.
   About a hundred years ago the situation was quite different (although even then you could talk about a constitutional monarchy). Queen Victoria, for example, had the possibility of choosing a prime minister according to her political sympathies, and her prime minister then had to look if he could find a majority in parliament. This was easier than it would be today as the party system had not evolved as we know it today, and royal patronage played quite important a role.
   So the term 'constitutional monarchy' only says that the monarch works within the framework of a constitution – but it does not define how much political power the monarch actually has in such a kind of monarchy.

3. The Crown (which represents both the Sovereign and the Government) is the symbol of supreme executive power, but in general its functions are exercised by ministers responsible to Parliament. The United Kingdom is governed by Her Majesty's Government in the name of the Queen. There are, however, many important acts of government which still require the participation of the Queen.
   The Queen summons, prorogues (discontinues until the next session without dissolving) and dissolves Parliament. Normally she opens the new session with a speech from the throne outlining her Government's programme. Before a Bill becomes a legal enactment, it must receive the Royal Assent.
   As the 'fountain of justice', the Queen confers peerages, knighthoods and other honours. She makes appointments to many important state offices, although on the advice of the Prime Minister or, in some cases, the appropriate Cabinet Minister. She

appoints and dismisses, for instance, government ministers, judges, members of the diplomatic corps and colonial officials. As Commander-in-Chief of the armed services she appoints officers, and as Supreme Governor of the established Church of England she makes appointments to its bishoprics and some other senior offices.
In international affairs, the Queen has the power to conclude treaties, to declare war and to make peace, to recognise foreign states and governments, and to annexe and to cede territory.

IV. Translation

Seit die Königin 1952 den Thron bestieg, hat sich die britische Monarchie während ihrer Regierungszeit an große Veränderungen in der britischen Gesellschaft und der britischen Stellung in der Welt angepaßt. Ein großer Teil der abhängigen Gebiete, (über) die sie bei ihrer Thronbesteigung regierte, sind unabhängige Mitglieder des Commonwealth – dessen Oberhaupt sie ist – geworden, und viele seiner Mitglieder erkennen sie weiterhin als Staatsoberhaupt an. Moderne Transport- und Kommunikationsmittel machen der Königin und der königlichen Familie mehr Besuche in Übersee möglich als jemals vorher. In Großbritannien hat das Fernsehen sie dem Volk viel näher gebracht, und Treffen mit Normalbürgern in Großbritannien und im Ausland haben die Entwicklung beschleunigt, die britische Monarchie zu einer weniger sich zurückhaltenden/erhabenen Einrichtung/Institution werden zu lassen, während sie noch immer die nationale Erinnerung an Jahrhunderte der Geschichte wachruft/wachhält. Die Königin verkörpert sowohl die Einheit der Nation als auch des Commonwealth, und die ganze königliche Familie übernimmt eine unterstützende Rolle und nimmt anstrengende Programme/Aufgaben auf sich. Eine Verbindung des Formalen und des Informellen ist ein besonderes Merkmal/Charakteristikum der heutigen Monarchie, die traditionellen Pomp und Zeremonie mit direktem Kontakt mit Menschen aller Klassen in deren Städten oder bei deren Arbeit verbindet. Sowohl in Großbritannien als auch bei Reisen im Commonwealth sind "walkabouts" – ein 'Bad in der Menge'/ein spontanes sich in die Menschenmenge begeben – eine beliebte Einrichtung geworden.

> **Leistungskurs Englisch (Baden-Württemberg): Textaufgaben Landeskunde**
> **Aufgabe 2: Religions in America**

If anyone were to ask you how many Americans belong to a church or temple or synagogue, you would probably say, "Almost all." But the facts are startling. Actually, 66,000,000 Amerikans – 35.4 percent of the population – are not church members.

Why are so many Americans members of no church? Has religion failed them?

There is no simple answer. Many of those who do not belong to any church have taken the hard rather than the easy road, for they have withstood great pressure in order to stay out of groups it is so easy to join, and for which high approval from neighbors and community is given.

We all know that many people join a church out of habit, or out of respect for their parents, or for family tradition. Some do so in order to wear the badge of respectability, or get a testimonial to good character. Businessmen and professional men often prize the "contacts" they make in a church or a temple; their careers are helped if they conform to the community's values. Some parents want their children to have a religious education, even though they themselves feel no strong need for a formal faith. Other parents want their children to "belong", to do what others in the group do, to associate with the "right" people, to make a good marriage with a decent and moral spouse. In addition, in these terrible days of anxiety and fear – with war and annihilation hanging over our heads – millions upon millions, not knowing where to turn or whom to trust, attend religious services which promise inner peace, salvation and life eternal. It is small wonder that ours is a day of a great religious revival.

Do the 66,000,000 Americans who refuse to "believe" in this way have anything in common – except the fact that they do not go to church? Yes. They share an important attitude – the idea that it is possible to be "religious", moral, decent, without joining a group and worshiping en masse. They believe the individual can get as close to the idea of God as any cleric or institution can bring him. They hold the high faith that men are responsible for what they do with their lives, how they think and live. They do not feel the need for "official" forgiveness or rituals or catechisms to make them men of virtue. They believe, as did some of the greatest men the human race has produced, that personal morality is not dependent on organized religion.

Is it bad for our country that so many Americans hold this independent attitude? The Founding Fathers did not think so: they created the First Amendment to the Constitution for the specific purpose of letting each man have the right to his own form of worship – or his own independence from religious groups.

The very richness and creativity of American life rests on the fact that people can and do think different thoughts, hold different beliefs, live in different ways. James Madison, "the Father of the Constitution", went so far as to say: "The best and only security for religious liberty in any society is a multiplicity of sects. Where there is such a variety of sects, there cannot be a majority of any one sect to oppress and persecute the rest."

Democracy means that people respect the rights of others, including the right to be different. Only dictatorships want everybody to think, feel, and act the same.

576 words
from: Religions in America, edited by Leo Rosten, copyright 1955, 1975 by Cowles,
Communications Inc.; renewed copyright 1983 by Cowles Broadcasting Inc.

Vocabulary:

line 2:	startling	–	surprising, shocking
line 6:	to withstand	–	to resist
line 11:	testimonial	–	attestation, confirmation
line 17:	annihilation	–	complete destruction
line 25:	cleric	–	clergyman, priest

I. Language

Deal with the following underlined words of expressions within their given context.

1. Vocabulary (ohne Wörterbuch zu bearbeiten)
   a) 10: "Some do so in order to wear the badge of respectability, ..."
   Paraphrase; the sentence structure may be changed. (2 VP)
   b) 17–18: "... – with war and annihilation hanging over our heads – ..."
   Paraphrase; the sentence structure may be changed. (1 VP)
   c) 30: "Is it bad for our country ..."
   Give a synonym; don't change the sentence. (1 VP)
   d) 35–39: "James Madison, 'the Father of the Constitution', went so far as to say: 'The best and only security for religious liberty in any society is a multiplicity of sects. Where there is such a variety of sects, there cannot be a majority of any one sect to oppress and persecute the rest'".
   Explain; you don't have to keep to the structure of the sentences. (5 VP)

2. Grammar and Style (ohne Wörterbuch zu bearbeiten)
   a) 1: "... how many Americans belong to a church (?) ..."
   Why is the auxiliary verb 'to do' not used in this question? (1 VP)
   b) 5–6: "Many of those who do not belong to any church have taken the hard ... road ..."
   Can the relative pronoun be left out? Explain why (or why not). (1 VP)
   c) 9: "... many people ..."
   Give the opposite. (1 VP)
   d) 28–29: "They believe, as did some of the greatest men the human race has produced, that personal morality is not dependent on organized religion."
   Explain the use of the tenses. (2 VP)

II. Comprehension

Please answer the following questions in complete sentences. Keep to the (direct or indirect) information given in the text when answering question 1; do not quote.

1. Which reasons are given in the text for joining a church; do you feel they are valid for you?
   (90–110 words) (4 VP)
2. Can you give examples of what is said in lines 34–35: "The very richness and creativity of American life rests on the fact that people can and do think different thoughts, hold different beliefs, live in different ways."
   (90–110 words) (4 VP)

3. If you look at modern life, how do you regard the influence of religion on people's lives?
(60–80 words) (2 VP)

III. Comment (10 VP)
Choose one of the following topics: (200–300 words)
1. The 1st Amendment begins: "Congress shall make no laws respecting an establishment of religion, or prohibiting the free exercise thereof; ..." What are your thoughts about that?
2. Why do quite a number of young people join sects or cults?
3. The text ends with the following sentences: "Democracy means that people respect the rights of others, including the right to be different. Only dictatorships want everybody to think, feel and act the same." Comment on that idea.

IV. Translation (30 VP)

Some people feel guilty because they do not belong to a church. Is there any reason for this? Of course there is. As children, they were taught to hold certain beliefs; but as they grew up they found that they no longer believed these things. This did not happen because they wanted to disbelieve or because they were "bad" people. It happened
5   because their experiences and development and intelligence led them to question or doubt their earlier beliefs. Often they long for the sense of security they got from their childhood faith. Often they would like to believe again what they once accepted. But they cannot honestly do so, and they feel uneasy about "betraying" the good people who taught them what a good life means.
10 Yet they have done nothing wrong. On the contrary, they refuse to give lip service to what they do not really believe. They have the courage to stand up for their own convictions and try to maintain their own integrity.
No, the nonconformist need not feel guilty. He is following some of the greatest visions of the human spirit – to seek dignity without dogma.
195 words   from: Religions in America, edited by Leo Rosten

Vocabulary:
line 8:   to betray – to be disloyal to, to act deceitfully towards
line 14: dignity   – the quality that earns or deserves respect

Lösungsvorschlag

I. Language
1. Vocabulary
   a) Some do so in order to be held in high esteem.
      Some do so in order to appear as citizens of (high) standing.
      Some do so in order to appear to be reputable citizens/people.
   b) – with war and annihilation threatening us –
   c) Is it negative/deplorable for our country?
   d) James Madison, 'the Father of the Constitution' even claimed/said: "The best and only security for religious freedom in any society is a great number of sects. Where there is such a number of different sects, there cannot be one sect which has so many members as to enable it to oppress and persecute the rest.'

2. Grammar and Style
   a) The interrogative adverb 'how', together with the adjective and noun 'many Americans' is the subject of the question; in such questions you must not use the auxiliary verb 'to do'. In indirect questions the interrogative form of the verb changes to the affirmative form.
   b) The relative pronoun 'who' cannot be left out because it is the subject of the defining relative clause.
   c) few people
   d) The past tense is used for activities that ended at a definite time in the past. The author uses the past tense 'did' because he is of the opinion that the 'greatest men' mentioned are all dead.
      The present perfect is used for activities that began in the past and still go on; obviously the author thinks that the human race might produce more great men as he uses the present perfect 'has produced'.

II. Comprehension
1. Many people join a church out of respect for their family, because their parents and grandparents belonged to it. Other people feel that if you want to be respectable you must belong to a church (otherwise you might be an outsider), and you may even profit from the contacts you make there.
   Some parents feel that their children should have a religious education and later decide if they want to belong to or leave the church; they don't want them to be outsiders as most of their friends belong to a chruch.
   Feelings of fear and uncertainty which pervade our world also make people join a church in the hope of attaining inner peace and finding a foundation to build their lives on. I think that those are valid reasons.

2. If you go to any bigger American city you can find many restaurants which serve ethnic food, and you can eat your way around the world, so to speak. This may be an unimportant and relatively trite example but it shows the variety of the American way of life.
   The same is true if you look at the various newspapers, magazines and books which are published in the US in many languages. This cultural diversity had much influence on American life although it is difficult to pinpoint single examples.
   The Americans have the richness of their varied cultural backgrounds, and the freedom to strike out on their own; this then accounts for the creativity and richness of American life.

3. In our modern life it seems that religion has very little real influence. Many people seem to belong to a church only because it is the proper thing to do. Even political parties with the adjective 'Christian' in their names do not have particularly Christian principles and programmes.
That there is a certain yearning for a religious life can be seen by the number of new sects which seem to attract quite large a following.

III. Comment

1. The first amendment expresses a sentiment which has been realized in very many countries; and it is an idea whose time had come some centuries ago.
For the citizen of a modern state it is an unbearable idea that one religion should be regarded as better than another, and subsequently have some official influence. Religion is something so personal and individual that it cannot and should not be decreed by any temporal power, be it the state or any other governmental agency.
History shows that as soon as religion and political power get mixed up you ultimately have conflicts and wars which are waged in the name of religion but the underlying motives normally are power and greed. Whether you look at the thiry-years' war or the inquisition, people were killed in the name of religion but the real interest of the people involved was power.
The most recent example of such a conflict is the trouble in Northern Ireland. Although the lines are drawn strictly along religious affiliation, everybody knows that religion as such is not at all the problem (even though Ian Paisley never tires of saying the opposite). The tragedy is that one group, the Protestants, have the political and economic power, and that the other group, the Catholics, want equal opportunities. The fact that the Protestants have the power has nothing to do with their religion as such but is the result of a long historical development.
I am of the opinion that something like the first amendment should be included in the constitutions of all states.

2. It seems to me that the text gives a hint which can help to find an answer. On line 16–19 it says that in our days of anxiety and fear many people turn to religion for inner peace.
Young people seem to be especially vulnerable as they are still looking to find their way through life, and the present-time situation does not offer them too much hope and security. It seems that in our apocalyptic situation there is not much to turn to, hardly anybody seems to be able to answer your questions. The world might be blown up tomorrow (if you think of the discussions as regards the deployment of new nuclear missiles in Europe, or if you look at the snail-paced disarmament negotiations where nobody appears to be willing to reduce the huge overkill capacity we have), either because of some aggression or – worse still – because of some misunderstanding, by accident, so to speak. Who can tell you – credibly – what you should do, which moral values can still be trusted?
This is the situation the sects and cults exploit. They offer the security of a life in a group with certain rules and taboos, and normally there is a guru who tells you what to believe. Your personal responsibility is taken away from you – but you are given security instead. It is understandable that young people succumb to this temptation but I doubt very much if this is a proper solution of their problems and difficulties.

3. This idea appears to sum up nicely the difference between a democratic and a totalitarian system of government.
A democratic system is much more complicated as it must reckon with many different points of view – the art of tolerance and compromise could be a motto of a de-

mocratically run society. Therefore the temptation to change to a totalitarian system is understandable; it is much easier to run a society where everybody thinks, feels and does the same.

But if you think of two books describing totalitarian systems, 'Brave New World' and '1984', you can see where such a society can lead to. Basic human rights are disregarded and those who do not conform are either spiritually broken or eliminated. Either solution is inhuman, and it really is a retrogression to times when a uniform and strictly organized society and state might have been acceptable and a good thing to have.

From the time of the French revolution, with its slogan of liberty, fraternity and equality, the development has been towards the rights of the individual as opposed to the rights of the state. This development has consequently led to democracy as we know it, with universal suffrage and a guarantee of basic human rights. It seems to me that this form of society is the best we have come to in the course of history (there might be better ones, of course, which have not been realized yet) and we should do our utmost to defend it against any attempt to impose a dictatorship.

IV. Translation

Einige Menschen fühlen sich schuldig/haben ein schlechtes Gewissen, weil sie keiner Kirche angehören. Gibt es dafür einen/irgendeinen Grund? Natürlich gibt es den. Als Kinder wurden sie gelehrt/wurde ihnen beigebracht, bestimmte/gewisse Glaubensinhalte zu glauben, aber als/indem sie aufwuchsen, stellten sie fest, daß sie an diese Dinge nicht mehr glaubten. Dies geschah nicht, weil sie nicht glauben wollten oder weil sie "schlechte" Menschen waren. Es geschah, weil ihre Erfahrungen, ihre Entwicklung und ihre Intelligenz sie dazu brachten, ihre früheren Glaubensinhalte in Frage zu stellen oder anzuzweifeln. Oft sehnen sie sich nach dem Gefühl der Sicherheit, das ihnen der Glaube ihrer Kindertage gab. Oft würden sie gerne wieder glauben, was sie (früher) einmal als wahr anerkannten. Aber dies können sie ehrlicherweise nicht tun, und sie fühlen sich unbehaglich/beunruhigt, die guten Menschen zu hintergehen/zu verraten, die sie lehrten, was ein gutes Leben bedeutet/heißt.

Jedoch haben sie nichts falsches/schlechtes getan. Im Gegenteil, sie weigern sich, ein Lippenbekenntnis von etwas abzulegen, was sie in Wirklichkeit nicht glauben. Sie haben den Mut für ihren eigenen Glauben geradezustehen/einzustehen/Sie ehren ihre eigenen Überzeugungen und versuchen, ihre eigene Integrität/Rechtschaffenheit zu erhalten.

Nein, der Nonkonformist braucht sich nicht schuldig zu fühlen/kein schlechtes Gewissen zu haben. Er folgt einer der größten/bedeutendsten Visionen des menschlichen Geistes – nach Würde ohne Dogma zu streben.

Leistungskurs Englisch (Baden-Württemberg): Textaufgaben Landeskunde
Aufgabe 3: New Arrivals: Dream and Reality

To German-born cardiologist Andreas Grüntzig, 42, America is the land of the free – and the home of the 15-hour workday. Grüntzig, who at 18 fled form East Germany to West Berlin before there was a wall, took a medical degree at Heidelberg University and eventually rose to be chief physician of a Zurich hospital before moving to Atlanta two years ago. He appears to be one of the few recent immigrants to be so completely happy. Whether they have arrived in the U.S. legally or illegally, on a permanent basis or temporarily, many other immigrants find their new life a mixed blessing: all too often, there is a sense of loss and uncertainty about the future. As it was for those who entered the U.S. before them in the great waves of 19th and early 20th century immigration, the transit is difficult, at times heart-breaking. Indeed, the new immigrants face complications that earlier arrivals never had to confront.

The difference for Grüntzig, perhaps, is that unlike most new arrivals, he was hastening toward something when he came to the U.S. rather than fleeing. Says Damian Smyth, 47, a San Francisco attorney who was born in Northern Ireland: "When a professional comes here, he gets a sort of immediate respect and he's not obliged to spend three generations climbing up the social ladder." Grüntzig explains: "It was never a question of money. There simply was not enough support for my work in Zurich. In America there is still a pioneering sense, a willingness to try something new. All over this country, there are the very best in my field. I like the competition, the challenge of knowing that I must do my finest work because others are doing their finest work."

In contrast, as TIME correspondents around the U.S. discover, many other immigrants, particularly the unskilled, are apprehensive about competition and challenge. Says a 22-year-old illegal entrant named Alfonso who escaped the El Salvador civil war eight months ago and now works in a Houston factory: "At home you are either rich or poor, that is the only discrimination. Here, bosses discriminate against workers, whites against blacks, legals against illegals. Even within the same race there is discrimination. I think it is because in America there is so much competition. People need any edge they can get to move ahead."

For almost all new arrivals, however, the greatest surprise is culture shock. Even American movies, books and television shows have not prepared them for U.S. reality. Lev and Zalina Gurevich, Soviet Jews who fled Rostov-na-Donu and landed in the U.S. in 1980, initially disagreed where to settle. Lev. 45, a conservatory teacher and violinist, wanted to remain in Europe because "we are European people." Zalina, 27, a pianist, insisted on the U.S. "because America is a country of refugees and immigrants and I wanted to be treated absolutely the same as other people." They have been, but their experience has been strange. The Gureviches had preconceptions about America from reading and listening to the Voice of America. The reality has been different. They hated New York: "Dirt. Danger. Crazy People." They like Orlando, Fla., where they have settled, but they remain uncomfortable with much that surrounds them.

544 words

by Spencer Davidson, in Time, February 22, 1982, abridged.

Vocabulary:

line 1:	cardiologist	–	a doctor specializing in heart ailments
line 32:	conservatory	–	school of music
line 36:	preconceptions	–	ideas or opinions formed in advance, before getting proper or enough knowledge or experience
line 37:	Voice of America	–	international American radio station, broadcasting in English and many foreign languages

I. Language

1. Vocabulary (ohne Wörterbuch zu bearbeiten)
   Substitute the words and expressions with synonymous words or terms; keep to the context.
   a) 4: "... and <u>eventually</u> rose to be chief physician of a Zurich hospital ..."
   Paraphrase; you may change the sentence. (1 VP)
   b) 5–6: "He <u>appears</u> to be one of the <u>few</u> recent immigrants to be so <u>completely</u> happy."
   Find synonyms; don't change the sentence. (3 VP)
   c) 6–7: "... on a <u>permanent</u> basis or temporarily, ..."
   Explain; the sentence may be changed. (2 VP)
   d) 7: "... many other immigrants find their new life a <u>mixed blessing</u>: ..."
   Paraphrase; you can change the sentence. (2 VP)
   e) 32: "... initially <u>disagreed</u> where to <u>settle</u>."
   Give suitable synonyms; don't change the structure of the sentence. (2 VP)

2. Grammar and Style (ohne Wörterbuch zu bearbeiten)
   a) 12–13: "... he <u>was hastening</u> toward something when he came to the U.S. ..."
   Why is the continuous form used here? (1 VP)
   b) 20: "... I must do my <u>finest</u> work ..."
   Give the opposite of 'finest'. (1 VP)
   c) 23: "... Alfonso <u>who</u> escaped the El Salvador civil war ..."
   Can the relative pronoun be left out? Say why (or why not). (1 VP)
   d) 37–38: "The reality <u>has been</u> different. They <u>hated</u> New York."
   Explain the use of the tenses. (2 VP)

II. Comprehension

Please answer the following questions (in complete sentences). When answering questions 2 and 3 keep to the direct or indirect information which is given in the text; no quotations, please.
1. Grüntzig says: "In America there is still a pioneering sense, a willingness to try something new." (line 17–18) Can you give examples of this attitude?
   (80–100 words) (3 VP)
2. What can new immigrants expect when they come to the USA?
   (90–110 words) (4 VP)
3. What effect does it have on a text if you have many quotations (in this text five new immigrants are quoted)?
   (80–100 words) (3 VP)

III. Comment (10 VP)

Choose <u>one</u> of the following topics: (200–300 words)
1. Why is the term "melting pot" more a myth than a reality?
2. What are the reasons that cause people to emigrate to another country?
3. If you had to emigrate, where would you emigrate to – why?

IV. Translation (30 VP)

The United States is not homogeneous; it is a pluralistic society, a nation of groups. The long cherished belief that the United States has been a great "melting pot" in which people from all nations and cultures have blended into what are called "Americans" is in many respects a myth. During the late 20th century a strong trend among minorities
5 (primarily among blacks and white ethnics) to organize groups to press for social change made the American people increasingly conscious of the characteristics of the various ethnic and racial groups that make up the national population.

Until about 1860 the population of the United States was relatively homogeneous. ... After the Civil War, however, larger numbers of immigrants began to arrive from the
10 countries of central and southeastern Europe. ... Most were non-English, non-Protestant, and markedly different in culture and language from the earlier Americans. The immigrants established their own neighbourhoods and rapidly developed ethnic societies, clubs, newspapers, and theatres; and their living areas became distinctive cultural and social enclaves within the larger society.

15 The immigrants, however separate, in large part were not denied access to the mainstreams of U.S. life. Those with ability and intelligence usually achieved success – and some achieved greatness.

202 words

from: "United States of America", in Encyclopaedia Britannica, 15th edition (1985), 29: 176–177

Vocabulary:

line 2:	to cherish	–	to keep (hope, feelings, etc.) alive in one's heart
line 7:	ethnic	–	hier: ethnisch
line 12:	neighbourhood	–	(people living in a) district
line 16:	mainstream	–	dominant trend, tendency

Lösungsvorschlag

I. Language

1. Vocabulary
   a) And finally/in the course of time/after some time rose to be chief physician of a Zurich hospital ...
   b) He seems to be one of the handful of/not numerous recent immigrants to be so totally/wholly happy.
   c) Whether they have arrived in the US in order to stay there for good/to live there forever or just for some time/for a certain length of time ...
   d) Many other immigrants find their new life is not only/just happy and successful, it also presents difficulties and problems.
   e) ... initially were not of one mind where to live permanently.

2. Grammar and Style
   a) The continuous form is used here as this form denotes (a state or) an action which is in progress and which is expected to come to an end.
   The continuous form is used here as the writer is concerned with action in progress, with action that has begun but not ended.
   b) most inferior/most awful/worst
   c) The relative pronoun of the defining relative clause cannot be left out as it is the subject of the clause.
   d) The present perfect tense 'has been' is used to show that an activity began in the past and extends into the present. The past tense form "hated" is used here because the activity had come to an end at a definite point in the past.

II. Comprehension

1. The legend that somebody starts washing dishes and ends up a millionaire still holds true in America – and not only as regards money.
   If you look at the number of inventions and discoveries the US is far ahead of the rest of the world; you can see that if you look at the number of Nobel Prizes awarded, for example. The space program is another case in point; the willingness and zest to cross new borders freed money and energies.
   A student raised a few thousand dollars and started tinkering in a garage – and in a few years' time this enterprise has become a multi-million dollar business – Apple Computers.

2. a) uncertainly, sense of loss, complication (line 6–11)
   b) respect and support (line 14–17)
   c) competition and challenge (line 18–20, 27–28)
   d) discrimination (line 24–28)
   e) culture shock (line 29–39)

3. Many quotations make a text more interesting because various points of view are presented with more immediacy and directness, and much more lively, straight from the horse's mouth, so to speak. (Though the choice of quotations is made by the author of the text and it can therefore still be biased.)
   Thus we do not only get the author's point of view. It is easier for the reader to follow the author's arguments if they are 'strengthened' by quotations from the people concerned.

III. Comment

1. The term 'melting pot' is more a myth than a reality because only the immigrants who came to the US till about 1860 were, more or less, homogeneous in their ethnic and religious background. They mainly came from Britain, Germany and the Netherlands, were of Germanic stock and almost exclusively Protestant. There was no difficulty of all of them becoming 'American' in a relatively short time. Later, when immigrants from other parts of Europe came to the US, the difference in religion, language and culture was much more pronounced. Many of these groups kept their separate cultural and religious identity up to the present, and they are proud of it.
   The latest group that has not 'melted' are the Spanish speaking Americans, mainly from Puerto Rico and Mexico. There is no great trend towards assimilation at the moment, but a valid judgement is not possible because most of them are 1st-generation immigrants. Religion plays a relatively minor role in the 'melting pot' as the example of the Irish shows; although predominantly Catholic they very soon became mainstream Americans.
   Racial minorities have always been excluded from the idea of the 'melting pot', and there are more such minorities now and a considerable percentage of the population belongs to racial minorities. They take a rather opposite view by stressing the differences (if you think of the slogan 'black is beautiful', for example).
   Thus one can say that the immigrants have not 'melted down' into a homogeneous group, but that America is a 'nation of nations' (or at least a nation of groups), a pluralistic nation.

2. Basically there are three reasons that cause people to emigrate: political, economic, and personal reasons.
   Political oppression often causes people to look for another country with more freedom to emigrate to. Thus, for example, Carl Schurz left Germany after the abortive revolution of 1848 and emigrated to the US where he played an important part in American politics, first as a US Senator and later as Secretary of the Interior under President Hayes. Other examples are the people who left Russia after the revolution in 1919, or the Jews and other 'unwanted' people after Hitler's rise to power in Germany, or the Vietnamese after the communist victory.
   In Germany, many sons and daughters of farmers who had no hope of ever getting a farm of their own decided to emigrate to the US where a homestead was theirs if they worked the land for five years. Many of the Mexicans who now – most of them illegally – immigrate into the US, hope to make a better living than before.
   A certain adventurism, or the hope of being able to realize one's plans and dreams in a new country also make some people emigrate. As the example of the German cardiologist shows, it need not be a question of money, but of better opportunities and a greater challenge. Of course there are other personal reasons, from an unhappy love affair to an unsavoury past, which can cause people to emigrate.

3. If I had to emigrate, and if I had a free choice, I think I would go to Australia. This country has quite a European flavour as it is a former British colony and most of its inhabitants are of British stock. On the other hand, Australia is in the southern hemisphere, and the Australian is quite a character in his own right, and not a European.
   The continent of Australia with its greatly differing regions also make it attractive; you have areas with a temperate climate and regular rainfalls, coastal areas with a warm maritime climate, and the wild and almost uninhabitable interior (where only the Aborigenes can survive).

All these features give a newcomer a very wide range of possibilities if he wants to start a new life there. If I went there I would first try to get to know the different parts of the country and then select a place where I would like to live and then try to find a job which would suit me. As Australia is such a fascinating country I cannot say which area this would be or what kind of job I would try to get.

IV. Translation

Die Vereinigten Staaten sind nicht homogen/einheitlich, sie sind eine pluralistische Gesellschaft, eine aus Gruppen zusammengesetzte Nation. Der lange hochgehaltene/geschätzte Glaube, daß die Vereinigten Staaten ein großer Schmelztiegel sind, in dem Menschen aus allen Nationen und Kulturen in das, was man "Amerikaner" nennt, verschmelzen, ist in vieler Hinsicht ein Mythos. Während des späten 20. Jahrhundert machte eine starke Neigung/Trend bei Minderheiten (hauptsächlich bei schwarzen und weißen ethnischen Gruppen), sich in Gruppen zusammenzuschließen, um auf soziale Änderungen zu dringen, dem amerikanischen Volk zunehmend die Charakteristika der verschiedenen ethnischen und rassischen Gruppen, aus denen sich die Bevölkerung zusammensetzt, bewußt. (machte ... aufmerksam ... auf.)

Bis ungefähr 1860 war die Bevölkerung der Vereingiten Staaten verhältnismäßig homogen/einheitlich. Nach dem Bürgerkrieg jedoch begann eine größere Zahl Einwanderer aus den Ländern Mittel- und Südosteuropas in die Vereinigten Staaten zu kommen. Die meisten waren keine Engländer, keine Protestanten und ihrer Kultur und Sprache nach deutlich von den früheren Amerikanern verschieden. Die Einwanderer richteten sich in eigenen Stadtteilen ein und entwicklten rasch ethnische Gesellschaften, Klubs, Zeitungen und Theater; und ihre Siedlungsgebiete/Stadtteile wurden besondere/deutlich kenntliche kulturelle und soziale Enklaven innerhalb der größeren Gesellschaft. Den Einwanderern, wie abgesondert sie auch waren, wurde großenteils der Zugang zum Hauptstrom des amerikanischen Lebens nicht verwehrt. Diejenigen mit Fähigkeiten und Intelligenz waren in der Regel erfolgreich – und einige erreichten große Bedeutung/wurden sehr bedeutend.

> **Leistungskurs Englisch (Baden-Württemberg): Textaufgaben Landeskunde**
> **Aufgabe 4: Britain: A Smouldering Anger**

Racial conflict has become almost a commonplace in Britain: in recent months, there have been racial clashes in London, Manchester, Birmingham and Liverpool. And in the Lancashire city of Blackburn there were 25 street assaults on Asians in May and June alone. But horrified as most Britons are by the upsurge in racial violence, a growing number of them are even more concerned by what they see as the very real prospect that the character of their nation will be changed by the swelling tide of colored immigrants, currently mostly Asian, that is flooding into the British Isles. And giving voice to this fear in the House of Commons recently, Tory M.P. John Stokes declared that continued immigration threatened "a takeover of this country by alien peoples ... a violation of our homes ... a rape of the English race."

Stokes's doom-filled language drew laughter from the government benches, but at a time when Britain is suffering from high unemployment, housing shortages, and rising costs of living, even some longtime Labor Party stalwarts have begun to wonder if it is not time to call a halt to immigration from black and Asian nations. "Enough is enough", says Robert Mellish, formerly the Labor Party's chief whip and M.P. for the working-class district of Bermondsey in London. "I am not a racist, but I am not a humbug. This tiny island of ours isn't much more than a dot on the map, and the time has come to face the problem ... We cannot take them all. We've done more than our share. Now we must go for the full integration of those who are already here."

Like so many of Britain's contemporary problems, the immigration issue grew out of the country's imperial heritage. Until 1962, a citizen of any Commonwealth nation could move to Britain and settle down there without formalities. At that point, alarmed by the influx of immigrants from the Caribbean countries and the Indian subcontinent, Parliament passed an act, that in essence restricted permanent residence in Britain to people who already held British passports, and the dependents of people already resident in the U.K.

Detached observers mostly agree that there is a very real – and mounting – tension between Britain's white and colored inhabitants, particularly in working-class areas of major cities where the various ethnic communities are pressed very closely together. Quite clearly, many Asians feel resentment over the treatment that they have received in Britain.

In rebuttal, many whites argue that, more and more, they feel like outsiders in their own country. In Dewsbury, a small Yorkshire mill town of 60,000, white residents complain about the Pakistanis who have settled among them and whose segregated life-style is so greatly different from their own. "We get children coming to school who have never mixed with white children, who have no toilet training, who have never held a knife or fork and who habitually speak nothing but Urdu at home", complains a local schoolteacher.

Appeals to tolerance and tradition by themselves seem unlikely to dispel the unease raised in the minds of many otherwise moderate Britons by the mutation that has already occurred in their country. "The question", said John Stokes in his speech to Commons, "is not of maintaining good relations but of preserving our national identity. A smouldering anger is building up among ordinary people against further immigrants."

567 words

from Newsweek, August 9, 1976, abridged and edited

Vocabulary:

line 3:	assault	–	violent and sudden attack
line 4:	upsurge	–	increase
line 11:	doom-filled	–	extremely pessimistic
line 13:	stalwart	–	loyal supporter (of a party etc.)
line 25:	dependent	–	hier: family member (depending upon an adult for home, food etc.), mainly children and old parents
line 27:	detached	–	impartial, not influenced by others
line 32:	in rebuttal	–	as a counter-argument

I. Language

1. Vocabulary (ohne Wörterbuch zu bearbeiten)
   Explain the underlined words or terms by using synonyms or paraphrases; keep to the given context.
   a) 1–2:   ... in <u>recent</u> months, there have been racial <u>clashes</u> in London...
   Find synonyms; keep to the sentence structure. (2 VP)
   b) 13:   ... Labor Party stalwarts have <u>begun</u> to <u>wonder</u> if...
   Give synonyms; don't change the sentence. (2 VP)
   c) 20:   ... Britain's <u>contemporary</u> problems, ...
   Paraphrase; the sentence can be changed. (1 VP)
   d) 39–40:   Appeals to tolerance and tradition by themselves <u>seem unlikely</u> to <u>dispel</u> the <u>unease raised</u> in the minds of many otherwise moderate Britons ...
   Paraphrase; you don't have to keep to the structure of the sentence. (5 VP)

2. Grammar and Style (ohne Wörterbuch zu bearbeiten)
   a) 1–4:   Racial conflict <u>has become</u> almost a commonplace in Britain ... And there <u>were</u> 25 street assaults on Asians in May and June alone.
   Explain the use of the tenses. (2 VP)
   b) 6–7:   ... The character of their nation will be changed by the <u>swelling tide</u> of colored immigrants ... that is <u>flooding</u> into the British Isles.
   What figure of speech is this?
   What does the author want to express? (2 VP)
   c)   Which linguistic indicators can be found in the text to show that this text is written in American English? (1 VP)

II. Comprehension

Please answer the following questions (in complete sentences, of course). Keep to the information which is given in the text when you answer question 1, but please do not quote.

1. Which problems do minorities face? (90–110 words) (4 VP)
2. Why do colored people come to Britain? (60–80 words) (2 VP)
3. In line 17 Britain is described as "... not much more than a dot on the map ...". In the time of the Empire, Britain was seen as the center of the world. Explain this change of attitude.
   (90–110 words) (4 VP)

III. Comment (10 VP)
Choose one of the following topics: (200–300 words)
1. Do you think the restrictions regarding the settlement of colored people in Britain (line 22–26) justified – or should there be absolute freedom of movement. Give reasons for your opinion.
2. What can be done to overcome prejudices against minorities?
3. Which are the connections Britain still has with the Commonwealth?

IV. Translation (30 VP)

As a member of the Commonwealth Britain participates in a system of mutual consultation and co-operation. While the nature of the Commonwealth normally precludes the formulation of central policies on, for example, economic and foreign affairs, the extent of the consultation and cooperation is not only of benefit to the member countries, but can also contribute generally to international understanding.

Diplomatic representatives exchanged by Commonwealth countries are called High Commissioners and are equal in status with Ambassadors. High Commissioners traditionally deal directly with a wider range of government departments than do their foreign counterparts, and Commonwealth High Commissioners in London have a particular relationship with Buckingham Palace deriving from the recognition of the Queen as head of the Commonwealth.

In addition to maintaining regular contact through normal diplomatic channels, heads of Government and other ministers meet regularly at conferences, and Commonwealth ministers hold discussions when attending international conferences or meetings of the United Nations. At the departmental level, senior civil servants and technical experts visit and consult directly with their opposite numbers. Trade and cultural exhibitions, conferences and conventions of judical, medical, cultural, educational and economic bodies are also held in various parts of the Commonwealth at frequent intervals. At all levels in the conduct of affairs between Commonwealth governments, there is informality and ease of contact helped by a common knowledge of the English language.

225 words
from: Britain and the Commonwealth, A Central Office of Information pamphlet, 1983

Vocabulary:

line 1:	mutual	–	wechselseitig, gegenseitig
line 2:	to preclude	–	to prevent, to make impossible
line 10:	to derive from	–	to have as a source/origin
line 15:	civil servant	–	Beamter

Lösungsvorschlag

I. Language

1. Vocabulary
   a) In the past few months there have been racial conflicts/riots/incidents in London.
   b) Labor stalwarts have started to ask (themselves) if ...
   c) The problems which Britain experiences at the moment.
      The problems which Britain goes through at present.
   d) It appears improbable that appeals to tolerance and tradition by themselves will remove/dissolve the uncomfortable/troubled feelings caused/created in the minds of many otherwise moderate Britons ...

2. Grammar and Style
   a) The present perfect tense 'has become' is used here to show that an activity began in the past and goes on at least until the present.
      The past tense 'were' is used here because the activity ended at a point in time in the past (the text was published in August, the 'were' refers to May and June).
   b) The expression 'the swelling tide ... flooding' is a metaphor. The author uses it to refer to the immense number of colored immigrants coming into Britain.
   c) American spelling: colored/couloured (line 6) Labor/Labour (line 13)
      American usage of the word: segregated (line 34)

II. Comprehension

1. Minorities face discrimination in many fields. Many Britons have difficulties in getting used to the strange and foreign customs and attitudes of the minorities in their country; this can even lead to violent incidents if members of minorities are blamed for problems or if the native population feels threatened.
   Discrimination is most obvious where getting decent housing or well-paid jobs are concerned; but on the other hand, if children come to school without having any idea of the British way of life (cf. line 35–38), it is understandable that they meet with difficulties at school – and without a good basic education it is difficult to get on in life.

2. The living standard in Britian is much higher than in almost all of the developing countries where most of the colored immigrants come from; and this economic fact is the strongest magnet attracting colored immigrants.
   They mainly come from Commonwealth countries because until 1962 they could settle in Britain without any formalities, and there are other ties between Britain and its former colonies. Political persecution at home also causes some people to come to Britain.

3. Before World War I Britain ruled over a vast Empire with colonies in America, Africa and Asia and could be regarded as 'the center of the world'. After giving the Dominions some measure of self-government, the Statute of Westminster in 1931 granted independent and equal status to the countries where European settlement had taken place on a large scale.
   After World War II almost all colonies became independent; e. g. India in 1947 and Ghana in 1957. There still are some small Dependencies and Associated States, but in general they are of not much importance.
   In the course of the 20th century, Britain thus changed from the center of a huge Empire to "... a dot on the map ...".

III. Comment

1. I am of the opinion that some restrictions regarding the immigration of colored people into Britain are justified.
   Unless you think that a country or a nation has no right to have and to keep its own distinctive character and way of life, the number of immigrants must be limited to such a number that does not change the national character. Only after these immigrants have become 'Englishmen' should new immigrants be admitted. (Colored immigrants face additional difficulties as regards assimilation, their color of skin will always make them conspicuous and 'different').
   Another aspect is the economy. If too many immigrants flood into a country there will be severe problems as regards unemployment. The economy of a country can only absorb a certain number of people looking for jobs – and Britain's economy has faced severe problems since the end of World War II (some of them due to the policy of decolonization). Thus there is a limit to the number of immigrants Britain can absorb.
   Theoretically, of course, the right to move to whichever country you want to and to settle there is an ideal which is widely held, and one should try to remove as many restrictions as possible – but, as I mentioned above, there are practical limits to that ideal.

2. Prejudices are – as the word says – premature judgements which are passed before sufficient evidence is in on a given problem. As regards minorities, many people don't take the trouble of getting to know members of a minority in order to come to valid conclusions. Thus one of the tasks would be to gather enough information to be able to come to a proper understanding of the beliefs, ways of life, customs and attitudes of any given minority. Then you might be able to understand those people and not be side-tracked by superficial impressions. That of course calls for a certain measure of compassion and willingness to learn.
   On the other hand, the members of a minority should themselves try to do everything they can to create an atmosphere of understanding so that it is easier for the people living around them to accept them and their special way of life. That does not mean that a minority must assimilate and adopt the life-style of the majority, thus losing its cultural, religious and perhaps racial identity. But an atmosphere of mutual understanding and trust should be created that no group need feel threatened or insecure.
   Parliament should also pass laws to get discrimination under control and try to prevent violent incident such as described in the text. Other organizations (for example trade unions) and the media could also play an important role; but individual action is the most relevant aspect to overcome this problem.

3. The Commonwealth is a voluntary association of some 40 independent sovereigns states which has evolved from the former British Empire. The only legal connection that binds all Commonwealth countries is their acknowledgement of the British monarch as Head of the Commonwealth. In some countries she is Head of State, some are republics and a few have their own monarchs.
   All other connections are of an informal nature, working through a system of consultation and co-operation.
   There are regular meetings of Heads of Government, permitting a frank exchange of views. While the nature of the Commonwealth normally precludes the formulation of central policies, however by trying to reach the highest measure of understanding of each other's point of view, Commonwealth members are able to make a special con-

tribution to the international efforts needed to find solutions to problems facing the world community, There are also meetings of finance, education health and law ministers.

As most Commonwealth countries originally based their parliamentary, legal, educational and many other organizations on the Britishs model (although much has been altered by now), there is co-operation and consultation in these fields, too.

Trade among Commonwealth countries is another strong tie – although it has fallen off during the last decades. Many Commonwealth countries have been brought into connection with the Common Market since Britain joined this organization in 1973.

But one of the strongest ties might be the English language which makes many of the above mentioned contacts possible. Though it is the native tongue only in some countries, it is spoken and understood in all of the Commonwealth.

IV. Translation

Als (ein) Mitglied des Commonwealth nimmt Großbritannien an einem System gegenseitiger Beratung(en) und Zusammenarbeit teil. Während die Natur/Struktur des Commonwealth normalerweise die Formulierung/Festlegung zentraler politischer Vorhaben in, z. B., wirtschafts- und außenpolitischen Angelegenheiten ausschließt, ist das Ausmaß/der Umfang der Beratung und Zusammenarbeit nicht nur von Nutzen/zum Wohl der/für die Mitgliedsländer, sondern kann auch allgemein zur internationalen Verständigung/Verständnis beitragen.

Diplomatische Vertreter, die zwischen/unter Commonwealthländern ausgetauscht werden, heißen High Commissioners und haben die gleiche Stellung wie Botschafter. Traditionellerweise treten High Commissioners mit einer größeren Zahl (von) Ministerien direkt in Kontakt als ihre ausländschen Kollegen; und Commonwealth High Commissioners in London haben eine besondere Beziehung zum Buckingham Palace/Königshaus, die sich aus der Anerkennung der Königin als Oberhaupt des Commonwealth ergibt/ableitet.

Zusätzlich zur Aufrecherhaltung regelmäßigen Kontaktes durch normale diplomatische Kanäle/auf normalem diplomatischen Wege treffen sich (die) Regierungschefs und andere Minister regelmäßig auf Konferenzen; und Commonwealthminister besprechen sich, wenn sie an internationalen Konferenzen oder Sitzungen der UN teilnehmen. Auf Ministeriumsebene treffen sich höhere Beamte und technische Fachleute und beraten direkt mit ihren Kollegen. In regelmäßigen Abständen werden auch Handels- und Kulturausstellungen, Konferenzen und Treffen juristischer, ärztlicher/medizinischer, kultureller, erziehungswissenschaftlicher und wirtschaftlicher Vereinigungen/Körperschaften in verschiedenen Teilen des Commonwealth abgehalten. In der Abwicklung von Angelegenheiten zwischen Commonwealthregierungen besteht auf allen Ebenen eine Ungezwungenheit und Leichtigkeit des Kontaktes, die durch eine gemeinsame/allgemeine Kenntnis/Beherrschung der englischen Sprache gefördert/unterstützt werden.

> **Leistungskurs Englisch (Baden-Württemberg): Textaufgaben Landeskunde**
> **Aufgabe 5: The Disintegrating Commonwealth**

What is the Commonwealth worth to us? Less and less in economic terms. We have been putting less into it and getting less out. Indeed, you could even argue that we would have been better off without it in recent years. Certainly we have suffered acute withdrawal symptoms.

5 As a trading area, which is the way most people see the Commonwealth, it is dying on its feet. The system of Commonwealth preferences – reduced or nil tariffs on goods imported from other Commonwealth countries – was set up in 1932, at the height of the Depression. The scheme was for the Commonwealth countries to help one another and protect themselves from outside competition.

10 At that time, Britain still took a third of the Commonwealth countries' exports and they took a third of our imports. But now, the old principle of complementarity, which was once the basis of British trade with the Commonwealth, has disappeared. Before the war, the Commonwealth supplied Britain with cheap raw materials and Britain used the Commonwealth as a captive market for its manufactured products. Now the developing
15 countries are building up industries of their own. And Britain, since the early 1950s, has introduced a series of measures designed to protect and encourage its own agriculture at the expense of some Commonwealth producers.

Trade among Commonwealth countries in recent years has been falling fast. In 1965 they sold about a third of all their exports to one another. Today they sell less than a
20 quarter – and the same has been happening to imports. As trade among Commonwealth countries has slumped, trade between them and the United States has bounded ahead.

Britain has followed the trend. We have nearly halved our exports to the Commonwealth countries in the last decade, and our imports from it are down by almost a third. In Britain's case it has not been the US that has been our fastest-growing market so much as
25 the Common Market. Britain has fast become less important as a trading partner for most Commonwealth countries. The proportion of Canada's exports sold to Britain has dropped by half and Australia's by a third. Among the main Commonwealth countries, only Nigeria is still dependent on Britain for as much as a third of its imports, and only three countries, Malawi, Zambia and Ghana, have recently been buying a larger share of
30 their imports from us.

Without a doubt, the reorientation of Commonwealth trade has added to Britain's economic troubles. Our share of world markets for manufactures has fallen throughout the decade – but it has fallen fastest of all in the Commonwealth.   433 words
from: 'Knocking the wealth out of the Commonwealth' by Frances Cairncross,
The Observer, 24 January 1971

Vocabulary:
line 3–4:	withdrawal symptoms	–	Entzugserscheinungen
line 6:	tariff	–	taxes on goods imported or exported
line 8:	Depression	–	time of very serious economic difficulties with much unemployment
line 11:	complementarity	–	cf. complement: that which makes something complete
line 14:	captive market	–	fester Absatzmarkt
line 21:	to slump	–	to fall steeply or suddenly

I. Language

1. Vocabulary (ohne Wörterbuch zu bearbeiten)
   Give synonyms or paraphrases for the following words and expressions; keep to the given context.

   a) 1–2: We have been <u>putting</u> <u>less</u> into it and <u>getting</u> <u>less out</u>.
   Paraphrase; the sentence may be changed. (2 VP)

   b) 5–6: As a trading area ... it is <u>dying on its feet</u>.
   Explain; you can change the sentence. (2 VP)

   c) 11–12: ... the old principle ... has <u>disappeared</u>.
   Find a synonym; don't change the sentence structure. (1 VP)

   d) Before the war, the Commonwealth <u>supplied</u> Britain with cheap raw materials; in the last <u>decade</u> this trade <u>has been falling</u> fast. Recently only some smaller countries have been buying a larger <u>share</u> of their imports from us.
   Give suitable synonyms; do not change the structure of the sentences. (5 VP)

2. Grammar and Style (ohne Wörterbuch zu bearbeiten)

   a) 1: <u>Less</u> and less in economic terms.
   Explain the underlined word grammatically; give the positive and the superlative forms. (2 VP)

   b) 2–3: ... we would have been better off without it in recent years.
   Start the sentence with: <u>If</u> ... (1 VP)

   c) 18–19: Trade among Commonwealth countries in recent years <u>has been falling fast.</u> In 1965 they <u>sold</u> about a third of all their exports to one another.
   Explain the tenses and their use. (2 VP)

II. Comprehension

Please answer the following questions. For the first question keep to the direct or indirect information which is given in the text; do not quote.

1. Explain the old principle of complementarity which was once the basis of British trade with the Commonwealth. Why does it not work any more?
   (90–110 words) (4 VP)

2. Why are many Commonwealth Countries more oriented towards the US while Britain has joined the Common Market?
   (60–80 words) (2 VP)

3. The text says that the Commonwealth is disintegrating. Which other links, besides economic links, could help to keep it together?
   (90–110 words) (4 VP)

III. Comment (10 VP)

Chose <u>one</u> of the following topics: (200–300 words)

1. Describe the development from Empire to Commonwealth.
2. Describe some British attitudes towards the Common Market (also known as EEC, European Economic Community).
3. What kind of an organization is the Commonwealth?

IV. Translation (30 VP)

The Commonwealth is a voluntary association of 44 independent sovereign states which has evolved from the former British Empire. The total population of member states, which vary in size from several hundred million people to a few thousand, is over 1,000 million, a quarter of the world's population. Their peoples are drawn from all the world's main races and from all continents. As some members are very rich and others very poor, the Commonwealth acts as a bridge between rich and poor nations. Britain participates fully in all activities of the Commonwealth and values it as a means of consulting and co-operation with peoples of widely differing cultures, thereby contributing to the promotion of international understanding and world peace. Membership of the Commonwealth involves no legal or constitutional obligations, finding its main expression in consultations between governments and in the large number of organisations concerned with cooperation in areas such as agriculture, health, law, economics, education and youth affairs.

Practically all Commonwealth countries are members of the United Nations, and many belong to other regional and political groupings. Since 1973 Britain has been a member of the European Community and a number of Commonwealth countries have been brought into a new partnership with the Community through the Lomé Conventions on aid, trade and development.

215 words
from: Britain and the Commonwealth, A Central Office of Information pamphlet, 1981

Vocabulary:
line 7: to participate in – to take part in; line 9: promotion – Förderung;
line 10: to involve – hier: mit sich bringen;
line 12: to be concerned with – hier: beschäftigt sein mit, zu tun haben mit

Lösungsvorschlag

I. Language

1. Vocabulary
   a) We have invested less and our profits/imports are shrinking/decreasing.
   b) As a trading area it is very much on the decline although it still works.
   c) The old principle ... has gone/vanished.
      The old principle ... is not valid any more.
   d) Before the war, the Commonwealth provided Britain with/sent Britain raw materials; in the last ten years this trade has been decreasing/slumping rapidly. Recently only some smaller countries have been buying a larger amount/part of their imports from us.

2. Grammar and Style
   a) Less is the comparative form; the positive form is little, the superlative form is least.
   b) If we had not had it in recent years we would have been better off.
   c) The present perfect "has been falling" is used here to describe an activity which started in the past and extends into the present (cf. 'in recent years'); the past tense "sold" must be used here because the activity was complete at a definite point in time in the past (cf. '1965').

II. Comprehension

1. The old principle of complementarity means that Britain used to import things it did not have (raw materials, some agricultural products) from Commonwealth countries, and exported its industrial goods to the Commonwealth countries which almost exclusively relied on British goods. But now the developing Commonwealth countries are in the process of building up their own industries and Britain loses access to some overseas markets; on the other hand, Britain's protectionist measures in agriculture hinder Commonwealth exports into Britain. These are the reasons why trade between Britain and the Commonwealth (and among other Commonwealth countries as well) is falling fast.

2. In the decades since the end of World War II certain shifts as regards trade have taken place. The USA trade mainly with Europe and Asia, and in Asia the US have geographical advantages over Britain. Britain's proximity to mainland Europe adds to the attraction of the Common Market which is one of the richest and most active trading areas of the world.

3. While economic links have weakened, there are many other links which could help to keep the Commonwealth together. Apart from a common knowledge of the English language in all Commonwealth countries (which in itself is a strong tie) the many conferences and consultations among these countries help to create mutual understanding and often lead to co-operation in many fields. Many Commonwealth countries have organized their political, judicial and educational systems along British lines which helps to keep relations alive. Britain also helps the developing Commonwealth countries in many areas; for example a great number of students from the Commonwealth study at British universities.

III. Comment

1. After Britain had built its empire during the last centuries and the beginning of this, World War I was an important point for the beginning development of the Commonwealth. The colonies where European settlement had taken place on a large scale (Canada, Australia, New Zealand and South Africa) had been granted a system of 'responsible government' before the war, but then the restrictions on the complete independence of the self-governing colonies (or 'Dominions' as they came to be known) gradually dropped away. The Dominions were autonomous communities within the British Empire, equal in status, unified by a common allegiance to the crown. This principle was legally formulated in the Statute of Westminster in 1931.
After World War II the process of decolonization started, with India and Pakistan becoming independent in 1947; and Ghana, the first African colony, in 1957. Since that day almost all the colonies which formerly had belonged to the British Empire have become independent. There still are some colonies left – mostly small islands with few inhabitants. These Dependencies and Associated States have considerable self-government, with Britain having general responsibility for defence, internal security and foreign relations. Thus the British Empire has become the Commonwealth, the development went from an empire governed by one nation to a group of independent nations which are equal in status – and the only formal link holding them together is their recognition of the British monarch as the head of the Commonwealth.

2. Quite a number of Britons are very enthusiastic about the Common Market because they feel that joining Europe is the only thing Britain can do. The economic ties with the Commonwealth have steadily become weaker in the past decades, the special Atlantic relationship with the USA has shown increasingly clearly that Britain definitely is the junior partner – in spite of Britain's independent nuclear deterrent. At the same time the Common Market has developed into one of the most important markets and trading blocks of the world – and it might even become something of a political power if the process of political unification finally gets under way as many people want. Thus it was only a logical step that Britain joined the Common Market in 1973 in order to make its voice heard in Europe – and many Britons were in favour. On the other hand, many Britons vehemently opposed – and still oppose – Britain's entry into the Common Market. They think Britain should not be drawn into Europe's squabbles (that had traditionally been Britain's policy for centuries) but should stay independent. They also see constitutional problems as the Common Market has its own decision-making process which may undermine the role of the British parliament and rob Britain of its sovereignty – vital problems might no longer be decided in the Houses of Parliament, but in Brussels or Strasbourg. The connections with the Commonwealth will become weaker and thus an important part of Britain's past might sooner or later come to an end.

3. The Commonwealth is a voluntary association of about fifty independent sovereign states which has evolved from the former British Empire. The Queen is acknowledged as head of the Commonwealth. Membership of the Commonwealth involves no legal or constitutional obligations. The Commonwealth Secretariat is the central co-ordinating body. As such the Commonwealth is an absolutely unique organization in many respects: an organization which has no clearly defined programm or binding legal obligations but still it works (and has been doing so for quite a number of years!); a group of states which includes the former ruler and its former colonies, but it works ; it includes very rich and very poor nations, very big and very small countries with widely differing interests – but it does not fall apart.
The main function of the Commonwealth is the consultation and co-operation among its members. This consultation and co-operation covers a wide range of subjects and

takes place on various levels; from meetings of heads of government to meetings of experts and private organizations. The English language is a strong common bond and facilitates contact, and as many former colonies have adopted some British ways of organizing their state and society there is a common basis to start from. The most important areas of consultation and co-operation are law, trade, aid, education, health, communication, defence and scientific co-operation.

IV. Translation

Das Commonwealth ist ein freiwilliger Zusammenschluß 44 unabhängiger souveräner Staaten, das sich aus dem früheren British Empire entwickelt hat. Die Gesamtbevölkerung der Mitgliedsstaaten – die in der Spanne/Größe von einigen 100 Millionen bis zu wenigen Tausend schwanken – umfaßt/beträgt über 100 Millionen, ein Viertel der Weltbevölkerung. Ihre Völker stammen aus allen großen Rassen/Hauptrassen der Welt und von allen Kontinenten. Da einige Mitglieder sehr reich und andere sehr arm sind, dient das Commonwealth als Brücke zwischen reichen und armen Nationen/Ländern. Großbritannien nimmt voll an allen Aktivitäten/Vorhaben des Commonwealth teil und schätzt es als ein Mittel, mit Völkern sehr unterschiedlicher Kulturen zu beraten und zusammenzuarbeiten und damit zur Förderung der internationalen Verständigung/Verständnis und des Weltfriedens beizutragen.

Die Mitgliedschaft des Commonwealth bringt keine rechtlichen/gesetzlichen oder verfassungsmäßigen Verpflichtungen mit sich. Sie findet ihren Hauptausdruck/wichtigsten Ausdruck in Beratungen zwischen Regierungen und in der großen Zahl (von) Organisationen, die mit der Zusammenarbeit auf Gebieten wie z. B. Landwirtschaft, Gesundheitswesen, Justiz/Rechtsprechung, Wirtschaft, Erziehung und Jugendfragen beschäftigt sind/zu tun haben.

Praktisch alle Commonwealthländer sind Miglied der UN, und viele gehören anderen regionalen und politischen Gruppierungen an. Großbritannien ist seit 1973 Mitglied der EG, und eine Anzahl Commonwealthländer sind durch die Lomé Konvention über (Wirtschafts)Hilfe, Handel und Entwicklung in eine neue Partnerschaft mit der EG gebracht worden/getreten.

Leistungskurs Englisch (Baden-Württemberg): Textaufgaben Landeskunde
Aufgabe 6: Parents scupper plans for grammar schools

Government hopes of bringing back grammar schools have foundered, partly because of opposition form parents who prefer to send their children to comprehensives.
When parents were asked whether, in principle, they would like grammar schools restored, 54 percent said yes, according to a national survey published last week. In practice, however, the evidence shows that most do not want to see their own children's comprehensives replaced by grammar schools.
Middle-class parents have found their children do well in comprehensives and fear new grammar schools would cream off the best pupils, leaving other schools at a disadvantage. Some have moved house to be near a successful comprehensive.
In some areas, Conservative councils are pressing ahead with comprehensive schemes to replace existing grammar schools – with the support of a majority of parents.
Gloucestershire County Council is to issue public notices for a comprehensive system in Stroud, including a sixth-form college. The closure of two voluntary controlled grammar schools is proposed.
Dorset County Council will vote this week on a proposal from its education committee to replace Sherborne's two grammar schools with a single comprehensive.
In Gloucestershire, the council overturned a proposal from the education committee for a 'super' grammar school in Stroud to take a small group of the ablest pupils. Polls of parents in the nonselective schools showed a majority of between 60 and 80 percent in favour of a fully-comprehensive system.
Mr. Martin Alder, a governor of one of the Stroud grammar schools and a member of the parents' group fighting for comprehensive education, claimed that only a minority of children would benefit from a selective system while the rest would be in secondary modern schools unable to offer the same breadth and depth of curriculum as a comprehensive.
Mr. Alder said parents had been particularly impressed by the fact that the A-level results of sixth-form colleges compared favourably with those of grammar schools. (The sixth-form colleges have maintained an A-level pass rate of 75 percent though their numbers have trebled since 1977.)
The Stroud grammar school lobby based its case on the contention that 'nothing promised by the comprehensives can match the overall performance and potential of the schools we have'.
In Dorset, parents voted by an average of 2:1 that Sherborne's selective schools should go. A county council official said the schools had to be reorganised because of falling rolls.
Though some attempts to save existing schools, such as Skegness, in Lincolnshire, and Cheltenham grammar school, have succeeded for the moment, efforts to introduce new ones have been a failure and have caused bitter divisions among Conservatives. In the London Borough of Richmond, a Tory councillor who advocated a return to grammar schools is believed to have cost the Conservatives control of the council. In the furore that followed, fellow Conservatives affirmed their support for the borough's highly successful comprehensive schools.
In Redbridge, London, plans to extend the selective system were dropped. A poll among parents showed 48 percent wanted a fully comprehensive system and 44 percent wanted selection in some form. About nine percent of the borough's pupils attend grammar schools.

In Hereford and Worcester, a proposal for a super grammar school to educate the ablest children was dropped after parents expressed fears that it would rob the surrounding schools of bright children.
50 In Solihull, the council also backed down from its plans for selection after a fierce campaign by parents whose children were prospering in the comprehensives.

581 words
Judith Judd, Education Correspondent, The Observer, Sunday 11 November 1984

Vocabulary:

	to scupper	–	to ruin
line 1:	to founder	–	to break down
line 30:	contention	–	argument used in a dispute
line 43:	poll	–	survey (line 4)
line 50:	to back down from	–	to give up

I. Language

1. Vocabulary (ohne Wörterbuch zu bearbeiten)
   Deal with the following underlined words or expressions within their given context.
   a) 8: "... would cream off the best pupils, ..."
   Paraphrase; the sentence can be changed. (2 VP)
   b) 21–23: "(Mr. Alder) ... claimed that only a minority of children would benefit ..."
   Paraphrase; you may change the sentence. (3 VP)
   c) 30: "The Stroud grammar school lobby based its case ..."
   Explain; you may change the sentence structure. (1 VP)
   d) 34–35: "... because of falling rolls."
   Find synonyms; don't change the sentence. (2 VP)
   e) 43: "... plans to extend the selective system were dropped."
   Give synonyms; do not change the structure of the sentence. (2 VP)

2. Grammar and Style (ohne Wörterbuch zu bearbeiten)
   a) 23–24: "... in secondary modern schools unable to offer the same breadth ..."
   What grammatical construction is "in secondary modern schools unable"?
   Rewrite by using a subordinate clause. (3 VP)
   b) 26–27: "... the A-level results of sixth-form colleges ..."
   Why is the abstract noun 'results' used with the definite article here? (1 VP)
   c) 37: "... have succeeded for the moment, ..."
   Explain to use of the tense. (1 VP)

II. Comprehension

Please anwer the three questions in complete sentences. When you answer questions 1 and 3 keep to the (direct or indirect) information in the text and do not quote.

1. Which reasons are given in the text for comprehensive schools and against the selective (tripartite) system? (about 100 words) (4 VP)
2. Describe the British system of education. (about 150 words) (5 VP)
3. How do Conservative politicians react to the trend towards a comprehensive system of education? (about 50 words) (1 VP)

III. Comment (10 VP)
Choose one of the following topics: (200 to 300 words)
1. What are some of the advantages and disadvantages of Britain's famous Public Schools?
2. Early specialization or a broad general education – what do you think more important, and why?
3. "We don't need no education", is the title of an rather well-known pop-song of some time ago.
What do you think about that?

IV. Translation (30 VP)

Scholarship has always been a magic word in education. It suggests a small intellectual élite, selected after rigorous examination to enjoy special status while at school or university. Almost as an afterthought has it been associated with money – and help with the cost of education.

5 This traditional approach to scholarship is slowly evolving into something quite different in the rest of the independent schools.

The emphasis is swinging away from the selection of an intellectual élite to the practical objective of helping parents with the rising cost of school fees. These have consistently risen above the rate of inflation. Independent schools are trying to move away from the
10 concept of a small élite, to widening the whole process to give financial help to as many as possible.

The increasing popularity of sixth-form colleges must concern the independent schools. Many schools now offer sixth-form scholarships both for current pupils and new pupils to enable them to finish their education in the independent sector. It may be argued that
15 the State-school-educated pupil from a family of limited means will thus be helped to acquire greater social self-confidence after enjoying two years in an independent school's sixth form, as well as an academic background for higher education at least as good as in sixth- form colleges.

214 words
compiled from: Clever way to pay the fees, by Julian Ayer, The Observer, Sunday 18 November 1984

Vocabulary:

line 1:	scholarship	–	Stipendium
line 1:	to suggest	–	hier: to bring (an idea) into mind
line 8:	consistently	–	ständig, beständig
line 13:	current	–	hier: derzeitig
line 16:	to acquire	–	go get, to gain

Lösungsvorschlag

I. Language

1. Vocabulary
   a) The grammar schools would select/take/absorb/attract the ablest/most intelligent pupils.
   b) Mr. Alder argued/maintained/said/was of the opinion that only a small number/not many children would profit/be helped/have any advantages ...
   c) The people working for/interested in the opening of the Stroud grammar school based their case ...
   d) ... because of the decreasing number of pupils.
   e) ... plans to enlarge the selective system were given up/abandoned/scrapped.

2. Grammar and Style
   a) It is a participle construction used to shorten the sentence (with 'to be' you can even leave out the participle 'being').
   "... in secondary schools which would be unable to offer the same breadth ..."
   b) The abstract noun 'results' is used with the definite article as it is defined by an 'of-clause'.
   c) The present perfect tense "have succeeded" is used here to show that the activity began in the past and still goes on.

II. Comprehension

1. Parents, expecially those from the middle class, have experienced that their children are successful in comprehensive schools and they are wary of the fact that new grammar schools would attract only the best pupils and lower the standard of existing comprehensives (line 7–9). Not only will just a minority of the children benefit from new grammar schools, the comprehensives might then have less depth and breadth of curriculum as a result (line 21–25). In addition, parents are quite impressed by the A-level results of sixth-form colleges as compared with those of grammar schools.

2. The British system of education can be divided into two sections, the state school system and the independent sector.
   The state school system offers primary schools for all children, and has two different systems in the secondary sector:
   a) The selective system offers three types of schools for a child; grammar schools (more oriented towards the classics and oriented towards a university education), technical schools (whose number is not very great) and secondary modern schools (for all children who cannot attend the first two). The eleven + exam (abolished in some areas) and other criteria decide which school a child can attend.
   b) The comprehensive system has differently gifted pupils in one school, and a streaming system then offers various possibilities to the pupils.
   The independent sector comprises a wide variety of schools which children can attend (after attending independent preperatory schools or state primary schools) after passing a kind of entrance examination.
   The Public Schools are the most famous and best known independent schools.

3. This trend has caused bitter divisions among Conservatives as they are actually more in favour of the selective system. However, they tend to follow the trend towards the comprehensive system as they see that the electorate – the parents – does not honour a trend back to the selective systems, as the comprehensive system is quite successful.

III. Comment

1. Most of the advantages Public Schools have can be summed up in two arguments: the pupils are at school for 24 hours each day, and the teachers are dedicated and are there for the pupils even after lesson and try to develop not only the pupils' intellectual faculties but also their characters and personalities. Thus school is the overwhelming influence in a pupil's life, and school education really has a chance to inculcate the pupil with the values it wants to transmit (of course you can also see that as a disadvantage if you do not agree with those values and feel that the pupils are being manipulated). Intellectually weaker students have better chances as there are tutorials and other possibilities of getting help with the homework and other tasks. Another advantage is the better chances you will have later in life when you want to go to a university or look for a job – if you went to a famous Public School, you will be accepted more readily.

   The disadvantages are that, for one thing, Public Schools have a certain snob-appeal and they have a reputation of mainly accepting upper-class children or children from rich families. The substantial fees are another insurmountable barrier for many people, although there are some scholarships available. Another argument against Public Schools is that it is not good for young people in their most formative years to be growing up away from their families. They lack the experience of growing up in a family and some of them later have certain difficulties to adapt to some aspects of adult life (if you think of the many broken-up marriages we have nowadays, however, it might be an advantage to be able to grow up in harmonious circumstances rather than face daily domestic quarrels).

   In conclusion, I would say that despite all the advantages I would not recommend the Public School to become the norm for all pupils – but their existence should be maintained to offer a wide variety of different kinds of schools.

2. I think a broad general education is better and more important because, basically, you can always specialize when having broad general knowledge – but when you only have specialized knowledge it is rather difficult to change to a new field.

   Apart from this fact it is necessary in our increasingly complex world that your knowledge covers various fields, otherwise you will be helpless in the face of problems outside your special field of knowledge. Thus people or governments might be able to manipulate you and lead you to where you didn't want to go in the first place. History is such a point in question. A famous man once said: "Those who don't know about history are condemned to repeat it." If you think of the struggles it took to secure the basic human rights for everybody, it would be a pity if people were not watchful so that we might finally end up in a society as described in Orwell's 1984. But if you don' know anything about history – how can you resist? Our culture in Europe is based on a long development, starting far back in pre-Christian times. If you want to be a cultured person and live a full life, your education should have such a broad basis that you are conscious of our culture and its roots.

   Even if you look at the situation concerning employment, a general education will help you a lot as there are prognostications that we all will have to change our jobs at least two or three times during our working life.

   So all arguments seem to be in favour of a broad general education, and specialization later in life.

3. The title of that song sounds rather seductive – and I suppose that many young people have come to that conclusion at some point in their lives (but luckily have given up on the idea before it was too late and ruined their lives). It appears that these words appeal to a feeling of wanting to be free, to be able to decide for oneself what to do and what not to do. This feeling may be strengthened when you look at the world

around us. On the one hand our world does not seem ideal (and education is supposed to prepare us to face the world), and on the other hand, many young people don't even get a job after finishing their education. So why bother?

But if you look at the world realistically, you will see that the rat-race for a job is even more difficult for you if you don't have a solid educational basis (although success in school does not guarantee success in life as many statistics show, but you do have better chances).

And if you should want to change the world because you think it is not ideal as it is – then you need a good education even more. Without knowing how our world became what it is now, and without developing clear – and practical – ideas about how to achieve what you want, you will work in vain.

Therefore I think that the idea of not needing education may be seductive, but if you really think about it you'll find that it is wrong.

IV. Translation

Das Wort 'Stipendium' war immer ein Zauberwort in der Erziehung. Es deutet hin auf eine kleine intellektuelle/geistige Elite, die nach (einer) strengen Prüfung ausgewählt wird, und sich (danach) einer besonderen Stellung erfreut, während sie an der Schule oder Universität ist. Fast erst in zweiter Linie hat man es mit dem Gedanken an Geld in Verbindung gebracht – und Hilfe bei den Kosten der Erziehung.

Diese traditionelle Haltung Stipendien gegenüber verwandelt sich langsam zu etwas ganz anderem in den übrigen Privatschulen/Schulen in freier Trägerschaft.

Die Betonung/Schwerpunkt/Nachdruck verschiebt sich von der Auswahl einer intellektuellen/geistigen Elite hin zu dem praktischen Ziel, Eltern mit den steigenden Kosten des Schulgeldes zu helfen. Diese sind ständig stärker gestiegen als die Inflationsrate. Privatschule/Schulen in freier Trägerschaft vesuchen, von der Idee einer kleinen Elite abzugehen/abzurücken, hin zu einer Erweiterung des ganzen Vorganges/Prozesses, um so viele wie möglich finanziell zu unterstützen.

Die zunehmende Beliebtheit der Sixth-Form Colleges muß die Privatschulen/Schulen in freier Trägerschaft beunruhigen/interessieren/betroffen machen/von Belang sein. Viele Schulen bieten jetzt Stipendien für die Prüfungsklassen an, sowohl für ihre eigenen/derzeitigen als auch für neue Schüler, um ihnen zu ermöglichen, ihre Erziehung im Privatschulbereich abzuschließen. Man könnte sagen, daß einem Staatsschüler aus einer ärmeren Familie auf diese Weise geholfen wird, ein größeres soziales Selbstbewußtsein zu erwerben/bekommen, nachdem er zwei Jahre in der Prüfungsklasse einer Privatschule/Schule in freier Trägerschaft erlebt hat; ebenso wie ihm geholfen wird, eine wissenschaftliche Grundlage/Hintergrund für die höhere Bildung zu erwerben, die zumindest so gut ist wie an Sixth-Form Colleges.

> **Leistungskurs Englisch (Baden-Württemberg): Textaufgaben Landeskunde**
> **Aufgabe 7: Values that can be bought**

The winds of change let loose by Sir Keith Joseph in the State education system in the last few months are whistling around the independent schools.

Sir Joseph's proposal to make parents pay for their children's tuition at universities or polytechnics may have been modified under public pressure, but the damage has been done.

The middle and higher income parents with children at independent schools have been reminded by the controversy that they have to budget for considerable expenses for the three or four years their children are at a university or polytechnic.

Is it surprising that many parents thinking of educating their childred at independent schools are increasingly questioning the benefits their children will receive from the £ 50,000 to £ 100,000 that has to be paid?

Would it not be better for parents to take their children out of school at 16 and have them study for their A levels in one of the increasingly well-regarded sixth-form colleges in the State system? The money saved could be used to cover the increasing expense of higher education. The independent school can, however, easily reassure parents about their general record of giving value for money by pointing out that independent schools do produce better examination results than State schools.

Independent schools have always been proud of the wide variety of schools in their ranks. To grade them according to examination results would tend to obscure this point in the minds of parents choosing schools.

The best independent schools have traditionally seen their main mission in British education to inculcate into pupils what are called 'traditional values'.

Tim Devlin, in his recently published book 'Choosing Your Independent School', restated this objective as follows:

"Traditional values: teachers and staff at independent schools aim to teach children to work hard and to take pride in their work; to pay attention to detail; to have good manners; above all, to consider other people's feelings and to grow up into a responsible adult who will be of use to the community.'

(after further discussing the problems of cost and of grading schools according to their examination results the text goes on:)

At the heart of the dispute about publishing exam results are the different interests of the newer, day independent schools and the traditional boarding schools.

Boarding schools, such as Harrow and Radlay, which drew pupils from all over the country and from abroad, can reasonably expect to 'educate the whole person'. They have the time. The pupil is at school for 24 hours a day, 30-plus weeks a year, over five years.

Day schools, fortified in recent years by the accession of powerful direct-grant schools like Dulwich college and Manchester Grammar School, see themselves as the heirs of the grammar school tradition – stresssing the virtues of the academic education they provide and their excellent examination results. They are less able, as day schools, to influence the values of their pupils.

Paradoxically, many parents are choosing independent day schools over boarding schools for social reasons rather than examination results. They believe that by keeping their children at home, in contact with the family and local life, they are instilling in them a realistic perspective of modern life.

Some consultants advise parents thinking of independent school education to give their children both boarding and day school education by changing schools at 16, so as to get the best of both the day school and the boarding school regimes.
But all career advisers are unanimous that examination success does not ensure success in life, and that personality in a competitve, swiftly changing world is increasingly important.
574 words

Julian Ayer in The Observer, Sunday 13 January 1985, abridged

Vocabulary:

line 13:	sixth-form college	–	classes for pupils being prepared for A-level examinations
line 22:	to inculcate	–	to fix (ideas) firmly
line 37:	to fortify	–	to strengthen
line 37:	accession	–	hier: something like addition
line 37:	direct-grant school	–	a school which is financed by the Ministry of Education and not by local authorities
line 39:	virtue	–	hier: excellence
line 49:	unanimous	–	completely in agreement

I. Language

1. Vocabulary (ohne Wörterbuch zu bearbeiten)
   Substitute the words and expressions with synonymous words or terms; keep to the context.
   a) 14:   "... to cover the increasing expense ..."
   Paraphrase; the sentence can be changed. (3 VP)
   b) 18–19:   "... the wide variety of schools in their ranks." Explain; you may change the sentence (3 VP)
   c) 31:   "At the heart of the dispute ..."
   Paraphrase the above expressions. (3 VP)
   d) 35:   "... 30-plus weeks a year."
   Give a paraphrase. (1 VP)
   e) 44–45:   "... they are instilling in them a realistic perspective of modern life."
   Find synonyms; do not change the sentence structure. (2 VP)
   f) 43:   "... for social reasons rather than examination results."
   Give a paraphrase; you do not have to keep to the sentence structure. (1 VP)

2. Grammar and Style (ohne Wörterbuch zu bearbeiten)
   a) 14:   "The money saved could be used ..."
   What construction is "The money saved"?
   Rewrite by using a subordinate clausel. (2 VP)
   b) 16–17:   "... independent schools do produce better examination results ..."
   Explain the use of "do" (1 VP)
   c) 18:   "Independent schools have always been proud of ..."
   Explain the use of the tense. (1 VP)
   d) 37–39:   "Day schools ... see themselves as the heirs of the grammar school tradition ..."
   Why is the abstract noun 'heirs' used with the definite article here? (1 VP)

II. Comprehension

Please answer the following three questions in complete sentences. In your answers to question one and two keep to the information given in the text; no quotations, please.

1. What are the main points of contention between day schools and boarding schools? (90–110 words) (4 VP)
2. In how far is it unfair to grade schools according to examination results? (60–80 words) (2 VP)
3. Is it fair to make parents pay for the education of their children? (90–110 words) (4 VP)

III. Comment (10 VP)

Choose one of the following topics (200–300 words)

1. How do you judge the 'traditional values' (line 25 to 28) independent schools try to teach their pupils?
2. Would you prefer a day school or a boarding school – give reasons.
3. Do you agree with the assessment of our present situation as given in the last paragraph of the text. Give examples.

IV. Translation (30 VP)

The educational system is the organized way in which every society transmits common values, beliefs, and understandings from generation to generation. Modern states have used education to further their own ends and to try to assure their continued existence. After the emergence of secularization in education about 1790, two major systems of
5   national education evolved. One of these was the decentralized system in which education, although a concern of the national government, was left largely to local jurisdiction and private institutions; the other was the centralized system, in which both educational policy and administration were controlled by the state. The decentralized system, regarded as English in origin, is closely associated with the democratic
10 tradition. Transplanted to the United States, it set the pattern of the locally administered, free, secular public school system, existing side by side with a system of private and parochial schools. The development of such systems as these in making education available to all is believed by many to be one of the distinguishing features of the democratic form of government as administered in the United States. The centralized
15 system of education usually has been associated with strong central governments and sometimes has been identified with totalitarianism.

201 words
from: The American Peoples Encyclopedia, reprinted with permission of the American Peoples Encyclopedia, Grolier, Inc.

Vocabulary:

line 1:	to transmit	–	to pass on, to hand on
line 4:	secularization	–	Säkularisierung, Übernahme durch den Staat
line 6:	concern	–	something in which one is interested
line 7:	jurisdiction	–	hier: Zuständigkeit
line 12:	parochial	–	hier: run by the church

Lösungsvorschlag

I. Language

1. Vocabulary
   a) The money saved could be used to pay for/to offset the rising cost of/the amount of money necessary for higher education.
   b) ... the very different schools among their number .../... the greatly varying curricula which the various/different independent schools offer ...
   c) The most fundamental problems .../The most important issues ...
   d) ... more than 30 weeks a year ...
   e) ... they are teaching them a realistic view/point of view of modern life.
   f) Social reasons are more important/of greater importance/carry more weight than examination results.

2. Grammar and Style
   a) It is a shortened subordinate clause using a participle construction.
   "The money which they saved could be used .../
   The money which was saved could be used ..."
   b) This is a case of emphatic use of to do.
   c) Present perfect is used to describe an activity that began in the past and still goes on (cf 'always').
   d) The definite article is used here as the noun 'heirs' is defined by an of-clause.

II. Comprehension

1. The main point of contention is the different attitudes day schools and boarding schools can instil in their pupils. Boarding schools have a better chance of making their pupils accept what they call traditional values (which are mentioned in the text, line 25–28) because the pupils are at school all day for most of the year. On the other hand pupils live outside of what you could call 'real life'. Day schools offer more possibilities of living a 'real life'; the pupils stay with their families, can take part in local life and have friends other than their school mates.

2. If you grade schools according to examination results this is unfair because all efforts at teaching the pupils any values goes unnoticed. for example, trying to teach pupils to grow up into a responsible adult can in no way be seen at an exam; other important characteristics such as creativity or compassion can neither be 'tested'.

3. It is unfair if being poor could prevent children from getting a proper education, but that problem could be solved by establishing a system of scholarships for poorer but gifted children who could then get a good education.
   On the other hand there are some arguments for making parents pay for the education of their children. Things which come free often are not appreciated. If parents had to pay school fees they might be more interested in the education their children get.
   If there is a choice of schools, why should rich parents not be able to send their children to independent schools?

III. Comment

1. The traditional values mentioned in the text are nowadays often called old-fashioned but if we want to survive as a human and compassionate society we need a certain amount of these values. If we don't work, and at the same time consider other people's feelings we shall revert to a kind of society where you cannot rely on your fellow-

man and you will have a kind of 'social Darwinism'. There everybody will try to get the upper hand at all costs and the weaker will not be considered.
That does not mean that you must accept all the 'traditional values' of our society. The text only says that you should be an adult "who will be of use to the community". That leaves you enough leeway to develop and change our society, only you should "consider other people's feelings".
Thus I think the traditional values are a very good basis to start your adult life from. They give you a solid foundation and you can build your life on that foundation and then go on to realize your plans and aspirations. Unfortunately it seems that many young people reject these values without having any viable alternatives.

2. I personally would prefer a day school. First of all I would miss my family if I could only see them during the holidays. I think living the everyday life of a family is important if you should ever want to have a family of your own. There is a difference between living with school mates and with brothers and sisters. There are different privileges you have, and other obligations and considerations to think of; there is the difference between friedship and love.
Secondly, I would miss the independence I have when attending a day school. If my parents let me, I can go to the treatre, to a concert, to the cinema, go on a hike etc. whenever I like. And I think there are many hobbies which you could not fully realize when at a boarding school. Your choice of friends also would be limited if you attended a boarding school.
On the other hand, if my parents separated, or if they quarrelled a lot and I did not get the inner security I do get and need, then I think a boarding school would be advantageous. Unfortunately, quite a number of children are in situations that make them feel insecure and unwanted, and for them, I think, a boarding school might be of help.

3. I do agree with this assessment of our present situation. Whenever you look for a job or an apprenticeship, or if you want to study, everybody tells you that you have to be flexible because you probably will have to change your job (or even your profession) twice or three times in the course of your life. A good examination result is a good way to start your career but that does not guarantee success in life. If you learn something you should try to do your best – but even that does not ensure a successful career; you may have to start anew in some years.
Your personality is important, expecially in our swiftly changing world. If you don't have values and abilities you can rely and depend on, you are relatively helpless if you are confronted with new and unusual problems and issues. The stronger your personality is, the better you can cope – and if you want to change the world (at least a little), your best asset is a strong personality. If you think, for example, of somebody like Albert Schweitzer – he would never have succeeded in becoming a doctor (after he had alreday been a famous organist) and in founding a hospital in Africa without a strong personality. And a lot of people, e.g. Bismarck, did not even have great examination success to start with, and later became great and famous persons.

IV. Translation

Das Erziehungssystem ist die organisierte Einrichtung, in der jede Gesellschaft gemeinsame Werte, Glaubensvorstellungen und Übereinkommen/Übereinkünfte von Generation zu Generation weitervermittelt. Moderne Staaten haben die Erziehung verwendet, um ihre eigenen Ziele zu fördern und um zu versuchen, ihr Weiterbestehen zu sichern. Nach dem Auftreten der Säkularisierung im Bildungswesen um 1790 bildeten sich zwei Hauptsysteme des nationalen Bildungswesens heraus. Eines davon war das dezentralisierte System, in dem die Erziehung – obwohl sie ein Anliegen der nationalen Regierung war – größtenteils der örtlichen Zuständigkeit und privaten Einrichtungen überlassen wurde; das andere war das zentralisierte System, in dem sowohl die Erziehungspolitik als auch die Unterrichtsverwaltung vom Staat kontrolliert wurde. Das dezentralisierte System, das in seinem Ursprung als britisch angesehen wird, ist eng mit der demokratischen Tradition verbunden. In die Vereinigten Staaten verpflanzt/übertragen, diente es als Vorbild des örtlich verwalteten/eingerichteten, freien, weltlichen öffentlichen Schulsystems, das Seite an Seite mit einem System privater und kirchlicher Schulen bestand. Viele glauben, daß die Entwicklung solcher Systeme, die Erziehung/Bildung für alle zugänglich/möglich macht, eines der hervorragenden/besonderen Züge der demokratischen Form der Regierung, wie sie in den USA ausgeübt wird, ist. Das zentralisierte System der Erziehung/Bildung wird gewöhnlich mit starken zentralen Regierungen in Verbindung gebracht, und wird manchmal mit Totalitarismus als identisch betrachtet.

> **Leistungskurs Englisch (Baden-Württemberg): Textaufgaben Landeskunde**
> **Aufgabe 8: Britain: Facing Up to Violence**

A 14-year-old Asian boy is beaten unconscious by a white gang; then his back is slashed to ribbons with a carpenter's knife. A striker is crushed to death on a picket line. These incidents – and more like them – happened this year in a land that once seemed the very embodiment of civility and respect for the law: Britain.

To be sure, Britain is still a relatively tranquil land in an increasingly brutalized world. Its violence does not begin to approach that of Lebanon; its murder rate is still far below that of the United States. Even so, terror and crime in Britain are rising rapidly. Every day newspapers and television tell of racist assaults, brutal muggings and what has become a running war between the police and the striking coal miners. Statistics show that violent crime of all kinds in Britain has doubled in the past decade. Though the number of murders has remained steady, serious injuries from assaults have almost doubled and violent robberies have tripled.

Britain's new ugliness also extends to racial violence, which has become endemic in many neighbourhoods. Assaults on immigrants from countries such as Pakistan, India and Bangladesh are clearly carried out for one reason: the victims are not white. "Any official figures for racial attacks in this area can be multiplied by at least 10", says Barbara Powis, a social worker in the racially troubled East London suburb of Tower Hamlets. "People have stopped calling the police because they know there is no point – the authorities simply don't do enough to help these people."

Even among the white middle class, acts of violence have become almost routine of late. A gang of young toughs was charged in a London court last week with torturing a shopkeeper and his wife to make them turn over their money. According to their own testimony, Cecily Tipple, 56, was humiliated before being battered unconscious. Her husband, Harry, 59, had half an ear sawed off by the alleged assailants; then they hacked off one of his toes and stuffed it in his mouth.

Such acts of savagery have begun to take a heavy psychological toll, even among those who are not the victims. In a recent survey, almost 60 percent of women who were polled said they felt "very unsafe" after dark. Inevitably, growing fears from virtually all segments of society have prompted experts to search for a reason for the rash of violence. One of the most frequently proposed theories might be called the "Clockwork Orange" syndrome – which contends that Britain's huge unemployment has widened the gap between the haves and have-nots, spawning gangs of alienated youths who commit crimes for monetary gains or just for kicks.

Many experts are sceptical of that theory. Criminologists point out that Britain suffered from massive unemployment during the Great Depression of the 1930s, yet the country never endured any dramatic upsurge in violence. Experts also cite the situation in Eastern Europe – which theoretically has no unemployment. Crime there also seems to be on the rise, they say. Those two facts have led experts to another explanation for Britain's current plight: that the country's population now contains the highest percentage ever of males in their late teens and early 20s, the demographic group that commits the most crimes. If that theory is correct, then the peace and safety that Britain enjoyed for so many years may be gone for the time being.

571 words

Newsweek, November 5, 1984, adapted and abridged

Vocabulary:

line 13:	endemic	–	common; often recurring in an area
line 21:	tough	–	a rough and violent person; often a criminal
line 24:	alleged	–	vermeintlich, angeblich
line 24:	assailant	–	attacker
line 29:	rash	–	outbreak
line 32:	to spawn	–	to produce in great numbers
line 32:	alienated	–	entfremdet
line 33:	just for kicks	–	just for fun

I. Language

1. Vocabulary (ohne Wörterbuch zu bearbeiten)
   Explain the underlined words or terms by using synonyms or paraphrases; keep to the given context.

   a) 5: "... Britain is still a <u>relatively</u> tranquil <u>land</u> in an <u>increasingly</u> brutalized world." Give synonyms but don't change the structure of the sentence. (3 VP)

   b) 10: "... violent crime ... has <u>doubled</u> in the past <u>decade</u>." Find suitable paraphrases. (2 VP)

   c) 19: "... the <u>authorities simply</u> don't do enough ..." Paraphrase; you can change the sentence. (2 VP)

   d) 31–32: "which <u>contends</u> that Britain's huge <u>unemployment</u> has <u>widened</u> the gap ..." Find paraphrases; you don't have to keep to the sentence structure. (3 VP)

2. Grammar and Style (ohne Wörterbuch zu bearbeiten)

   a) 2: "A striker is crushed to death on a picket line." Why is the passive voice – without the by-agent – used here? (1 VP)

   b) 26: "Such acts ... <u>have begun</u> to take a heavy psychological toll, ..." Explain the use of the tense. (1 VP)

   c) 27–28: "... almost 60 percent of women <u>who were polled</u> ..." Can the relative pronoun be left out? Say why (or why not). (1 VP)

   d) 31–33: "... Britian's huge unemployment has widened the gap between the haves and havenots, <u>spawning gangs of alienated youths</u> who commit crimes ..." What grammatical construction is 'spawning gangs of alienated youths'? Rewrite by using a subordinate clause. (2 VP)

II. Comprehension

Please answer the following three questions in complete sentences. In your answers to question 1 and 2 keep to the direct and indirect information given in the text and do not quote.

1. Which explanations are given for the increasing violence in Britain? (90–110 words) (4 VP)

2. How does the increasing violence influence people's lives? (60–80 words) (2 VP)

3. Is a policy of "law and order" a positive reaction to the problems mentioned in the text? (90–110 words) (4 VP)

III. Comment (10 VP)

Choose one of the following topics: (200–300 words)
1. How would you explain the increasing violence against members of minorities (cf line 13–16)?
2. Some people think that capital punishment would help to stop the increase in violent crime.
   What do you think about that?
3. The younger generation is strongly engaged in the movement for peace and disarmament – on the other hand a proportionally large number of young people commit violent crimes.
   Can you explain this contradiction?

IV. Translation (30 VP)

The criminal law persumes a person to be innocent until he has been proved guilty beyond reasonable doubt, and every possible step is taken to deny the prosecution any advantage over the defence. An accused person cannot be compelled to give evidence at his trial; if he remains silent, the prosecution is not allowed to comment on the fact,
5 although the judge may do so. Witnesses normally give evidence in open court.
Every accused person has the right to employ a legal adviser for his defence. If he cannot afford to pay his legal costs, he may be granted legal aid from public funds. Anyone found guilty of a crime usually has the right of appeal to a higher court either against conviction or against the sentence imposed.
10 Proceedings in court are normally held in public except in cases involving children (where the child's right of privacy is considered paramount) or matters of State security. Court proceedings are normally reported in the press. Comments may also be published after the end of a trial, but not before, provided that they are not calculated to bring a court or a judge into contempt, or to interfere with the course of justice.

199 words

from: Criminal Justice in Britain, a General Office of Information pamphlet, 1978

Vocabulary:

line 2:	do deny	–	to refuse to give
line 3:	to compel	–	to force
line 8:	appeal	–	to take a question (to a higher court) for rehearing and a new decision
line 11:	paramount	–	of highest importance
line 14:	contempt	–	hier Mißachtung, Verächtlichmachung

Lösungsvorschlag

I. Language

1. Vocabulary
   a) Britain is still a comparatively tranquil country in a more and more brutalized world.
   b) In the past ten years violent crime has increased twofold.
   In the past ten years twice as many violent crimes have ben committed.
   c) The police and other officials just don't do enough.
   d) Which says/maintains/claims that the huge number of people out of work/people on the dole has made the gap much larger.

2. Grammar and Style
   a) The passive voice is used here because only the fact that a striker is crushed to death is of importance – who did it is of no concern here.
   b) The present perfect tense 'have begun' is used here to describe an activity which began in the past and still goes on.
   c) The relative pronoun 'who' cannot be left out because it is the subject of the defining relative clause.
   The relative pronoun 'who' cannot be left out because there is no other subject of the defining relative clause.
   d) The construction 'spawning gangs of alienated youths' is a shortened subordinate clause using a participle construction.
   "... which has spawned gangs of alienated youths ..."

II. Comprehension

1. The most widely held belief is that the great number of people who are out of work has made the difference between rich and poor people even greater and more conspicuous; and therefore more crimes are committed for monetary gains. But many people do not believe in that theory as there were other times with much unemployment but not so much crime.
Another theory contends that the high crime-rate simply has a demographic background: the number of males in their teens and early twenties is at an all-time high: and this age group commits the most crimes.

2. The increasing violence produces insecurity.
Many members of minorities do not even bother to call the police after violent incidents because they feel that not enough is done to help them.
Another sign of this insecurity is that 60 percent of women who were polled said that they felt 'very unsafe' after dark – although most of them have never been victims of crimes themselves.

3. A policy of 'law and order' alone can do nothing to solve the problems because it only tries to cure the symptoms and does not get at the root of them. It is a very good policy to make people feel safe again if, at the same time, investigations are being undertaken to find out the root causes of the problems, and then measures are taken to eliminate the causes of this increasing violence. Therefore a policy of 'law and order' can play only a secondary and supporting role – on its own it will utterly fail.

III. Comment

1. If an economy is in a recession or if a great number of people is on the dole, there always is a danger that the increasing restlessness, disaffection and discontent seeks some way of expressing itself; in other words, people look for a scapegoat.
Expecially racial minorities are very conspicuous – you can see at once that they are no Englishmen; they are different. In addition, quite often they do not only have another colour of skin, they also might speak a different language, have a different culture and religion. Anything that is different from what people are used to makes them feel uncomfortable – and if a situation gets difficult they might even feel threatened. 'The Indians (or members of any minority, for that matter) came to England and took away our jobs – we are unemployed but they have got jobs', this attitude (which quite a number of people think to be a very reasonable one to have) can easily lead to violence against members of minorities.
People tend to forget that those immigrants (or guest-workers, as we call them in Germany) came because there were some low-paid, dirty, menial jobs nobody else wanted. London's public transport, for example, would totally collapse if all coloured personnel should be laid off.
Unless people realize that in a democracy violence is no means of settling differences, and that everybody has a right to be different and still be accepted, there always will be a danger that, in difficult times, violence against members of minorities will increase.

2. Capital punishment is an Old Testament solution. The underlying idea is that as a murderer took a life, his life must be taken; society takes revenge. Another argument is that if everybody knows that he will be executed if he takes somebody's life or commits another hideous crime, he will not do it. Statistics show that this idea is a fallacy; no great changes in the numbers of murders or violent crimes could be detected when capital punishment was introduced or abolished in any given country. This can easily be explained: normally no murderer or kidnapper ever really expects to be caught and to be brought to judgement – or else he would not commit his crime. Thus one can see that capital punishment is no instrument to reduce violent crime.
Another aspect of this problem is the theory that only very few crimes are rooted solely in the personality of the criminal; society also has to bear some responsibility for its deviating members – as it is no perfect society. Therefore society is under the obligation of giving the miscreant a chance to change and improve his character. (A more theological argument along those lines says that a criminal should be given time and a chance to repent and do penance.)
Capital punishment is an absolute and irreversible measure, and although society must protect itself, it seems to me that it is not the ideal solution.

3. I think that this is not really a contradiction, it only seems to be one.
On the one hand, young people are very idealistic and therefore want to change the world – and if you want the world changed, you must have a world to change. With the overkill capacities in the two military blocks there is quite a chance that very soon there won't be a world any more where human beings can live. Therefore we must have real peace – and not a balance of terror – if we want to go on living. Young people are very much aware of this fact and therefore they are strongly engaged in the movements for peace and disarmament.
On the other hand, if you look at statistics, people in their teens and early twenties are criminally most active. These young people have not yet settled down and have not yet come to accept the society they live in. If frustrations become unbearable (or better, seem to become unbearable), younger people are more apt than older people to vent their anger violently (one example would be the young people who turned to

violence and terrorism after they could not change society as they wanted to). Young people seem to be less tolerant of compromises and therefore turn to violence more easily.

This possible (and, on the whole, too simplistic) explanation cannot explain the underlying causes, nor does it explain why there always is a certain percentage of people who commit violent crimes.

IV. Translation

Das Strafrecht nimmt an/vermutet/setzt voraus, daß ein Mensch unschuldig ist, bis bewiesen ist, daß er jenseits jeden vernünftigen Zweifels schuldig ist; und jede mögliche Maßnahme wird getroffen, der Anklage jeglichen Vorteil über die Verteidigung zu nehmen. Ein Angeklagter kann nicht gezwungen werden, bei seinem Prozess auszusagen; wenn er schweigt, darf die Anklage diesen Punkt/diese Tatsache nicht erwähnen, allerdings kann/darf es der Richter. Zeugen sagen normalerweise in öffentlichen Verhandlungen aus.

Jeder Angeklagte hat das Recht, zu seiner Verteidigung einen Rechtsberater/ Rechtsanwalt zu nehmen. Wenn er seine Anwaltskosten nicht bezahlen kann, kann ihm Rechtshilfe aus öffentlichen Mitteln gewährt werden. Jeder der eines Verbrechens schuldig gesprochen wird, hat normalerweise das Recht, ein höheres Gericht anzurufen/ Berufung bei einem höheren Gericht einzulegen, entweder gegen die Verurteilung oder gegen die ausgesprochene/verhängte Strafe.

Gerichtsverhandlungen/Gerichtsverfahren sind normalerweise öffentlich, außer in Fällen, in denen Kinder beteiligt sind (wo das Persönlichkeitsrecht des Kindes als ausschlaggebend/von höchster Wichtigkeit betrachtet wird) oder in Staatsschutzverfahren. Über Gerichtsverfahren wird in der Regel in der Presse berichtet. Kommentare können/ dürfen auch nach dem Ende eines Verfahrens veröffentlicht werden – aber nicht vorher – vorausgesetzt, daß nicht beabsichtigt ist/sie nicht darauf angelegt sind, ein Gericht oder einen Richter verächtlich zu machen oder den Ablauf des Rechts/der Justiz zu behindern/beeinträchtigen.

Leistungskurs Englisch (Baden-Württemberg): Textaufgaben Landeskunde
Aufgabe 9: War and Peace in Northern Ireland

(...) It is the dawn of the Glorious Twelfth of July, and Belfast's Prostestants are celebrating the victory of William of Orange over the Catholic King James II at the battle of the Boyne almost 300 years ago – a victory that made England irrevocably Protestant.

At daybreak more than 100,000 primly bowler-hatted members of the Orange Order will parade, beginning a holiday season in which two-thirds of Northern Ireland's 1.5-million population proclaim their Protestant heritage and their loyalty to the British crown. But tonight belongs to the street crowds, and there's a manic edge of menace to the holiday mood.

In the Catholic ghettos of West Belfast things are quiet. British troops in battle gear partrol the rubbled streets of Turf Lodge, Ballymurphy, and the Clonard. Indoors, people remember another night of fire, that in August 1969, when Protestant mobs burned dozens of Catholic homes, forcing hundreds of panic-stricken families to flee.

Since the mid-19th century, scores of similar riots have flashed and faded during the summer solstices of sectarian pride, but 1969 was different. It ignited a vicious war of terror bombing and assassination that in 12 years has killled more than 2,000 men, women and children, injured more than 17,000 and cost about a billion dollars in property damage. Some 8,000 people have been jailed for terrorist crimes under emergency laws that suspend many of Britain's most precious civil rights.

(...) West Belfast is the battle zone, where a grotesque "peace line" of steel and concrete slashes through an eerie wilderness of shattered buildings, separating the modest neighborhoods of "Prods" (Protestants) and "Taigs" (a contemptuous term for Catholics). Sheltering among them, the terrorists of the Irish Republican Army and the Protestant Ulster Volunteer Force and Ulster Defense Association refresh their hatred at the same poisoned well of Irish history.

(...) But todays violence had a very modern cause. Northern Catholics – and moderate Protestants – began a civil-rights campaign to overturn laws and policies that had kept them poor and powerless. Peaceful street protests turned into riots, and the ancient bonfires flared again. And no amount of bloodshed seems likely to quench them.

(...) There are severe economic problems. Unemployment is more than 15 percent – nearly double that of Britain – and ranges above 30 percent among males in Catholic ghettos. The "troubles" have cost thousands of jobs. And in Belfast, violence and intimidation have forced thousands of working-class Catholics and Protestants to leave their homes in one of Europe's largest refugee movements since World War II.

(...) "NO SURRENDER!" identifies the loyalist Protestant majority, which clings stubbornly to union with Britain and swears never to accept union with the Catholic-dominated Irish Republic to the south.

"BRITS OUT!" is the battle cry of the Provisional IRA, or Provos, and its (...) political wing, Sinn Fein, which forecast unending violence until British troops and government are withdrawn, leaving the island's inhabitants to sort out things for themselves. While this reflects a profound hope to some, most fear it would bring immediate civil war. (...)

In March 1978 the UDA issued a manifesto calling for a negotiated independence from Britain and an Ulster government based on a constitution and bill of rights similar to the American codes. It also contained this stark appraisal of northern affairs: "Without the

45 evolution of proper politics," the manifesto said, "the people of Northern Ireland will continually be manipulated by sectarian politicians who ... fan the flames of religious bigotry for self-gain and preservation." – It was another way of saying that the war need not have happened. (...) 583 words
(excerpts from: 'War and Peace in Northern Ireland' by BrianHodgson, in National Geographic, April 1981, Vol. 159, No. 4)

Vocabulary:

line 8:	manic	–	violently mad
line 15:	solstice	–	time (around 21 June) when the sun is farthest north; the longest day of the year
line 21	eerie	–	causing a feeling of mystery and fear
line 42:	UDA	–	Ulster Defense Association (line 24); a Protestant organistation

I. Language

1. Vocabulary (ohne Wörterbuch zu bearbeiten)
   Give synonyms or paraphrases for the following words and expressions; keep to the given context.
   a) 15: "It <u>ignited</u> a vicious war ..."
   Find a synonym; don't change the sentence. (1 VP)
   b) 18: "<u>Some</u> 8,000 people have beem <u>jailed</u> ..."
   Find synonyms; don't change the sentence. (2 VP)
   c) 23: "<u>Sheltering</u> among them ..."
   Find a synonym; don't change the structure of the sentence. (1 VP)
   d) 28–29: "<u>Peaceful</u> street protests <u>turned into riots</u>, and the ancient bonfires <u>flared</u> again."
   Find synonyms; don't change the sentence. (4 VP)
   e) 29: "And no amount of bloodshed seems <u>likely</u> to quench them." Give a paraphrase; you may change the sentence. (2 VP)

2. Grammar and Style (ohne Wörterbuch zu bearbeiten)
   a) 21–22: "..., separating <u>the</u> modest neighborhoods of 'Prods' .. and 'Taigs' ..." Why is the definite article used here? (1 VP)
   b) 29: "and no amount of bloodshed seems <u>likely</u> to quench them".
   What part of speech is 'likely'? (1 VP)
   c) 39–40: "... Sinn Fein, which forecast <u>unending</u> violence until British troops and government are withdrawn, <u>leaving</u> the island's inhabitants to sort out things for themselves."
   Give a full explanation of the -ing forms. (2 VP)
   d) 46–47: "... who ... <u>fan the flames</u> of religious bigotry ..."
   What figure of speech is 'fan the flames'? (1 VP)

II. Comprehension

Please answer the following questions in complete sentences. Keep to the (direct of indirect) information given in the text; use your own words as far as possible, but do not quote.
1. Describe some of the causes underlying the conflict in Northern Ireland.(80–100 words) (4 VP)
2. What have been some of the consequences of the "troubles" in Northern Ireland? (70–90 words) (3 VP)
3. Why is the term "peace line" (line 20) put in quotation marks, and why has it the adjective 'grotesque' in front of it? (70–90 words) (3 VP)

III. Comment (10 VP)

Choose one of the following topics: (200–300 words)
1. What possibilities do you see for a solution of the difficult situation in Northern Ireland?
2. How do you judge terrorism and bloodshed as a means for the solution of political (or other) problems?

IV. Translation

Ulster: Will for peace but fear runs high

According to some veterans, this week has seen the worst sectarian fighting in Belfast since the state of Northern Ireland was set up in 1920.

For anyone who saw the high heroic beginnings of the civil rights campaign last autumn – the determined non-violence, the appeals by the young leaders for an end to ancient religious divisions – the past week here must have tasted very bitter.

After the rioting and the looting came the intimidation of families in their homes. Threatening letters arrived, written in large, childish writing on cheap lined paper. The bullies came in groups of twos and threes and refused to identify themselves, giving families 24 hours notice to quit, so that the police could in some cases do nothing but advise that it might be safer to move. More often, no one thought to ask the police for protection, for this week the distaste for the Royal Ulster Constabulary, which has been general among Catholics for some time, has spread to the Protestant working-class of Belfast.

In this situation the omens of hope are pitifully few.

194 wods.

(by Mary Holland, in: The Observer, 10 August, 1969)

Vocabulary:
line 1:	sectarian fighting	–	fighting between religious groups
line 6:	to loot	–	plündern
line 8:	bully	–	person who uses his strength or power to frighten or hurt those who are weaker
line 11:	Royal Ulster Constabulary	–	not to be translated

Lösungsvorschlag

I. Language

1. Vocabulary
   a) It started/set off/led to a vicious war ...
   b) Approximately/roughly/about 8000 people have ben imprisoned/arrested/taken into custody ...
   c) Hiding among them ...
   d) Non-violent street protest became/changed into revolt/violent incidents/rebellion and the ancient bonfires burned/were fuelled/started again.
   e) Probably no amount of bloodshed will quench them. It is probable that no amount of bloodshed will quench them.

2. Grammar and Style
   a) The definite article is used here because the abstract noun is defined by a possessive case/by an of-clause.
   b) 'Likely' is an adjective.
   c) 'Unending' is a present participle used as an adjective.
      'Leaving' is a present participle used to shorten a subordinate clause.
   d) It is a metaphor.

II. Comprehension

1. The English conquest of Ireland led to the plantation of Protestants in the north of Ireland. Catholics were disenfranchised and the Protestants had all the political power and absolutely dominated the economy.
   Moves for Home Rule and a politically independent role for Ireland led to the Easter Rising in 1916 and – after World War I – civil war. Ireland was partitioned, and in Northern Ireland the Catholic population (which makes up about 1/3 of the total population) has lived under Protestant supremacy ever since.
   The Protestants want Northern Ireland to remain part of the United Kingdom while most Catholics advocate a united Ireland, or at least want the discriminatory laws repealed.

2. The gap between Protestants and Catholics has widened, and in some areas even walls between Catholic and Protestant neighbourhoods were erected.
   More than 2000 people have been killed, many of them innocent bystanders, and many more have been injured. The economic situation is very bad, with almost twice the number of people on the dole than in Britain. Extensive property damage and the civil war-like situation and atmosphere have greatly reduced new investment.

3. The term 'peace line' is an ironic euphemism. Normally you would expect a 'peaceline' to be something which creates or keeps the peace, while in this case it is only a demarcation line between two warring factions.
   It might help reduce hostilies by keeping the two fighting groups apart, but as such it only can reduce the symptoms – the bloodshed – but does nothing about the underlying causes – the bitterness caused by Irish history.
   Thus to call such a wall a 'peace line' really is grotesque.

III. Comment

1. Many people have tried to find a solution for the problems of Northern Ireland, and at least the political attempts at a solution have failed so far.
   The attitudes of the adult population seem to be so inflexible and unchangeable that there seems to be only one way which a small group of idealistic people hopes will find many followers. They run a school where Catholic and Protestant children are educated together. They learn and play together and learn to be tolerant towards each other. I am of the opinion that this is the only long range measure that promises any hope of success: to make children break the old vicious cycle of prejudices leading to the unjust treatment of "the others".
   Other possible and necessary measures which should be undertaken are the repeal of all laws and ordinances which discriminate against one group.
   Another possibility of finding a solution might be the concept of finding a political framework which enables the groups to find a democratic way of dealing with their difficulties. But as past attempts have shown, there doesn't seem to be one solution which can be accepted by both groups.

It seems that both the British and Irish governments will have to be involved in any solution, although even that does not guarantee any smooth transition as the last few attempts at coming to an understanding have shown.
Britain's withdrawal of its troops from Northern Ireland would not be a solution as it most probably would lead to an all-out civil war which would draw the Republic of Ireland into the fighting.
It is very difficult to find a viable solution – and almost impossible to find one which is acceptable to all groups concerned – it is a classical no-win situation.

2. Terrorism and bloodshed are means which are used to intimidate people who are of different opinions and who are not so 'radical' to resort to force to reach their aims. I am of the opinion that – with hardly any exeptions – it is not an acceptable means for the solution of any problem.
In any civilized society there should be other possibilities to vent one's grievances than the use of brutal force, and in most countries these possibilities exist.
Normally terrorists are fanatical radicals who see no other possibilities to impose their will upon an unwilling or hostile society. They may be honestly convinced that they are right – but if they have to rely on brute force they probably will not convince anybody, even if they should rise to power. They probably would have to resort to terrorism to stay in power – and probably provoke counter-terrorism.
Another ugly aspect of terrorism is its randomness. Even if terrorists strike directly against whatever or whoever stands in their way they very often are cynically indifferent as to what may happen to innocent bystanders. Quite often they even use innocent people to blackmail their adversaries.
Because of all the above mentioned reasons I do not think that terrorism and bloodshed are a means to solve problems; in a civilized society the use of force should be outlawed completely so as to give nobody an excuse to become a terrorist.

IV. Translations

Ulster: Friedenswille, aber große Furcht/Angst

Laut/nach einigen erfahrenen Beobachtern sah diese Woche die schlimmsten Kämpfe/ Auseinandersetzungen zwischen den religiösen Gruppen in Belfast seit der Errichtung des nordirischen Staates im Jahre 1920/seit der nordirische Staat 1920 errichtet wurde.

Für jeden, der die überaus/positiven heldenhaften Anfänge der Bürgerrechtsbewegung im letzten Herbst gesehen/beobachtet hat – die entschiedene/nachdrückliche Gewaltlosigkeit, die Bitten/Appelle/Aufrufe der jungen (An)Führer, den alten religiösen Trennungen ein Ende zu machen – muß die vergangene Woche hier sehr bitter gewesen sein.

Nach dem Aufruhr und dem Plündern kam die Einschüchterung von Familien in ihren Häusern/Wohnungen. Drohbriefe kamen (an)/trafen ein, mit großer kindischer Schrift auf billigem liniertem Papier. Die Randalierer kamen zu zweit und zu dritt/in Gruppen von zweien und dreien und weigerten sich, sich auszuweisen/ihre Namen zu sagen und gaben den Familien eine Frist von 24 Stunden um auszuziehen/die Wohnung zu verlassen; so daß die Polizei in manchen/einigen Fällen nichts (anderes) tun konnte, als den Rat zu geben, daß es sicherer/besser sei, umzuziehen. Noch öfter dachte man nicht/ niemand daran/kam man nicht auf den Gedanken/Idee, die Polizei um Schutz zu bitten, denn in dieser Woche hat die Abneigung gegen die Royal Ulster Constabulary – die (schon) seit einiger Zeit unter den Katholiken allgemein verbreitet ist – auf die protestantische Arbeiterklasse in Belfast übergegriffen/sich auf ... ausgebreitet.

In dieser Situation/Lage gibt es (nur) erbärmlich/bedauerlich wenige Zeichen der Hoffnung.

> Leistungskurs Englisch (Baden-Württemberg): Textaufgaben Landeskunde
> Aufgabe 10: Defusing the 'Jobs Bomb'

Defusing the 'Jobs Bomb'

Despite hesitant signs of economic growth in Britain and West Germany, Europe's postwar employment prospects have never been more bleak. The traditional smokestack industries that powered its economies into the 20th century are falling by the wayside; yet they are not being replaced by new industries of the 21st. As a result, Europe's jobless rolls have swelled, almost without interruption. More than 18 million people are now out of work – roughly 12 percent of the work force. By the end of next year, reports the Paris-based Organization for Economic Cooperation and Development (OECD), another 2 million people will be without jobs. Beyond any doubt, unemployment in Europe has entered a new dimension. Realizing, finally, that the disease is chronic, European leaders are discarding the quick fixes of the past and are now searching for new cures, ranging from shortened workweeks to early, and sometimes forced, retirement. They are implementing job-training programs and experimenting with a slew of new "entrepreneurial" programs to help unemployed workers become self-employed small businessmen. The efforts come none too soon. By any measure the jobless figures are numbing. But the stakes are not just economic; the human toll exacted by Europe's joblessness is beyond calculation. More than a third of Britain's unemployed workers are under 25; many have never had a chance to get the first job needed to start a career.

Not surprisingly, social disaffection and political alienation are mounting. As policy-makers come to grips with unemployment as a structural problem that Europe will have to live with – perhaps for decades – they are rethinking the old notions about employment, and doing so at considerable political risk. Strikes by French auto- and steelworkers have disrupted the government's plans to streamline its smokestack industries. Voters consistently rank unemployment as their most pressing concern – ahead of pollution, nuclear disarmament, inflation and crime in the streets. European political leaders clearly recognize the gravity of the situation, but their dilemma leaves them little room for maneuver. In almost every country, deficit-ridden governments are adopting tough-line solutions, cutting welfare and unemployment payments and generally reining in the socialist programs of recent decades.

This growing sense of realism has had extraordinary consequences. From Madrid to Copenhagen, governments are grappling for new ways to create, or at least save, as many jobs as possible. Most governments no longer even think about trying to find jobs for people over 55. Instead, they place their emphasis on training – and retraining – unemployed youths. Hundreds of thousands of Europeans have been coaxed into early retirement.

The demographics of Britain's joblessness are expecially troubling. As elsewhere in Europe, unemployment has fallen particularly hard on the young. Jobless youths seem increasingly adrift, a kind of "aimless generation" that lacks the purpose and material well-being of its more fortunate elders. In France, where nearly 40 percent of the unemployed are between 16 and 25, the "primary goal is to get young people off the streets and into a job," says Jean-Cyril Spinetta, a senior government official. Then, too, there is an alarming trend toward longer unemployment. People who have been out of work for more than three years constitute one of Britain's fastestgrowing social groups. Were this phenomenon peculiar to Britain, it might not be quite as disturbing. In fact, however, the same thing is happening elsewhere. In West Germany, for example, 1 out of 25 persons unemployed in 1982 had been out of work for two or more years,. Today the figure is one in nine.

579 words

from Newsweek, April 22, 1985, abridged

Vocabulary:

line 10:	fix	–	hier: solution
line 12:	to implement	–	to carry into effect;
line 12:	slew	–	a large number
line 27:	tough-line	–	strong, unpopular
line 28:	to rein in	–	to restrain, to reduce
line 37:	adrift	–	hier: at the mercy of circumstances

I. Language

1. Vocabulary (ohne Wörterbuch zu bearbeiten)
   Deal with the following underlined words or expressions within their given context.
   a) 2–3: "The traditional <u>smokestack</u> industries ..."
   Explain; you can change the structure of the sentence. (1 VP)
   b) 4–5: "... Europe's <u>jobless rolls</u> have swelled, ..."
   Paraphrase; you can change the sentence. (1 VP)
   c) 6: " – <u>roughly</u> 12 percent ..."
   Give a suitable synonym; do not change the structure of the sentence. (1 VP)
   d) 9: "Realizing, <u>finally</u>, that ..."
   Give a synonym; don't change the sentence. (1 VP)
   e) 9: "... that the <u>disease</u> is <u>chronic</u> ..."
   Paraphrase; you may change the structure of the sentence. (2 VP)
   f) 10–11: "... are now searching for new <u>cures</u>, ..."
   Give a synonym; do not change the sentence. (1 VP)
   g) 20: "... <u>decades</u>."
   Explain this word. (1 VP)
   h) 36: "... unemployment has <u>fallen particularly</u> hard on the young."
   Paraphrase; you may change the structure of the sentence. (2 VP)

2. Grammar and Style (ohne Wörterbuch zu bearbeiten)
   a) 12: "They are implementing job-training programs ..."
   Put into the Passive Voice. (1 VP)
   b) 18: "Not surprisingly, social disaffection and political alienation are mounting."
   Start the sentence with: It is ... (1 VP)
   c) 11: "... new cures rang<u>ing</u> from shortened work-weeks ..."
      12: "They are implement<u>ing</u> ... programs ..."
      23: "... their most press<u>ing</u> concern ..."
      32: "... they place their emphasis on train<u>ing</u> ..."
   Explain the -ing forms. (2 VP)
   d) 43: "Were this phenomenon peculiar to Britain, ..."
   Start the sentence with: If ... (1 VP)

II. Comprehension

Please answer the following questions in complete sentences. Keep to the information given in the text, but do not quote, please.
1. Which are the main economic reasons for Europe's problems with unemployment? (70–90 words) (3 VP)
2. What solutions do politicians propose? (50–70 words) (2 VP)
3. How are the young affected? (50–70 words) (2 VP)
4. What does the future look like? (70–90 words) (3 VP)

III. Comment (10 VP)
Choose <u>one</u> of the following topics: (200–300 words)
1. "A person should have a job as a right." Discuss this statement.
2. "We live to work" – "We work to live". Which of the two statements do you agree with, and why?

IV. Translation (30 VP)

The unspoken consensus seems to be that little can be done for Europe's hard-core unemployed, apart from a return to the now discredited welfare policies of the past. Bleak as that picture is, however, there is some reason for optimism. Toward the end of this decade, Europe's demographics will begin to change. As its postwar baby-boom generation grows older, there will be fewer entrants to the work force. And sweeping structural changes now taking place – deregulation, the decline of the steel and coal industries, the automation of automaking and electronics – will have been completed.

In the meantime, though, Europe must create 12,000 jobs a day to keep unemployment from rising. For a network of economies that has lost more jobs than it has generated over the past decade, that seems an insuperable challenge. To some extent, Europe will be split ever more deeply between those who work and those who do not. Some of the pain will be cushioned by Europe's still-generous welfare institutions. But as benefits are whittled down, more and more people will feel the bite. Plainly, the rigidities built into economic and social systems will not quickly be overcome. Europe's best hope may be that the steady rise in joblessness can be arrested, or even turned back a point or two. Until then, Europe has little choice but to live with a disease it may be able to contain but cannot cure. *239 words*

from Newsweek, April 22, 1985, abridged

Vocabulary:

line 4:	demographics	–	the relation of the dynamic balance of population (hier: with regard to the relation between the old and the young)
line 10:	insuperable	–	(something) that cannot be overcome
line 13:	to whittle down	–	to reduce (the amount of)
line 13:	rigidity	–	inflexibility
line 16:	to contain	–	hier: to keep under control

Lösungsvorschlag

I. Language

1. Vocabulary
   a) The traditional manufacturing industries – especially those producing or using steel – ...
      The traditional heavy industries ...
   b) ... the number of unemployed people/people on the dole/people out of work/people without a job in Europe has swelled, ...
   c) ... – about/around/approximately 12 percent ...
   d) Realizing, ultimately/at last, that ...
   e) ... that it is a long-term problem ...
      ... that it is not a short-term problem ...
   f) ... are now searching for new solutions/methods of overcoming the problem.
   g) A decade is the time of ten years.
      ... of the past ten or twenty years or so.

h) ... unemployment has hit the young especially hard.
   ... unemployment is an especially difficult problem for the young.
   ... unemployment has affected the young especially badly.
   ... the young suffer especially badly from unemployment.
2. Grammar and Style
   a) Job-training programs are being implemented (by them).
   b) It is not surprising that social disaffection and political alienation are mounting.
   c) 1. Present participle, used to shorten a subordinate clause.
      2. Present participle used in the present continuous form.
      3. Present participle used as an adejective/attribute.
      4. Gerund used after noun + preposition.
   d) If this phenomenon were peculiar to Britain, ...

II. Comprehension

1. It seems that Europe is not innovative enough and has not replaced its old industries with more future-oriented ones. Therefore unemployment is endemic in Europe, and there is no quick cure as the process of innovation takes some time.
   Another reason is that the high welfare costs drove taxes very high and that gives the governments little room for giving economic incentives.
   Wages and fringe benefits are quite high in Europe and that makes competition difficult with countries that have lower labour costs.

2. Politicians have proposed different solutions; one is to persuade people over 55 to retire early and thus reduce the number of those on the dole.
   Another measure is to put a stronger emphasis on training people entering the job market, and retraining those who are unemployed.
   Programs to help unemployed people start their own businesses is another measure expected to help reduce unemployment.

3. The young are especially hard hit, they make up a large group of those out of work. Those who don't find work after finishing school or job training seem to develop into an "aimless generation" with no goal in life. They are frustrated and frequently turn to violence. Europe experiences increasing social disaffection and the young unemployed are alienated, they feel that society has failed them.

4. The future looks bleak as the problem of unemployment appears to be chronic and the number of people out of work has entered a new dimension. The "quick fixes" of the past do not seem to work any more and new, convincing solutions are hard to come by. It is politically difficult to implement tough solutions as everybody realizes that the problem must be tackled but does not want to be affected by negative side-effects. As the OECD projection shows, unemployment will increase in 1986.

III. Comment

1. If you look at this question from a more theoretical point of view, of course everybody should have a job as a (at least moral) right. Work is an important part of our lives – insofar as it enables us to earn our living and insofar as it shows us to be useful members of our society which just would not work if nobody worked. Apart from giving us a chance to earn a living, work should have, and in most cases has, a central role in our lives (we spend about a third of our lives working – and that's quite a lot!) and many people find satisfaction in what they do.
   Unemployment poses many problems, both economically and as regards the psychological problems of the people who are out of work (social problems, feelings of alienation, frustration etc). But in our society and free enterprise economy it is impossible to guarantee that everybody has a job. That can only be done in a state-run

economy – but there you have other problems, such as a lack of freedom and 'hidden unemployment', i.e. more jobs than work, and central planning.
The statement does not say anything about having the job one wants or likes – and if the price for a guaranteed job is that somebody tells you what job you are going to get, I think most people would rather not have a job as a right.
2. Both statements are partly true – but if you take them unconditionally and absolutely, they are both wrong and absurd. "We live to work." Yes, I think that we live here on earth to fulfil a certain task, that we work to further the cause of humanity and, if we can, to help our fellow men. Life as we know it in our Western society, our culture and living standard are impossible without work. And each of us has his special gifts and constributions to make which nobody else is able to.
But that does not mean that work is the only thing we can expect from life, there is more to it than drudgery and hard labour. "We work to live." One aspect of working – whatever your job or profession and however high or low your station in life – is to earn your living. So we really work that we can pay the rent, buy food and clothes and whatever else we need to live – to keep the wolf from the door.
But it would not be very satisfactory if you looked at your job only as a means to earn money. (Unfortunately that probably is the case in many jobs in our economy where we have much dull and unsatisfying work.) If that should be the case, alienation from your work will be the result – and the increasing importance of hobbies and other leisure activities shows how real this problem has become. So each statement – taken with a grain of salt – will provide you with a proper view of work and life.

IV. Translation

Es scheint (die) stillschweigende Einigkeit/Übereinkunft (darüber) zu herrschen/ bestehen, daß für die schwer zu vermittelnden Arbeitslosen in Europa/daß für die hartnäckigen Fälle der Arbeitslosigkeit in Europa wenig getan werden kann, außer eine Rückkehr zu der jetzt/nun unglaubwürdigen/in Verruf geratenen Wohlfahrtspolitik der Vergangenheit. Es gibt jedoch einige Gründe, optimistisch zu sein, so trostlos das Bild (auch) ist/aussieht. Gegen Ende dieses Jahrzehnts wird sich Europas Bevölkerungsstruktur anfänglich verändern. Während die geburtenstarke Nachkriegsgeneration älter wird, werden weniger junge Arbeitssuchende auf den Arbeitsmarkt drängen. Und (die) durchgreifenden/radikalen Strukturänderungen, die derzeit ablaufen/stattfinden – der Abbau von Verordnungen/Vorschriften, der Niedergang der Stahl- und Kohleindustrie, die Automatisierung in der Automobil- und Elektronikindustrie – werden (dann) abgeschlossen sein.
Inzwischen muß Europa jedoch jeden Tag 12000 Arbeitsplätze schaffen, nur um die Arbeitslosigkeit am Zunehmen zu hindern/nur um eine Zunahme der Arbeitslosigkeit zu verhindern. Für eine Gruppe von Volkswirtschaften, die im letzten Jahrzehnt mehr Arbeitsplätze abgebaut/verloren hat als sie (neue) schuf, scheint dies eine nicht zu bewältigende Herausforderung zu sein. In gewissem Ausmaß/Maß wird Europa noch tiefer gespalten werden/sein in diejenigen, die Arbeit haben und die Arbeitslosen. Einige der negativen Auswirkungen/Schmerzen werden gemäßigt werden durch Europas immer noch großzügige Wohlfahrtseinrichtungen. Aber indem/während die Leistungen reduziert/ zurückgenommen werden, werden immer mehr/mehr und mehr Menschen die schmerzlichen Auswirkungen spüren. Es ist deutlich/klar, daß die Starrheit/Unbeweglichkeit, die in den wirtschaftlichen und politischen Systemen vorhanden ist/zu eigen ist, nicht schnell/rasch überwunden werden wird. Europas beste Hoffnung wird/mag wohl sein, daß die ständige Zunahme der Arbeitslosigkeit eingedämmt, oder sogar ein oder zwei Prozentpunkte verringert werden kann. Bis dahin hat Europa eigentlich keine andere/ kaum eine andere Wahl als mit einer Krankheit zu leben, die es vielleicht eindämmen/ zum Stillstand bringen, aber nicht heilen/überwinden kann.

> **Leistungskurs Englisch (Baden-Württemberg): Textaufgaben Landeskunde**
> **Aufgabe 11: International Relations**

International Relations

The two world wars of this century are the decisive factor in the decline of Europe as the political center of the world. At the same time as they weakened the main European nations in their human and material resources, they brought non-European nations to the fore, the United States and Japan after the First World War, the United States and the Soviet Union after the Second. These two world wars differ not only in their consequences but also in their intrinsic character from the wars that have been fought in the Western world in modern times. Most previous wars were limited: only a fraction of the total human and material resources of the belligerents was committed to the war, only a fraction of the total population was morally identified with the war and suffered from it, and the war was waged only for limited objectives. The two world wars and those for which the most powerful nations prepare today are total in all these respects. The actuality and threat of total war are indeed the most important distinctive characteristics of contemporary international relations. This threat of war is caused by an unpreedented accumulation of destructive power in the hands of the most powerful nations and the incentive to use that power for national purposes.

The trend toward the concentration of more and more power in the hands of fewer and fewer states has continued and at the end of the Second World War the number of nations of the first rank was reduced to two – the United States and the Soviet Union.

Whereas traditionally the international relations of the Western world were carried on within the framework of common moral principles and a common way of life, which imposed effective limitations upon the struggle for power, in our age international relations are dominated by the conflict between democracy and communism, each putting forth a message of universal salvation, each trying – with differing intensity – to extend its dominion to all mankind, and each identified with one of the two great powers left in the world. Thus international relations today are characterized not only by the traditional threat and use of military force on behalf of the aspirations of individual nations but also by a struggle for the minds of men through which the proponents of the two antagonistic philosophies and ways of life – using the instruments of propaganda, foreign aid, and foreign trade – endeavor to gain the allegiance of uncommitted nations. By the same token, the traditional methods of diplomacy are in eclipse; although nations can negotiate and bargain about their interests and conclude compromises concerning them, they feel that they cannot yield an inch where their philosophies and ways of life are at stake.

However, the search for a more effective method of preserving peace than diplomacy can provide – a search that has occupied humanity to an ever-increasing extent since the beginning of the nineteenth century – reflects the new and ever-increasing urgency that the problem of peace has taken on in our time. The political, technological, and moral revolutions of our time have transformed war from the rational instrument of foreign policy which it once was into an instrument of universal destruction. It is one of the great paradoxes of our age that the preservation of peace has become a matter of survival for Western civilization, while the traditional instruments of preserving it have become less effective and more effective ones have not yet been devised.

580 words

from: International Relations, by Hans J. Morgenthau, in: American Polities andGovernment, Voice of America Forum Lectures, shortened and edited.

Vocabulary:
line 6:	intrinsic	–	belonging naturally, essential, inherent
line 15:	incentive	–	motivation, sth. that constitutes a motive
line 24:	dominion	–	supremacy, overriding influence, supreme power
line 30:	token	–	evidence, indication
line 33:	to be at stake	–	to be won or lost

I. Language

1. Vocabulary (ohne Wörterbuch zu bearbeiten)
   Please give synonyms or paraphrases for the following expressions or words – keep to the given context.

   a) 7: "Most <u>previous</u> wars were limited ..."
   Please give a paraphrase, you may change the sentence structure. (1 VP)

   b) 7–8: "... only a <u>fraction</u> of the ... resources ..."
   Give a synonym, don't change the sentence. (1 VP)

   c) 8: "... <u>belligerents</u> ..."
   Paraphrase, you can change the sentence. (1 VP)

   d) 10: "... the war was waged only for limited <u>objectives</u>."
   Find a suitable synonym, do not change the sentence. (1 VP)

   e) 12: "... <u>indeed</u> ..."
   Give a fitting synonym but do not change the structure of the sentence. (1 VP)

   f) 12–13: "... the most important distinctive <u>characteristics</u> of contem<u>porary</u> international relations."
   Explain, you can change the sentence. (2 VP)

   g) 13–14: "... by an <u>unprecedented</u> accumulation ..."
   Explain, you may change the structure of the sentence. (1 VP)

   h) 30: "... the traditional methods of dipolmacy are <u>in eclipse</u> ..."
   Please explain, you may change the sentence. (1 VP)

   i) 34–36: "... the search ... <u>reflects</u> ... the new urgency ..."
   Find a synonym, do not change the structure of the sentence. (1 VP)

2. Grammar and Style (ohne Wörterbuch zu bearbeiten)

   a) 16–18: "The trend ... <u>has continued</u> and at the end of the Second World War the number of nations of the first rank <u>was reduced</u> to two ..." Explain the use of the tenses. (2 VP)

   b) 14: destructive
      21: effective
      Give the verbs to these adjectives. (1 VP)

   c) 5–6: "These two world wars differ not only in their consequences ..."
   Start the sentence with: Not only ... (1 VP)

   d) 34–36: "However, the search for a more effective method ... reflects the new ... urgency ..."
   What part of speech is 'however' in this sentence? (1 VP)

II. Comprehension
You are to deal with the following questions, in complete sentences. Keep to the direct and indirect information given in the text, no quotations, please.

1. What are the differences between the old 'traditional' wars and the two world wars?
   (60–80 words) (3 VP)
2. How has Europe's role changed since the beginning of the 20th century?
   (60–80 words) (3 VP)
3. Which new role have the USA assumed after the end of the Second World War?
   (90–110 words) (4 VP)
4. Can you give one or two examples of "the decline of Europe as the political center of the world" (line 1–2)?
   (100–120 words) (4 VP)

III. Comment (10 VP)
Choose one of the following topics: (200–300 words)

1. "It is one of the great paradoxes of our age that the preservation of peace has become a matter of survival for Western civilization, while the traditional instruments of preserving it have become less effective and more effective ones have not yet been devised." (line 39–42) Comment on that idea.
2. People say West Germany has become Americanized since 1945. Can you give some examples for that phenomenon.
3. America's role as the leader of the Western world has sometimes presented difficulties and problems for Europe. Can you describe some of them.

IV. Translation (30 VP)

The question remained in the latter years of the 20th century as to what new configurations might emerge in world politics in consequence of America's decline as a world power, of Communist polycentrism, and of the seeming rise to prominence of a new Third World. Would the international system, in becoming more diffuse and
5 decentralized, become more anarchic or more stable? Would the diminution of America's international commitments encourage a healthier multipolar world or invite new threats to peace? Or were the perceived changes themselves deceptive, concealing the persistence of the Cold War?
One permanent change was clear to any close observer of international politics; world
10 politics now was wholly global; more than ever before in human history, local events in any part of the world could gain worldwide significance as elements in an interlocking whole that was regulated by no single centre of authority. The Western democratic nations were now a small minority of states in a world otherwise dominated by authoritarian or totalitarian regimes, their influence over world events largely deriving
15 from their continuing economic vitality. Above all of this remained the vivid awareness of the potential destructiveness of nuclear war, inspiring both prudence and fear.

198 words

from: "International Relations", in Encyclopaedia Britannica, 15th edition (1985), 21: 823

Vocabulary:

line 3:	polycentrism	–	Polyzentrismus
line 4:	diffuse	–	vague, uncertain
line 6:	commitments	–	Verpflichtungen
line 8:	persistence	–	hier: continuation
line 12:	regulated	–	controlled, ruled

Lösungsvorschlag

I. Language

1. Vocabulary
   a) Most wars of the past were limited ...
      Most wars in former times were limited ...
   b) ... only a (small) part of the resources ...
   c) ... of those/the nations waging war/being at war/being involved in a war ...
   d) ... the war was waged only for limited aims/goals.
   e) ... really/in fact ...
   f) ... the most important distinctive features/typical qualities/signs of the international relations of our time/of the present time.
   g) ... by an accumulation of destructive power which has never before existed ...
   h) ... the traditional methods of diplomacy are losing importance/becoming less important/getting less significant ...
   i) ... the search ... shows/makes clear ... the new urgency ...

2. Grammar and Style
   a) The present perfect is used in the first case because a process is described which began in the past and the results of this process are still valid now.
      In the second case the past tense is used as the process began and ended in the past (at the end of the Second World War ...)
   b) to destry
      to effect
   c) Not only do these two world wars differ in their consequences ...
   d) In this sentence 'however' is a conjunction.

II. Comprehension

1. They differ in two aspects from the world wars. The old, 'traditional' wars normally left the system of the states which waged war basically intact and unchanged, although there were territorial gains and losses. And in those wars the warring states and nations were not totally committed; neither as regards their resources nor as regards the moral commitment or the suffering of their population.

2. At the beginning of the 20th century Europe was the political centre of the world. The First World War brought about a change in this role: Europe was weakened (especially Germany and Russia; the Austrian empire broke up; and to a certain extent even France became weaker) and the USA became a great power and so did Japan – to a certain extent.
   The Second World War brought even more sweeping changes; only the USA and the USSR are left as the two great superpowers.

3. After World War II the USA was the one superpower, the Soviet Union the other. As the cold war developed, the USA assumed the role of the leader of the Western World. As such they feel responsible for the political and military safety of the coun-

tries in their sphere of influence, and they try to contain (or roll-back, depending on the political doctrine of the day) the influence of communism. In this struggle the instruments of propaganda, foreign aid, and foreign trade are used – as well as military threats (if you think of the Cuban missile crisis) and military action (e.g. Vietnam, Grenada).
4. One good example of "the decline of Europe as the political center of the world" is the development of the former British Empire.
At the end of the 19th century a huge empire was ruled from London and contributed to Britain's political, economic and military power.
After the colonies with a substantial number of white settlers were given more and more political power, their relatively independent dominion status was formally recognized in the Statute of Westminster in 1931. After World War II practically all of the British colonies successively became independent; the British Commonwealth being a very loose institution based on consultation – but London has no power any more to really influence the policies of its former colonies.

III. Comment

1. Since the Second World War ended in Japan with the explosion of the two first atom bombs, the threat of total destruction of the earth has become a real possibility. Since the USSR also has nuclear weapons and since the beginning of the cold war in the late 1940s with the bi-polar system and its conflicts between democracy and communism, the threat of the total destruction of our planet has become not only a possibility but a grave danger. This possibility of the destruction of the whole world is a totally new phenomenon – each armed conflict since that point in time has a new quality (and the parties concerned must show much more responsibility) which no war in the past ever had.
On the other hand, the traditional instruments of preserving peace – and that normally was diplomacy – have become less effective. The main reasons seem to be that the basic understanding of the nations of the world has been shattered. Since 1917 the political ideology of socialism and communism has taken root and since 1945 a large part of the world has been ruled by socialist or communist governments. The communist ideology and democracy are fundamentally opposed as regards all sectors of political life – therefore diplomacy has lost some effectiveness as even fundamentals cannot be agreed upon any more.
The two above mentioned factors – total destructive power and less dipomatic understanding – characterize the paradox and perverse situation of our endangered planet. We need strong efforts at finding new ways of coming to genuine and universally accepted measures of keeping and securing peace.
2. I would say that it is a fact that Germany became Americanized in many respects – but this is a phenomenon which is not particular to Germany but can be seen in all parts of the Western World, and to a certain extent even in some communist countries. If you look at what young people wear, Blue Jeans have almost become a must for young people – if they want to be "in", Jeans normally are part of the dress code; and not only in Germany and Western Europe but also in Communist countries where Jeans are the most sought after black market commodity.
Other aspects are the ubiquity of the fast food chains – such as McDonalds –, chewing gum and other facets of our youth culture. If you turn on the radio you'll mostly hear English language pop-songs, mostly from America.
Many words have become part of our language which can be traced to postwar American influence, and the most impressive fact about that is that you find them in all areas of life (e. g. cash-flow, cash-and-carry, input and output if you think of

economics; pre-bleached, sun-top, T-shirt, sweat shirt etc. if you think of fashion; almost all technical terms in the computer business; etc). There are other instances where you can remark this strong American influence in the Federal Republic of Germany – and it is no surprise if you consider the strong political, economic, and military ties which developed after the end of the Second World War.

3. Apart from any examples regarding US – European problems I think one should first take a look at the psychological situation if you have a (relatively strong) leader and a group of followers. In such a situation you are bound to come across conflicts between the leader and the others; especially if the group which is led feels independent and self-confident, and if questions concerning conflicting interests crop up. One of the recent problems concerns the deployment of medium-range missiles and cruise missiles in Europe. The US (and Nato) think these missiles should be stationed in Europe to keep the USSR in check, but some European governments and a large part of public opinion disagree as these missiles would only be used in the case of a European war (and therefore affect only Europe and not the USA), and they might invite retaliatory strikes.

The Vietnam war was another instance when many Europeans disagreed with the US who planned to bomb North-Vienam into submission, supporting a corrupt regime in South-Vietnam. As the downfall of South Vietnam showed they were probably right.

The development of the EEC into an economic juggernaut has also presented problems in the relations with the USA, especially in times of recession. Both sides try to protect their economies and every now and then resort to protectionist measures which are incompatible with free trade agreements. But although those conflicts lead to heated exchanges of arguments, and sometimes to counter-measures (retaliatory tariffs and taxes) they have always been overcome.

There will always be difficulties and conflicts such as the above-mentioned – but they can be solved without too many complications as those of the past were solved.

IV. Translation

In den letzten/späten Jahren des 20. Jahrhunderts blieb die Frage (bestehen), welche neuen Konfigurationen/Konstellationen/Strukturen in der Weltpolitik auftauchen könnten/mögen als Folge/Konsequenz von Amerikas Niedergang als Weltmacht, des kommunistischen Polyzentrismus und des anscheinenden Aufstiegs/in den Vordergrund treten einer neuen dritten Welt. Würde das internationale politische System – indem es undifferenzierter und dezentralisierter wurde – anarchistischer/labiler oder stabiler werden? Würde die Abnahme/Abschwächung der amerikanischen internationalen Verpflichtungen (die Entwicklung) eine gesündere, multipolare Welt fördern oder neue Bedrohungen des Friedens herausfordern/hevorrufen? Oder waren die Veränderungen, die man bemerkte, selbst/in Wirklichkeit eine Täuschung, welche die Fortsetzung/das Andauern/ die Fortdauer des kalten Krieges verbargen/vertuschten?

Eine endgültige Veränderung war für jeden aufmerksamen Beobachter der internationalen Politik deutlich/klar: die Weltpolitik umfaßte nun/jetzt (wirklich) die ganze Welt; mehr denn je in der Geschichte der Menschheit konnten örtliche Ereignisse/Geschehnisse in irgendeinem Teil der Welt weltweite Bedeutung erhalten als Teile in einem interdependenten/miteinander verflochtenen Ganzen, das nicht von einem einzigen Machtzentrum regiert/bestimmt wird. Die westlichen Demokratien waren nun eine kleine Minderheit von Staaten in einer Welt, die ansonsten von autoritären oder totalitären Regierungen/Regimes beherrscht wurde und deren Einfluß auf Weltereignisse/ Ereignisse in der Welt hauptsächlich/größtenteils auf ihrer weiter andauernden wirtschaftlichen Kraft beruhte. Alle diese Probleme/Phänomene überlagerte das deutliche/ lebendige Bewußtsein der potentiellen Zerstörungskraft des Atomkriegs, was sowohl Besonnenheit/Vernunft als auch Furcht hervorrief.

> **Leistungskurs Englisch (Baden-Württemberg): Abiturprüfung 1986**
> **Textaufgabe und Übersetzung**

The evolution of Golding's reputation in the United States traces and parodies our intellectual drift. In the course of the last ten years, controversy over his famous book has raged through urban and rural school boards across the land, and more than one chapter of the Parent-Teacher-Association has become alarmed over their reading of the unhappy island adventure. In some school libraries *Lord of the Flies* was put under lock and key. It has been declared both subversive and obscene. Both the Radical Right and the New Left have published official condemnations stating that Golding is too old-fashioned and pessimistic for properly oriented young moderns.

Arthur Simpson, writing in "Mainstream", tells us that Golding believes "evil is inherent in the human mind itself", while every good socialist revolutionary knows that evil is, in Simpson's words, "the product of a particular organization of society." Golding, he concludes, has written a book which takes the opposite view and therefore supports "the ruling class" and "the hydrogen bomb ideologists". A similar interpretation is offered by Juliet Mitchell writing in the "New Left Review". She argues that Golding is a banal Christian theologian who believes in the fundamentmental evil of the human being; and, naturally, if one believes that, then there is no point in committment to the New Left politics, or any other politics as a means of improving the behavior of men. The Radical Right has offered no more sophisticated arguments than these, since it usually confines itself simply to pointing out that Golding undermines the confidence of the young in the American Way of Life – that wonderfully convenient phrase which sums up so much glorious folly. One has only to point to Ralph to suggest some of the objections from this quarter: here is an elected leader, chosen by the sacrosanct democratic procedure, yet he fails to save his constituency; here is a young man – blond, blue-eyed, stalwart, a hard worker, a good sport, a believer in adult integrity and adult authority, who even has a father in the navy – and, well, he lets his hair grow and just doesn't see things through to a desirable conclusion.

As these views suggest, the political conservative and the political revolutionary hold at least one thing in common: both predicate their theories and hopes on the thesis that human problems and ills may be controlled and eventually overcome through adjustments in the social and economic environment.

Golding's belief, insofar as it is spelled out in the events on his island, is indeed something quite different. Social and economic adjustments, he believes, treat only the symptoms instead of the disease. The troubles manifested in the social world are a direct outgrowth of human deficiencies we have not mastered in the course of our evolution as biological and moral beings. This strikes us as a very unfashionable idea, a discouraging estimate of human nature and cultural progress. Golding gives only two cheers for democracy because it has failed to evolve into an ideal community, and because it is certainly not moving in that direction now.

This qualified evaluation of the modern mind and the social establishment it has built is the very antithesis of the popular view which has stood for at least a hundred and fifty years. According to Golding, we have been reared in a tradition of optimism about man and his potentials, and as a consequence we suffer from "an appaling ignorance" of our real nature.

574 words   *James R. Baker*

Vocabulary:

line 3:	chapter	–	local branch of an association
line 23/24:	stalwart	–	strong
line 28:	to predicate on	–	to base on
line 41:	to rear	–	to bring up, to educate

I. Language

1. Vocabulary (Ohne Wörterbuch zu bearbeiten)
   In the following you are to deal with the underlined words/expressions within the given context.

   a) 16–17: "... There is <u>no point in commitment to</u> the New Left politics ..."
   Explain; you may change the sentence structure. (2 VP)

   b) 20: "... that wonderfully <u>convenient</u> phrase ..."
   Find a suitable substitute; keep to the sentence structure. (1 VP)

   c) 20–21: "... which sums up to the most <u>glorious</u> folly ..."
   Find a suitable substitute; keep to the sentence structure. (1 VP)

   d) 25–26: "... he ... just doesn't see things <u>through to a desirable conclusion</u>."
   Explain; you may change the sentence structure. (2 VP)

   e) 33–34: "The troubles ... are a direct <u>outgrowth</u> ot human deficiencies ..."
   Find a suitable substitute; keep to the sentence structure. (1 VP)

   f) 36–37: "Golding <u>gives only two cheers</u> for democray ..."
   Explain; you may change the sentence structure. (2 VP)

   g) 40: "... the <u>very</u> antithesis of the popular view ..."
   Find a suitable substitute; keep to the sentence structure. (1 VP)

   h) 42–43: "... we suffer from an '<u>appalling</u> ignorance' of our real nature."
   Find a suitable substitute; keep to the sentence structure. (1 VP)

2. Grammar and Style (ohne Wörterbuch zu bearbeiten)

   a) 6: "It has been declared both subversive and obscene."
   Change into the active voice. (1 VP)

   b) 10: "... in the human mind itself ..."
      18–19: "... it usually confines itself ..."
   Explain the use of "itself" in each case. (2 VP)

   c) 17–18: "The Radical Right has offered no more sophisticated arguments than these ..."
   Which word does "more" refer to? (1 VP)

   d) 28: "... on the thesis that ..."
      31: "(his) belief, insofar as it is ..."
   Give the plural forms of the nouns. (1VP)

II. Comprehension

Answer the following questions in complete sentences. In your answers to questions 1, 2 and 3 keep to the information given, but do not quote.

1. How did the American New Left and the American Radical Right understand Golding and why did each side object to his views?
   (80–120 words) (4 VP)
2. What views on Golding did the two sides, in spite of their different convictions, have in common?
   (40–60 words) (2 VP)
3. What is Goldings's belief according to J.R. Baker?
   (40–60 words) (2 VP)
4. "In some school librairies *Lord of the Flies* was put under lock and key. It has been declared both subversive and obscene."
   Choose a characteristic scene from the novel that might have shocked the American public and explain why that effect was possible.
   (50 – 70 words) (2 VP)

III. Comment (10 VP)

Choose <u>one</u> of the following topics: (200–300 words)

1. *Lord of the Flies* has been labelled a "wholly pessimistic story". Discuss this view.
2. The opponents Jack and Ralph: compare their characters, aims and methods.
3. Choose two or three symbols from the novel and show their significance.

IV. Translation (30 VP)

During the post-war years the whole process of "decolonisation" mattered for Britain in two main respects: in so far as it raised issues that split public opinion at home – about the rights of white settlers in Kenya or Rhodesia, or the degree of tolerance to be extended to terrorist leaders; and in so far as it interacted with foreign affairs – such as in the
5 safeguarding of naval and air bases overseas or preventing Communist intrusions. the problems, desires, and needs of underdeveloped countries had never before impinged so directly on British politics nor received so much attention from British politicians. Events happened fast, and the climate of British opinion was so favourable to colonial emancipation that little resistance was offered to each new claim for larger self-go-
10 vernment or for sovereign independence. The essential problems – whether self-government would lead to military dictatorship, sovereign independence to social injustice – were too seldom discussed. The values of nationalism were assumed to be absolute, their righteousness taken to be self-evident.
   Yet historical experience has often shown that the principle of national self-determina-
15 tion, carried to extremes, makes for the tyranny of demagogues or generals.

188 words   David Thomson

Vocabulary
line 5:   to safequard   –   to protect
line 6/7:   to impinge on   –   to have an effect on
line 13:   righteousness   –   cf. adj. righteous: morally justified

Lösungsvorschlag

I. Language

1. Vocabulary

a) ... it doesn't make sense/it's useless to struggle and work for the New Left politics/to support the New Left politics.
There is no reason for supporting the New Left politics.
b) ...that wonderfully appropriate/useful/suitable/fitting phrase ...
c) ... which sums up so much wonderful/triumphant/splendid/brilliant folly.
d) ... he just isn't able to bring things to a successful/positive ending.
... he just isn't able to handle things so as to come to a positive result.
e) The troubles... are a direct product/result/consequence of human deficiencies.
f) Golding is not very enthusiastic/optimistic about democracy ...
Golding does not think too well of democracy ...
g) ... the real/direct/exact antithesis of the popular view ...
h) ... we suffer from a shocking/(an) abominable/(an) awful/terrible/horrible ignorance of our real nature ...

2. Grammar and Style

a) They/People have (One has) declared it both subversive and obscene.
b) ... in the human mind itself ...: This is a case of emphatic use of 'itself' (emphasizing 'human mind').
... it usually confines itself ...: Itself is a reflexive pronoun used with a (reflexive) verb.
c) 'more' refers to the adjective 'sophisticated'.
d) theses – beliefs

II. Comprehension

1. The American New Left objected to Golding's opinion that evil is an inherent quality in the human mind and cannot be overcome by man himself.
The leftist ideology says that man's life is determined by the material and social conditions and that thus a change of these conditions can and will change and improve man's nature. As Golding's view of man is different, the New Left saw him as a supporter of the ruling class.
The radical Right accused Golding of being too pessimistic and of weakening the confidence of the young people in American values. Ralph's failure to manage things successfully as the democratically elected leader is the most obvious example of this attitude.

2. Both sides criticized Golding for being too pessimistic. They thought that his book does not offer any characters which are positive models for the young Americans.
Most important, both sides objected to Golding's view that man cannot be changed by improving the economic and social conditions under which he lives.

3. Man's troubles which one can see in the social and economic world are a direct consequence of deficiencies in his evolution; man has not overcome or learned to control his primitive instincts.
Therefore economic and social improvements can only treat the symptoms – not the root causes – and cannot create a perfect society.

4. One scene that might have shocked is Piggy's death. After Piggy's glasses had been stolen, Ralph and Piggy tried to reason with Jack to return the glasses. In cold blood Roger levered a rock free from above which hit Piggy and smashed the conch.
The American public might have felt the brutal murder committed by a boy and the graphic description of Piggy's death to be subversive and obscene.

III. Comment

1. There are good reasons to label *Lord of the Flies* a wholly pessimistic story.
Even the background – an atomic war – is a rather nasty situation; and whenever the adult world enters the picture it also is only negatively; the dead parachutist who lands on the island was shot in aerial combat, and the ship which rescues the boys is a war ship.

If you look at the overall development of this group of boys you could say that the situation changes from bad to worse. After trying to organize the semblance of a democratic system of government the majority of the boys become savages and form an autocratically run tribe.

The conch, the symbol of democracy, and free speech, is smashed and the spears as instruments of killing and torture could be seen as the new symbols of the tribe. The bloodlust of the boys becomes stronger and develops into a decisive factor in the story. At the beginning even Jack hesitates to kill a pig, later on the boys kill Simon in their frenzy, Piggy is killed in cold blood, and at the end the tribe arranges an organized hunt for Ralph – to capture, torture and probably kill him – which is only interrupted by the arrival of the officer.

There are a few things, however, which one could look at as hopeful and optimistic signs. Ralph tries, although relatively unsuccessfully, to uphold a civilized society. And he, Piggy and Samneric too, show considerable courage when they go to Castle Rock to get back Piggy's glasses. But Ralph's struggle gets more and more hopeless as the novel progresses; and Piggy is killed when they argue with Jack about the glasses.

So one could say that *Lord of the Flies* is a "wholly pessimistic story".

2. Jack seems to be more ambitious than Ralph. He likes to exercise power and to have a group of boys who depend on him. Although he appears to be co-operative at the beginning, he becomes impatient when he does not succeed. His bloodthirst as the leader of the hunters strengthens the darker sides of his character, and as the masked chief of his tribe he personifies absolute, primitive power and enjoys his power.
He aims to wrest power from Ralph; and he does so by luring the boys into his tribe. He wants to live in the present (rescue is no aim of his) and to satisfy his desires here and now – as he himself says, he wants to have fun on the island.
His methods are that he offers the boys to have some fun, such as the parties with a fire, meat and dancing (his providing meat is another important point). He also suc-

ceeds – at least in part – in easing the fear of the boys by introducing primitive rituals (if you think of the painted bodies, the mask, and the offering of the pig's head to the beast).

Ralph is more of a dreamer, and not very quick in grasping the important facts – but he is the most helpful of the boys, he shows hardly any egoistical features. He shows tenacity in trying to uphold a civilized community even when he fails, and never gives up the hope of being rescued. His aim is to form a little England on the island, an orderly democratic and civilized society – until they are rescued; and that is why the signal fire is so important to him.

He tries to implement some clear rules to organize their life on the island (not like Jack who wants to have rules only that he can punish the offenders), the best instance for this endeavour are the meetings and the various duties (the group building the shelters, the hunters, and those guarding the signal fire).

3. The conch is the symbol of what Ralph tries to realize on the island. When Piggy and Ralph find it, it belongs to the natural harmony of the island; later it is used to call the boys together, and whoever holds the conch at a meeting can speak and the others (should) listen. You could call it a symbol of democracy. When the community breaks up and Jack's more primitive and atavistic tribe takes over it is only fitting that this symbol of order and democracy is smashed when Piggy is killed.

The mask which Jack wears could be seen as the symbol of a primitve way of life. As soon as Jack wears it he becomes much more assertive as the absolute chief of his tribe; he can hide his insecurity and the remnants of civilization behind this mask, and the reversal to a primitive and atavistic society progresses much faster and Jack becomes bolder and even resorts to torture.

The fire is a symbol which has no clear and unambiguous meaning. On the one hand, the signal fire can be seen as the symbol of hope for the boys, a symbol of the hope of being helped by the adult world. But quite early in the novel this fire burns out of control and a part of the forest is destroyed – and afterwards one of the littluns is missing. This foreshadows the destructive side of the fire which finds its climax in the final fire destroying the whole island (which was started to flush out Ralph from his hiding place when the tribe wanted to catch, torture and perhaps even kill him). Paradoxically, this destructive fire also gets the boys rescued. Thus the fire is a symbol of hope – but when it gets out of control it symbolizes destruction.

IV. Translation

Der gesamte/ganze Vorgang/Prozess der Entkolonialisierung war während der Nachkriegsjahre für Großbritannien in zweierlei Hinsicht von Bedeutung (...spielte ... eine Rolle): insofern als er Probleme/Fragen aufwarf, die die öffentliche Meinung im eigenen Land/in Großbritannien spalteten – über die Rechte der weißen Siedler in Kenia oder Rhodesien oder über das Maß/Ausmaß an Toleranz, das Terroristenführern gewährt/entgegengebracht werden sollte; and insofern als es außenpolitische Auswirkungen hatte – so wie z. B. bei der Sicherung überseeischer Marine- und Luftwaffenstützpunkte oder bei der Verhinderung/dem Verhindern des Eindringens des Kommunismus. Die Probleme, Wünsche und Bedürfnisse/Forderungen der unterentwickelten Länder hatten sich niemals vorher so direkt auf die britische Politik ausgewirkt, noch hatten sie jemals zuvor so viel Aufmerksamkeit/Beachtung bei britischen Politikern gefunden. Die Ereignisse liefen sehr rasch ab/überstürzten sich, und die Einstellung/das Klima der öffentlichen Meinung in Großbritannien war für die Entlassung der Kolonien in die Unabhängigkeit so günstig, daß jeder neuen Forderung nach mehr innerer Selbstverwaltung oder nach völliger Unabhängigkeit wenig/kaum Widerstand entgegengesetzt/geleistet wurde. Die wichtigen/wesentlichen Probleme/Fragen – ob Selbstverwaltung zur Militärdiktatur führen oder völlige Unabhängigkeit zu sozialer Ungerechtigkeit führen würden – wurden zu selten diskutiert/erörtert. Die Wertvorstellungen des Nationalismus wurden als absolut hingenommen/gesetzt, ihre moralische Berechtigung für selbstverständlich gehalten. Jedoch hat die geschichtliche Erfahrung oft gelehrt/gezeigt, daß das Prinzip der nationalen Selbstbestimmung, wenn es übertrieben wird/wenn es auf die Spitze getrieben wird, zur Diktatur von Demagogen oder Generälen führt/tendiert (die Diktatur von ... fördert).

> **Leistungskurs Englisch (Baden-Württemberg): Abiturprüfung 1987**
> **Textaufgabe und Übersetzung**

Up to the events leading to the Treaty of 1921 which created the Irish Free State and kept Ulster within the United Kingdom the British emotional involvement in Ireland was as great as that of any of the Irish. Not only for many centuries had there been the closest personal, cultural and economic ties between people living in the two islands, but in the 120 years after the Act of Union, this connection seemed, for the British, to have become something like an inseparable part of their own personality. The great Empire they had built for themselves had been won to a considerable extent by the active participation of Irish soldiers and sailors of all ranks. Descendants of old colonists in Ireland or of the earlier Gaelic settlers, or of a mixture of the two, had merged often indistinguishably into the cultural, administrative and political life of the British nation.

The anglicization of Ireland itself during this period, in which the Gaelic language at last ceased to be the language of the majority of the inhabitants, confirmed the illusion for the British that the Irish, charmingly different in many ways as they might be, were also one with them. This explains the passionate British attachment to the Union or later to the idea of Home Rule – the latter being, as its supporters believed, a device for preserving the inseparable polity of the two islands while allowing the Irish to maintain their identity within it. When the Union had to be abandoned and Home Rule proved unworkable it was for Britain a traumatic experience. So traumatic was the rupture at the time that after the Treaty of 1921 the British people acted in the only way in which it is possible to survive a deep wound: they awaited the inevitable formation of scar tissue which finally enabled that wound to be forgotten.

In 1968–9, when Ireland once again came to the forefront of Britain's problems with the Civil Rights marches in Ulster there was small emotional involvement left. It was a different problem now: for the government a tedious one, and for the British people themselves a bore. A referendum held in Britain today on the issue of whether or not Britain should surrender sovereignty over Northern Ireland would very possibly result in a 'Yes' vote – not because the electorate had carefully thought the matter out, but because they wanted to get rid of Northern Ireland and its apparently insoluble problems. Such indifference on the part of the British public would have seemed inconceivable in the days when even the prospect of Home Rule could excite the fiercest passions.

Any British government, however, and particularly a Conservative one, is bound by a moral and, under an Act of Parliament of 1949, legal obligation not to allow Northern Ireland to become part of the Republic of Ireland unless the Parliament of Northern Ireland wishes this to happen. But this is an obligation not supported by that passionate sense of commitment which was once attached to the Act of Union. Perhaps the most positive reason for continued involvement is that, were the British government to withdraw, it would look like surrender to terrorism and thus lead to a loss of authority and credibility of governmental purpose elsewhere. It would be surrender to terrorism, too. But it could be pointed out that an earlier British government withdrew from a much larger area of Ireland by surrendering to terrorism sixty years ago.

581 words *Robert Kee (1980)*

Vocabulary:

line 5:	Act of Union	–	Act passed by the British and Irish parliaments to form the United Kingdom of Great Britain and Ireland
line 15:	Home Rule	–	self-government in internal affairs by the people of Ireland
line 16:	polity	–	a nation or other politically organized society
line 18:	rupture	–	breaking apart
line 20/21:	formation of scar tissue	–	the healing of a wound

I. Language

1. Vocabulary (ohne Wörterbuch zu bearbeiten)

   In the following you are to deal with the underlined words/expressions within the given context.

   a) 4: "... cultural and economic <u>ties</u> between people ..."
   Find a suitable substitute; keep to the sentence structure. (1 VP)

   b) 8–10: "Descendants of old colonists ... had <u>merged</u> often <u>indistinguishably</u> into the ... life of the British nation."
   Explain; you may change the sentence structure. (2 VP)

   c) 15–16: "... a <u>device</u> for preserving the inseparable polity ..."
   Find a suitable substitute; keep to the sentence structure. (1 VP)

   d) 22: "... Ireland once again <u>came to the forefront</u> of Britain's problems ..."
   Explain; you may change the sentence structure. (1 VP)

   e) 27: "... not because the <u>electorate</u> had carefully thought the matter out ..."
   Explain; you may change the sentence structure. (1 VP)

   f) 29: "<u>Such indifference on the part of</u> the British public ..."
   Explain; you may change the sentence structure. (2 VP)

   g) 40–41: "... an earlier British government <u>withdrew</u> from a much larger area ..."
   Explain; you may change the sentence structure. (1 VP)

   h) 41: "... by <u>surrendering</u> to terrorism ..."
   Find a suitable substitute; keep to the sentence structure. (1 VP)

2. Grammar and Style (ohne Wörterbuch zu bearbeiten)

   a) 3–4: "Not only ... had there been the closest ... ties ..."
   37–38: "... were the British government to withdraw ..."
   Why is inversion used in each of the two sentences? (1 VP)

b) 14–16: "This explains the passionate British attachment to the Union or later to the idea of Home Rule – the latter <u>being</u> ... a device for preserving the inseparable polity of the two islands while <u>allowing</u> the Irish to maintain ..."
Rewrite the sentence by replacing the underlinded -ing-forms. (1 VP)

c) 20–21: "... the inevitable formation of scar tissue <u>which finally enabled that wound to be forgotten</u>."
Rewrite the clause, changing the passive into the active voice. (1 VP)

d) 34–35: "... unless the Parliament of Northern Ireland wishes this to happen."
Replace 'unless' and rewrite the clause without changing its meaning. (2 VP)

II. Comprehension

Answer the following questions in complete sentences. Keep to the information given in the text, but do not quote.

1. Characterize the relations between the British and the Irish before 1921.
   (80–120 words) (4 VP)
2. In what way has the attitude of the British towards Ireland changed since the end of the Union?
   (60–90 words) (3 VP)
3. What arguments against British withdrawal from Ulster does the author put forward?
   (60–90 words) (3 VP)

III. Comment (10 VP)

Choose <u>one</u> of the following topics: (200–300 words)

1. The conflict in Northern Ireland has been called a religious war.
   Discuss this view.
2. Apart form the Northern Irish conflict Britain is confronted with other social and political problems.
   Write about two of them.
3. The Civil Rights marches in Ulster remind us of similar events in the United States in the 1960s.
   Describe some of the causes, methods and achievements of the American Civil Rights Movement.

IV. Translation (30 VP)

Certainly the civilisation created by Golding disintegrates in the course of the story. And if we take the children separately as representing certain qualities within any individual, the book becomes hardly less gloomy. For Piggy shows us that rationality alone will not sustain us; Ralph shows us that good intentions, a capacity for leadership, and a commitment to social order will not suffice to prevent a reversion to savagery under pressure; and Jack shows us that the fears, cruelty, and lust for power which inhabit every one of us can gain dominance all too easily. But Simon seeks to confront his fears and comes to accept the evil that inheres in him as well as in the other children, though he pays with his life for what he discovers. By thus struggling against and yet recognizing his limitations as a person, Simon engages in that ever-lasting human task which is the source of man's defeats as of his triumphs – whether one regards man from the Christian perspective suggested by certain details in the novel or from a predominantly secular perspective.

180 words   *Howard S. Babb*

Vocabulary
line 1:   to disintegrate   –   to break up
line 4:   to sustain   –   to keep up, to support
line 5:   to suffice   –   to be enough

Lösungsvorschlag

I. Language

1. Vocabulary
   a) ... cultural and economic connections/links/bonds between people ...
   b) Descendants of old colonists ... had often been totally/completely integrated into the ... life of the British nation.
      Often there wasn't any discernable difference between the descendants of old colonists and the British.
      Descendants of old colonists ... had often become completely British.
   c) ... a means/tool/instrument for preserving the inseparable polity ...
   d) ... Ireland once again became one of the most important/crucial issues on the British political agenda ...
      ... Ireland once again became one of Britain's most pressing political problems ...
      ... the Irish question once again came to the attention of the British ...
   e) ... not because those who could vote had carefully thought the matter out ...
      The electorate are all the people in any given country who have the right to vote; and those people in England had not carefully thought the matter out ...
   f) the fact that the British public was (were) hardly interested/concerned ...
      The fact that the British public showed such lack of concern/interest ...
   g) ... an earlier British government gave up/retreated from/ended its occupation of a much larger area ...
   h) ... by giving in/yielding/capitulating to terrorism ...

2. Grammar and Style
   a) The first sentence begins with a negative adverbial/In the first sentence the negative adverbial is in front position; in such cases inversion is mandatory.
      The inversion in the second sentence expresses a condition ("if" has been omitted).
   b) This explains the passionate British attachment to the Union or later ot the idea of Home Rule – (as) the latter was ... a device for preserving the inseparable polity of the two islands while it allowed the Irish to maintain ...
   c) ... the inevitable formation of scar tissue which finally enabled people/them/the British to forget that wound.
   d) ... if the Parliament of Northern Ireland does not wish this to happen.
      ... exept in the case/except for the possibility that the Parliament of Northern Ireland wishes this to happen.

II. Comprehension

1. Before 1921 the British felt that Ireland really and truly was a part of the United Kingdom. There had been close ties for many centuries – economic, political, cultural and personal connections; and these ties had become even closer after the Act of Union in 1801.
In the course of history Ireland had become increasingly anglicized and many Irish actively took part in Britain's affairs. So there was a passionate attachment of the Bri-

tish to the Union – the British simply couldn't imagine that the Irish should not belong to the United Kingdom.

As the events in the 19th century and especially those leading up to the creation of the Irish Free State showed, the majority of the Irish had quite different ideas of their relations with the British.

2. The Treaty of 1921 was a shock for the British, a shock which numbed them. To overcome this shock they waited for that cut to heal – and in the process the close – and often emotional – attachment to Ireland decreased substantially.

This fact can be seen when looking at the situation which began in the late 1960s; it is very probable that the British electorate would vote for an unconditional withdrawal from Ireland just to be rid of the problem.

3. The author says that any British government must honour an Act of Parliament of 1949 which stipulates that the Parliament of Northern Ireland must consent to Northern Ireland becoming a part of the Republic of Ireland.

Furthermore there is a moral obligation which – especially a conservative – government should feel bound to.

A withdrawal from Northern Ireland would in effect mean giving in to terrorism and losing face – but that is what already happened in 1921.

III. Comment

1. I think the conflict in Northern Ireland is not a religious conflict, although the question who belongs to which side normally runs along religious lines. And if you read studies about the conflicts, it usually is only the Prostestant extremists who talk about religion, and only to incite their followers. There are no conflicts about religion as such. The conflict is the result of a long and cruel history in whose course politics and religion were mixed; and belonging to one religion meant having political and economic power, and belonging to the other meant having none.

Although Ireland became anglicized to a certain extent, the Catholics were treated as second class citizens – they had no right of citizenship and few of ownership and were in the control of largely absentee landlords – at least until 1829 when Parliament passed the Catholic Emancipation Act and Catholics could be elected to the Commons. During these times the word 'Protestant' became associated with 'oppression', and 'Catholic' was a synonym for 'oppressed'.

Therefore, whenever the Catholics wanted to improve their situation and wanted a share of the political power and the economic opportunities, they met with the resistance of the ruling class – and for centuries the ruling class in Ireland had been the Protestants. They tenaciously clung to power (and even opposed Home Rule as it would have meant giving up some power) which resulted in all the greater pressure by the Catholics.

Because of this historical background you always have Protestants pitted against Catholics in all political struggles in Northern Ireland – but it is not a religious war because religion as such plays no role; it only decides which side you are on.

2. I am of the opinion that the two most important conflicts Britain is confronted with at the moment are the problems with the coloured minorities living in Britain, and the gap between the stagnant north and the properous south.

After World War II a lot of people from Britain's former colonies came to the United Kingdom – mainly in the hope of finding better economic opportunities there. They were welcomed during the post-war boom and found work in industry and in the public sector (if you think of the National Health Service and public transport). The first generation immigrants were satisfied with the menial and badly paid work they usually got, but the second generation immigrants have 'normal' expectations which leads to tensions if these expectations are not realized. In addition to this, massive unemployment has intensified the latent prejudices racial minorities often encounter. This led to some very nasty riots in some English cities. The integration of the racial minorities in Britain is a very grave problem and a great task.

Unemployment in Britain is a great problem but some underlying causes are even more worrying. The decline of heavy industry is common to all industrialized countries, but Britain is especially hard hit. (Owing to its post-war policy of sheltering its nationalized industries from competitive market forces and thus destroying them in the long run.)

Thus Britain suffers from structural unemployment; the old industrial heartland in the north is economically depressed while the south shows signs of high-tech ventures and activities in the world of finance leading to a new prosperity. This gap between north and south is increasing steadily; with the north sinking into an economic depression with all its social consequences (alcoholism, domestic violence, broken homes, drugs, etc.) A newspaper even headlined an article about this problem "The two Britains"; and a Conservative MP wrote that Britain is about to "become a society of two nations".

3. In the late 1950s the Civil Rights Movement started as a movement in order to redress some of the grievances of the negroes in the USA.

The negroes were discriminated against, especially in the former slave states in the south. They had very great difficulties registering to vote and most public and private institutions were segregated, that means there were designated areas for whites and for blacks. This also led to discrimination in education and other areas of life, though the motto was "separate but equal".

The methods of the Civil Rights Movement were strictly non-violent and Martin Luther King succeeded in transforming a spontaneous racial protest (after Mrs. Rose Parks was arrested on December 5, 1955 for refusing to move to the negro section of a bus in Montgomery, Ala.) into a massive resistance movement. Patterned on Ghandi's methods the movement used boycotts, picketting, sit-ins and non-violent demonstrations (the climax being the great March on Washington, D.C. in August 1963) to desegregate public facilities and to get equal rights.

The achievements of the Civil Rights Movement are quite remarkable. Apart from desegregating many institutions directly (the economic results of boycotting – "hit them in the pocket book where it really hurts"), the politicians reacted. In 1960 both the Democratic and Republican parties adopted strong civil rights platforms, and during the Kennedy and especially during the Johnson administrations far-reaching civil rights bills were passed by Congress. The implementation of those laws has not brought total equality for the negroes, but substantial steps have been taken towards improving the situation.

IV. Translation

Gewiß/Sicherlich zerfällt die von Golding geschaffene Zivilisation/die Zivilisation, die Golding geschafften hat, im Verlauf der Erzählung/Geschichte. Und wenn wir die Kinder einzeln nehmen/betrachten als Verkörperung/Repräsentanten gewisser Eigenschaften/Qualitäten, die in jedem einzelnen Menschen/Einzelnen vorhanden sind, wird das Buch kaum weniger düster/bedrückend. Denn Piggy zeigt uns, daß die Vernunft allein uns nicht aufrecht hält/halten wird; Ralph zeigt uns, daß gute Absichen/Vorsätze, Führungsqualitäten und eine innere Verpflichtung, die soziale/gesellschaftliche Ordnung aufrecht zu erhalten/und ein Eintreten für soziale/gesellschaftliche Ordnung nicht genügen/ausreichen (werden), um unter Druck/Bedrängnis einen Rückfall in die Barbarei zu verhüten/vermeiden; und Jack zeigt uns, daß die Ängste, die Grausamkeit und der Machtkitzel/Machtgier, die in jedem von uns vorhanden sind/innewohnen, nur allzuleicht die Oberhand gewinnen können. Aber Simon versucht/strebt an, seinen Ängsten in's Auge zu blicken/sich seinen Ängsten zu stellen, und er kommt soweit/dazu, das Böse, das in ihm wie in den anderen Kindern lebt/verwurzelt ist, anzunehmen – obwohl er mit seinem Leben für seine Entdeckung/für das, was er entdeckt, bezahlt. Indem er so gegen seine Unvollkommenheiten/Grenzen als Mensch ankämpft und sie dennoch anerkennt, nimmt er jene ewige/immerwährende menschliche Aufgabe auf sich, aus der sich die Niederlagen wie auch die Siege/Triumphe des Menschen ergeben – ob man den Menschen (nun) von christlichen Gesichtspunkten aus betrachtet, wie gewisse Einzelheiten in dem Roman nahelegen, oder von einem hauptsächlichen weltlichen Standpunkt/Blickwinkel aus.

Leistungskurs Englisch (Baden-Württemberg): Abiturprüfung 1988
Textaufgabe und Übersetzung

We hear the sound of the Shell again, as Ralph summons a second meeting to try to clarify and set right what has gone wrong. Half way through the novel we get a measure of how far we have come; Ralph, discovering his dirt and realizing how much of his time he spends watching his feet to escape falling, 'smiles jeeringly' as he remembers 'that first enthusiastic exploration as though it were part of a brighter childhood'.

This assembly has to be not fun, but business. Ralph is having to realize what it means to be a leader, to take decisions in a hurry, to think things out step by step. This brings out a new scale of values, whereby he sees how little fatness, asthma, myopia and laziness weigh against Piggy's one great quality – his ability to think. But thinking is complicated by the fact that things look different in different lights, and from different points of view. 'If faces were different when lit from above or below – what was a face? What was anything?'

Ralph produces a workmanlike programme to put things straight: a plan for better sanitation, for keeping the fire going, for never cooking except on the mountain-top. But at a level deeper than any programme can reach, things are breaking up because the children are frightened. So the meeting becomes a testing-ground for Ralph's faith that what is wrong can be cured by talking things over reasonably, and coming to a democratic decision on fear itself, on whether or not there is a 'Beast'.

Jack's experience as hunter tells him that there is no fearsome animal on the island, but it also tells him why the littluns are frightened and have nightmares. They are frightened 'because you're like that', because it is human nature to be frightened of the world and of life when it is dark and man is by himself. But for Jack, 'fear can't hurt you any more than a dream'. Fear can be lived with, and any Beast can be hunted and killed.

Piggy disagrees about fear. For him, everything can be explained and anything wrong, even in the mind, can be cured. Life is scientific. There is no Beast to fear, and there is no need to fear anything 'unless we get frightened of people'. This rationality, however, is greeted with scorn by those whose experience seems to tell them otherwise. Maurice wonders whether science has, in fact, explored the whole of existence and rendered everything explicable and known. The littlun who claims that the Beast comes from the water, and Maurice's memory of great squids only fleetingly glimpsed by man, are both pointers to a sea that may contain a great unknown.

The worst contempt of the meeting, however, is resevered for Simon, who thinks that there may be a Beast that is not any kind of animal: 'What I mean is ... maybe it's only us.' He is trying to say that man may fear darkness and solitude because they rob him of the world he builds with his daylight mind, and force him to live with his own interior darkness. Perhaps there is something bestial, something absolutely dirty, not external to man but present deep in himself. But Simon is howled down even more than Piggy; and when the vote comes to be taken Ralph is forced to realize that fear cannot be dispelled by voting.

568 words   *Kinkead-Weekes/Gregor (1984)*

Vocabulary:

line 4:	jeeringly	–	mockingly
line 8:	myopia	–	short-sightedness
line 30:	squid	–	Tintenfisch
line 30:	to glimpse	–	to have a quick look at, to see quickly

I. Language

1. Vocabulary (ohne Wörterbuch zu bearbeiten)

   In the following (items a-g) you are to deal with the underlined words/expressions within the given context.

   a) 1: "..., as Ralph <u>summons</u> a second meeting ..."
   Explain; you may change the sentence structure. (1 VP)

   b) 6: "Ralph is having to <u>realize</u> ..."
   Find a suitable substitute; keep to the sentence structure. (1 VP)

   c) 13: "Ralph produces a workmanlike programme to <u>put things straight</u> ..."
   Find a suitable substitute; keep to the sentence structure. (1 VP)

   d) 20: "... why the littluns ... have <u>nightmares</u>."
   Find a suitable substitute; keep to the sentence structure. (1 VP)

   e) 22: "... and man is <u>by himself</u>."
   Find a suitable substitute; keep to the sentence structure. (1 VP)

   f) 27–28: "Maurice <u>wonders</u> whether science has, ..., explored ..."
   Find a suitable substitute; keep to the sentence structure. (1 VP)

   g) 35–36. "... his own <u>interior</u> darkness."
   Explain; you may change the sentence structure. (1 VP)

   Find the corresponding abstract nouns (not the -ing-forms):

   | Examples: | explore | exploration |
   | | different | difference |

   h) 3: discover
   4: remember
   7: think
   8: see
   29: explicable
   31: contain (3 VP)

2. Grammar and Style (ohne Wörterbuch zu bearbeiten)

   a) 2: "... and set right what <u>has gone wrong</u>."
   15: "... things <u>are breaking up</u> ..."
   Define the verb forms and explain their use. (2 VP)

   b) 25: "<u>Life</u> is scientific."
   26: "... 'unless we get frightened of <u>people</u>'."
   Why are both nouns used without the definite article? (1 VP)

c) 32: "The worst contempt ..., is reserved for Simon, <u>who thinks</u> ..."
34–35: "... because they rob him of the world <u>he builds</u> ..."
Name the underlined clauses and explain the differences between them. (2 VP)

II. Comprehension

Answer the following questions in complete sentences. Keep to the information given in the text, but do not quote.

1. Things have changed since the first meeting. What challenges will Ralph have to face and what programme does he consider necessary now?
   (40–60 words) (2 VP)
2. What was Ralph's attitude towards Piggy at the beginning and how does he see him now?
   (40–60 words) (2 VP)
3. Describe the different attitudes of Ralph, Jack, Maurice and Simon concerning the Beast.
   (120–180 words) (6 VP)

III. Comment (10 VP)

Choose <u>one</u> of the following topics: (200–300 words)

1. Characterize Piggy and describe his role in the novel.
2. Why does William Golding choose young schoolboys as characters and a desert island as a setting for his novel?
3. Analyse the last scene beginning with the sudden appearance of the naval officer and show how it contributes to the understanding of the novel.

IV. Translation (30 VP)

The Boer War, with which the nineteenth century ended and the twentieth began, brought the last major addition of territory to an empire which, in the next sixty years, was to be transformed from a <u>collection</u> of more-or-less dependent countries into an <u>association</u> of equal partners. During the reign of Edward VII the British were immensely proud of having built an empire and were deeply conscious of their responsibility for protecting and administering it. Their grandchildren were less sure of themselves: some were angry and ashamed that Britain's power and prestige had been given away; others rejoiced that they had been so progressive and unprejudiced.

The process of change was sometimes smooth and cordial, sometimes violent. There was seldom a direct clash between Britain's attempt to retain her possessions and the colonies' demands for independence. Rather was there disagreement over the rate of change. The leaders of the Indian and, later, African nationalist movements naturally wanted to be free as soon as possible, whereas British politicians and colonial governors wanted to prepare the subject peoples for independence and feared that a premature British withdrawal might lead to disaster.

190 words W. Robson

Vocabulary:

line 1: Boer War (1899–1902) – Burenkrieg (zwischen den Buren und Briten in Südafrika)
line 4: Edward VII – britischer König von 1901–1910

Lösungsvorschlag

I. Language

1. Vocabulary
   a) ... as Ralph calls a second meeting ...
      ... as Ralph assembles/musters/gathers the boys for a second meeting ...
      ... as Ralph calls the boys together ...
   b) Ralph is having to understand/see/recognize/become conscious of/become aware of ...
   c) Ralph produces a workmanlike programme to solve the problems/deal (successfully) with the situation/organize matters/cope with the situation/find solutions for the problems: ...
   d) ... why the littluns ... have bad/terrible/horrible/shocking/frightening dreams.
   e) ... and man is (all) alone.
      ... and man is on his own.
   f) Maurice asks himself/is not really sure/asks/doubts/puzzles whether science has ... explored ...
   g) ... the darkness in his soul.
      ... his own inner darkness.
      ... the darkness within himself.
   h) discovery
      remembrance, memory
      thought
      sight
      explanation (explication; very rarely used)
      containment, contents, content

2. Grammar and Style
   a) "Has gone wrong" is a present perfect (simple form), used here to describe something that began in the past and is still relevant.
      "Are breaking up" is a present continuous which is used to describe an action in progress.
   b) "Life" is an abstract noun, used in a general sense. "People" is a plural noun, also used in a general sense.
   c) The first clause is a non-defining relative clause (cf. the commas).
      The second clause is a defining relative clause. In defining relative clauses the relative pronoun can be left out when it is used in the object case.

II. Comprehension

1. As the leader of the group of boys Ralph must understand what it means to be in a leadership position; he must take quick decisions, and plan things slowly and logically.
   The programme he thinks necessary now is to organize their lives properly – such things as improvements in sanitation, keeping the fire going and deciding on a place for cooking.

2. At the beginning Ralph's attitude was strongly coloured by Piggy's physical defects (his being fat, his asthma, myopia, and clumsiness) and his laziness. Now – as Ralph realizes the challenges of leadership – he comes to admire and accept Piggy's one great quality: his intellectual faculties, his ability to think.

3. Ralph believes that all problems can be solved reasonably by talking about them; and that by taking a vote on whether the "Beast" exists or not (which would be a democratic decision on fear as such!) the problem would be taken care of. But when it comes to the vote, Ralph realizes that life is not that simple and that voting is no help against fear.

Jack knows that there is not "Beast" on the island; but he also knows (from his experience as a hunter) that fear exists and is a reality, and it must be lived with.

Maurice isn't sure whether science has all the answers – and by what he remembers about animals living in the sea he can well imagine that the littluns are right about the beast coming from the water.

Simon thinks that the "Beast" is not an animal but an expression of the interior darkness of Man's soul. Whenever man is confronted with this dark, bestial, dirty, side of his soul, fear of darkness and solitude may result.

III. Comment

1. Piggy is a fat, asthmatic boy who cannot take part in most of the activities of the boys because of his physical deficiencies. But he also hides behind his asthma whenever there is work to be done (for example the building of the shelters). On the other hand he is very intelligent and the only one who can really think straight. As he tends to tell the others after the fact "I told you so", he is not very popular. Many of the boys make fun of him (even Ralph does at the beginning) and in certain respects he is an outsider. In order to find a secure place in the group he befriends Ralph who accepts him after he recognizes the inner qualities of Piggy.

In the novel Piggy is the thinker. His plans and proposals make sense and help to establish a certain order (e. g. he finds the conch and tells Ralph how to use it – and the conch becomes the symbol of democracy and order). Ralph who has difficulties in formulating his vague ideas which he feels more than he can clearly put into words is greatly helped by Piggy's faculties of being reasonable and articulate. When Piggy is killed (and the conch is smashed) the last vestiges of order disappear and the savage tribe of Jack's rules unopposed.

2. Golding wants to show that the inherent evil in man is stronger than the values of civilisation and culture which rule our lives.

If you want to show how this evil manifests itself you need a setting where there is as little external influence as possible. Thus a tropical desert island is an ideal setting, as the boys can survive without having to worry too much about food and shelter, and there is not much influence from the outside (although the dead parachutist plays an important role in creating dissent and chaos). The author then can concentrate on the development and interplay of the forces of good and evil.

The age of the protagonists also is of great importance. Adult people already have (or should have) found a way of living with the forces of good and evil and therefore less development can be expected and a reversal to savagery is less probable. Younger children would not be able to survive on the island, and social interaction would not be possible on a conscious level. Thus young schoolboys are an ideal group – they have not yet fully developed their personalities but are old enough to see and deal with (on their level) the problems having to do with the forces of good and evil.

3. The appearance of the naval officer puts everything back into its proper perspective. When he appears, the boys become boys again (although he underestimates what has been going on when he says that the boys had been "playing games"), and Ralph really weeps for the first time in the novel.

In no way do the boys try to go on playing their roles (though Jack starts forward to assume a leadership role, but then shrinks back), and the savage tribe which hunted Ralph and scared him to death (he knew that a "stick sharpended at both ends" had been prepared for him) becomes a goup of dirty, bedraggled boys waiting for the decision of the officer.

The officer could be seen as the force (the adult world) which can help the boys to suppress or overcome the inherent evil in themselves. They are too young to avoid falling victims to the evil forces, they still need the adults. In the adult world these forces are held in check by the rules of society (rules, mores, laws; things which "simply are not done", etc), although the adult world is far from perfect (the officer carries a revolver, there is a sub-machine gun in the boat, and the world is at war).

The last chapter with the terrible fire which renders the island a barren rock, and with the merciless hunt for Ralph is the climax of savagery to which the boys reverted. The group of schoolboys who were looking forward towards having a nice, adventurous time on the island succumb to the evil forces within them and hunt Ralph (the last person who believes in and clings to reason) as if he were the beast they are afraid of.

IV. Translation

Der Burenkrieg, mit dem das 19. Jahrhundert endete und das 20. begann, brachte die letzte größere Gebietserweiterung/zuwachs für ein Weltreich, das sich in den nächsten/ folgenden 60 Jahren von einer Ansammlung mehr oder weniger abhängiger Länder/ Gebiete zu einer Vereingiung gleicher/gleichberechtigter Partner wandeln sollte. Während der Regierungszeit/Unter Edward VII. waren die Briten ungeheuer stolz darauf, ein Weltreich aufgebaut zu haben/daß sie ... aufgebaut hatten, und (sie) waren sich ihrer Verantwortung, es zu beschützen und zu verwalten/für seinen Schutz und Verwaltung vollauf/zutiefst bewußt. Ihre Enkel waren sich weniger sicher/weniger selbstsicher/selbstbewußt: einige waren zornig und beschämt/schämten sich, daß Großbritanniens Macht und Ansehen/Prestige verschenkt/preisgegeben worden waren; andere freuten sich sehr/waren sehr froh, daß sie so fortschrittlich und unvoreingenommen/ vorurteilsfrei/ohne Vorurteile gewesen waren.

Der Übergang/Umwandlungsprozeß war/verlief manchmal glatt/reibungslos und freundschaftlich, machmal gewaltsam/mit Gewalttaten verbunden. Es gab selten einen direkten Zusammenstoß zwischen/wegen Großbritanniens Versuch, seine Gebiete/Besitzungen zu behalten und den Forderungen der Kolonien nach Unabhängigkeit. Es gab eher/Schon eher gab es Uneinigkeit darüber, wie rasch der Wandlungsprozeß vollzogen werden sollte. Die Führer der indischen, und später der afrikanischen Nationalbewegungen wollten natürlich so schnell/bald wie möglich frei sein; während/wohingegen (die) britischen Politiker und (die) Gouverneure der Kolonien die unterworfenen/abhängigen Völker auf/(für) die Unabhängigkeit vorbereiten wollten und Bedenken hatten/fürchteten, daß ein vorzeitiger/zu früher/ verfrühter britischer Abzug zu einer Katastrophe führen könnte.

> **Leistungskurs Englisch (Baden-Württemberg): Abiturprüfung 1989**
> **Textaufgabe und Übersetzung**

Perhaps more than any other American play, Death of a Salesman captures the confusions and contradictions at the heart of the American experience - between the past and the present, illusion and reality, idealism and materialism, promise and loss. Without his knowing it, Willy speaks for the mass of Americans whose dreams have not been realized, whose hopes have ended in despair. But it is not merely an American play. It has universal impact in its portrayal of human disintegration under the pressures of modern life, in its lament for a vanished past and its criticism of an inadequate present, in its insistence on understanding and compassion. Attention must be paid, Linda tells her sons. If failure and despair are tragic, then Willy Loman is a tragic figure deserving our attention.

It is not so much that Willy Loman is in fact a failure but that he reckons himself one. He comes to the end of his life and looks back over what is to him nothing. He feels he has done nothing, accomplished nothing, achieved nothing. He has always, he admits, felt temporary. By what terms do we reckon a man who does his work, maintains a family, pays off a mortgage, elicits deep emotional response from wife and children a failure? We reckon him a failure only if we judge him by the terms with which Willy judges himself. By material standards, by modern definitions of success he is a failure. But surely one of Miller's intentions in this play is to call into question those standards, those definitions. We are not to be as confused as Willy is. We are to understand, as he does not, what is and is not possible in modern life.

And we are to take heart from Biff's development. It does not take his father's death to make Biff realize his own errors. Before Willy's death Biff is able to see his father as a human being and judge him accordingly. He has finally recovered from his shock at discovering his father was not perfect. He is able to love the man he once loved and pity the man he now is. He can criticize his father without relegating him to some inhuman category.

And he is able to do all that because he has finally begun to look at himself, has finally begun to confront his own petty dishonesties, his own inadequacies as a human being, has finally been able to accept himself for what and who he is. At this point he no longer needs to blame others, to act as judge, jury and executioner. He has moved beyond blame, beyond judgment to understanding and acceptance.

Willy Loman is the center of Death of a Salesman but Biff Loman is the hero, the man who grows and develops and comes out on the side of life, on the side of reality and honesty and compassion. His is the journey Miller insists we all must make, the journey from innocence to experience, from illusion to reality. Never to make that journey is, as we see in Willy's case, totally self-destructive. Willy is the object lesson we must not become, a portrait in confusion and self-delusion and, finally and inevitably, self-destruction. But Biff is what we all must do – the need to see things and people as they are, the commitment to accept what is acceptable, the absolute necessity of self-knowledge.

568 words *Barry Gross (1971)*

Vocabulary:

line 7:	to vanish	–	to disappear
line 11:	to reckon	–	to consider
line 15:	to elicit	–	here: to get
line 21:	to take heart from	–	to be encouraged by
line 25:	to relegate	–	to put into a lower position

I. Language

1. Vocabulary (ohne Wörterbuch zu bearbeiten)

   In the following (items a-g) you are to deal with the underlined words/expressions within the given context.

   a) 2: "... contradictions <u>at the heart</u> of ..."
   Explain; you may change the sentence structure. (1 VP)

   b) 5–6: "But it is not <u>merely</u> an American play."
   Find a suitable substitute; keep to the sentence structure. (1 VP)

   c) 6: "It has <u>universal impact</u> in ..."
   Explain; you may change the sentence structure. (2 VP)

   d) 7–8: "... of an <u>inadequate</u> present, ..."
   Explain; you may change the sentence structure. (1 VP)

   e) 14–15: "..., <u>maintains</u> a family, ..."
   Find a suitable substitute; keep to the sentence structure. (1 VP)

   f) 23: "He has finally <u>recovered</u> from his shock ..."
   Explain; you may change the sentence structure. (1 VP)

   g) 37–38: "... self-delusion and, finally and <u>inevitably</u>, self-destruction."
   Explain; you may change the sentence structure. (1 VP)

   Find the corresponding **abstract** nouns (not the -ing-forms):

   h) 13: admit
   28: confront
   33: grow
   34: insist (2 VP)

2. Grammar and Style (ohne Wörterbuch zu bearbeiten)

   a) 4: "<u>Without his knowing it,</u> Willy speaks ..."
   Explain the -ing-form and replace the underlined phrase by a subordinate clause. (2 VP)

   b) 12–13: "He feels he has done nothing, accomplished nothing, achieved nothing."
   Describe the stylistic device used in this sentence and explain its function. (1 VP)

   c) 30–31: "He has moved beyond blame, ..."
   Explain the use of the tense. (1 VP)

   d) 36–37: "Willy is the object lesson <u>we must not become</u>, ..."
   Why can the relative pronoun be left out? (1 VP)

II. Comprehension

Answer the following questions in complete sentences. Keep to the information given in the text, but do not quote.

1. In how far does this play, according to the author, reflect typical traits of life in America and of modern life and its deficiencies in general? (70–90 words) (3 VP)
2. Why must Willy Loman consider himself a failure, and how do Gross and Miller judge his performance? (70–90 words) (3 VP)
3. The author calls Biff Loman the hero of <u>Death of a Salesman</u>. What reasons does he give for this view, and what lesson are we to learn? (100–120 words) (4 VP)

III. Comment (10 VP)

Choose <u>one</u> of the following topics: (200–300 words)

1. How do you judge Willy's role as a father?
2. In the course of the play Willy frequently recollects the past, and the action takes place partly in the present and partly in the past. Give one or two examples of these time shifts and explain their function.

IV. Translation (30 VP)

In 1963 Martin Luther King published an impassioned essay called "Why We Can't Wait". The subject was segregation, but even at that early date King understood that his real mission was broader social and economic change. "In that separate culture of poverty in which the half-educated Negro lives, an economic depression rages today," he
5 wrote. The solution for that, King realized, would be very complicated.
Twenty years after his death, millions of Americans, black and white, have given up waiting altogether. The war on poverty – one aim of the civil rights movement – has almost been lost. Worse, the moral energy to continue the battle has been weakened by complacency and an appalling game of finger-pointing. Year after year, the agony of
10 the underclass has been seen as the blacks' problem, the government's problem, but not everyone's. The long road back to commitment will not be easy. Ronald Reagan, who owes his two electoral victories almost exclusively to white voters, was determined to leave the issue alone when he came to office. He will retire with a huge budget deficit, which means that large-scale efforts to improve the condition of the underclass will be
15 difficult for his successors.

196 words   *From Newsweek, March 7, 1988*

Vocabulary:

line 9:	complacency	–	a feeling of satisfaction with oneself
line 9:	appalling	–	shocking, disgusting
line 9:	finger-pointing	–	here: mutual accusations

Lösungsvorschlag

I. Language

1. Vocabulary

   a) ... contradictions which are at the center of ...
      ... contradictions which are a central part of ...

   b) But it is not simply/just/only an American play.

   c) It is of importance for people everywhere in ...
      It matters greatly to people all over the world in ...
      It is very important for people wherever they may live in ...

   d) ... of a present which needs to be improved, ...
      ... of a present which is by no means ideal/perfect, ...

   e) ... supports a family, ...
      ... provides for a family, ...
      ... provides food and housing for a family, ...

   f) He has finally got over his shock ...
      He has finally regained control over himself after his shock ...

   g) ... self-delusion and, finally and inescapably/unavoidably, self-destruction.
      ... self-delusion and self-destruction which is inescapable.

   h) admission, admittance
      confrontation (confrontment)
      growth
      insistence (insistance, insistency)

2. Grammar and Style

   a) 'Knowing' is a gerund (used after a preposition, to replace an adverbial phrase).
      Although he doesn't know it, Willy speaks ...

   b) The gradation of the three verbs do, accomplish and achieve, together with the repetition of 'nothing' could be called a climax. It is used to emphasize the fact that Willy really has accomplished nothing.

   c) The present perfect is used here to describe the result of a development (resultative use).

   d) It can be left out as the underlined clause is a defining relative clause, and the relative pronoun would be in the object case.
      It can be left out as the underlined clause is a defining relative clause, and the subordinate clause has a subject other than the relative pronoun.

II. Comprehension

1. The play shows typical traits of life in America insofar as it presents the sharp contrasts and confusing experiences of life in America – the contradicitons between the past and the present, between reality and dreams, between the idealistic and material aspects of life, and between hope and failure. Willy is somebody whose "American Dream" did not come true, someone who ends in despair.

The play shows the difficulties of modern life; it shows a nostalgia for the "good old days", and it insists on the values of a more human and compassionate society (1st paragraph).

2. Willy must consider himself a failure because he judges himself solely by material standards. According to those standards he did not achieve anything: he lost his job, he did not amass material riches, he did not get on in the world, he is not a successful businessman.

Gross and Miller see Willy differently. They think that working hard all his life, building a house, supporting a family and winning the family's affection are respectable achievements which cannot be called a complete failure (2nd paragraph).

3. Biff is called the hero of the play because the develops into a mature character. he can overcome his childish notions that the shock of discovering that his father is not perfect is the underlying reason for all he has become. He learns to confront himself honestly and to accept himself for what he is – and that enables him to love and pity his father even while criticizing him. He has learned to be honest and compassionate.

We are to learn Biff's lesson. We all should learn to confront our weaknesses and be honest with ourselves, make "the journey from innocence to experience, from illusion to reality" (line 34–35); thus we can also learn to understand and show sympathy for our fellow men (the last three paragraphs).

III. Comment

1. Willy tries hard to be a good father, to make his sons love him, and to give them some values for their future life. His main fault seems to be that he apparently has the wrong values; and that causes problems.

When the boys were young, Willy must have done something right for the boys adored and idolized him. When he came home from his business trips they came running to him, and he brought them something (e.g. a punching ball); they simonized the car for him and eagerly awaited his approval.

But even in those early days he overestimated the shallow values of appearances, and he told his boys that popularity and being well-liked (the ability to impress – and then use – people) was more important than solid work. You can see that when you look at the scene when Willy talks about young Bernard. He at least half condoned the unethical action of his boys (when Biff brings home the football from the lockerroom, and when the boys steal some sand from a building site).

Another point is that it appears that Biff was favoured above Happy. A father should not have favourites among his children. (This is all the more paradox as Happy turns out much more of a 'success' if you apply Willy's values.)

Now that Biff has grown up, his father still pesters him with expectations. Willy obviously does not (perhaps cannot) understand that children must live their own lives once they have grown up. This misunderstanding is one cause of the constant friction between Willy and Biff.

The other reason is that Willy failed Biff (in a way, but not as gravely as Biff takes it) as a father when Biff discovered that his father was not an ideal person (when he was unfaithful to his wife in Boston and Biff caught him with the woman in his hotel room). But it seems more of a weakness on Biff's side that he cannot overcome this disappointment – as all children must discover that their parents have weaknesses (albeit perhaps not such bad ones as Willy).

One could say that Willy tried hard to be a good father – but he failed rather badly. Only at the end of the play does it seem that Biff can find his own way; Happy seems to be stuck in his situation.

2. When Willy and his sons meet in a restaurant for dinner (act 2), Willy relives the scene from the past where Biff travelled to meet his father in Boston after he had failed maths. Willy doesn't (or cannot, as he 'lives' in two time zones simultaneously) listen properly to what Biff is trying to tell him: that he failed in his interview with Oliver. Willy and Biff cannot communicate, Biff leaves dejectedly, and Willy lives through the scene in the past (where Biff had caught him being unfaithful to Linda; this had shattered Biff's belief in his father, and it made him lose his sense of direction in life).

This flashback (as some of the others) is used here for exposition, that is, to give background information to make the play as a whole intelligible. The Boston hotel scene accounts for some of the quarrels between Biff and Willy, and explains Willy's feelings of guilt; it explains why Bernard asks what had happened there as Biff apparently seemed to have come back from Boston a completely different person.

But more importantly, these time-shifts are a reality for Willy. They torment him so much and are so real to him that he cannot even drive his car anymore and has accidents. The pleasant scenes make the present appear even more unbearable; and the unpleasant ones (his painful memories, his feelings of guilt, and his frustrations) distort his thinking and almost unsettle his mind, reinforcing the anxieties for the present. Thus these flashbacks are very much a part of Willy's present situation and are, in a certain way, just as important as his final meetings and quarrels with Howard and Biff. One could even say that, psychologically, these flashbacks explain Willy's character and what sort of man he is – and perhaps why he is finally driven to commit suicide.

IV. Translation

1963 veröffentlichte Martin Luther King einen leidenschaftlichen Aufsatz/Essay mit dem Titel "Warum wir nicht warten können". Das Thema war (die) Rassentrennung, aber bereits/schon zu diesem frühen Zeitpunkt verstand King, daß sein eigentlicher/wirklicher Auftrag eine weitergehende/breitere gesellschaftliche/soziale und wirtschaftliche Veränderung war. Er schrieb: "In jener eigenen/selbständigen/separaten Kultur der Armut, in der der wenig gebildete Neger lebt, herrscht/wütet heute eine wirtschaftliche Depression." Die Lösung dafür, das war King klar/deutlich, würde sehr kompliziert sein.

Zwanzig Jahre nach seinem Tod haben Millionen schwarze und weiße Amerikaner das Warten völlig/ganz aufgegeben. Der Krieg/Kampf gegen die Armut – ein Ziel der Bürgerrechtsbewegung – ist fast verloren. Noch schlimmer, die moralische Kraft, den Kampf aufrechtzuerhalten/weiterzuführen, ist durch Selbstzufriedenheit und ein widerwärtiges Spiel gegenseitiger Schuldzuweisung/Beschuldigung geschwächt worden. Jahr für Jahr ist das Leiden/die schweren Probleme der Unterklasse als das Problem der Schwarzen, das der Regierung nicht jedoch als das Problem jedes einzelnen angesehen worden.

Der lange Weg zurück zu engagiertem Handeln wird nicht leicht sein. Ronald Reagan, der seine beiden Wahlsiege fast ausschließlich weißen Wählern verdankt, war entschlossen, das Problem nicht anzugehen/anzufassen, als er sein Amt antrat. Er wird mit einem riesigen Haushaltsdefizit abtreten, was heißt/das bedeutet, daß weitreichende Bemühungen, die Lebensbedingungen/Umstände der Unterklasse zu verbessern, für seine Nachfolger schwierig sein werden.

**Leistungskurs Englisch (Baden-Württemberg): Abiturprüfung 1990
Textaufgabe und Übersetzung**

Dark Side of the Dream

The names and the nationalities change but the same heartwarming story keeps appearing in American newspapers and magazines and on television. Most often it is about a Korean or Vietnamese or Latin American family. After scratching and clawing their way to the United States, these poor but proud, energetic and hardworking immigrants
5 succeed in realizing their dream of a better life and, in the process of advancing themselves, contribute new vigor to their adopted country.
Children of immigrants like myself are not inclined to criticize these newcomers. Why should they be denied the same opportunities that led our parents to abandon their native land? Still, there is something about these stories that I find offensive. In a subtle,
10 indirect way, they transmit the message that native-born American workers are lazy and stupid, and that black families, in particular, that have labored in this land for nearly two centuries are perhaps not as American as the newcomers.
A recent story in a large-circulation weekly extolled the virtues of Vietnamese immigrants who not only succeeded but also "saved the neighborhood." The opening
15 sentence describes the "Uptown" Chicago area they moved into as a place where "a few years ago, the most active business people were muggers, drug dealers and street-corner prostitutes." You do not have to be a Chicagoan or a sociologist to presume that the "muggers, drug dealers and prostitutes" were mostly black. And when the head of this upward-mobile Vietnamese family of eight tells the reporter, "We had Vietnamese pride
20 and did not want to take public aid. We wanted the American community and authorities to respect us, " we are given the distinct impression that American citizens who do accept public assistance have no pride and deserve no respect.
The dark side of these upward-mobility tales is never discussed. Using child labor in the family business is not just condoned but praised, and the willingness to accept poor
25 working conditions and substandard pay is admired. By implication, Americans who insist on decent wages, health and pension benefits and employee rights are regarded to be just too lazy or unmotivated to deserve a job. Sweatshop employers and agricultural entrepreneurs claim that American workers do not want the jobs they can fill with legal and illegal immigrants. But it is not the work itself that Americans object to. It is the
30 miserable pay and working conditions.
The people who are most enthusiastic about immigration tend to be those who are not directly affected by it. They do not compete with the newcomers for jobs or housing, and their warm welcome springs more from an abstract belief in the United States as a melting pot and a land of opportunity than from any direct experience of immigration's
35 effects on the economy.
Working Americans who may want to limit immigration have no surplus funds and little political power. They are motivated not by racism but by clear evidence that the new immigrants' gains are being made at their expense. By opening the U.S. work force to foreigners whose standards are far below those of American citizens, employers have
40 reduced the once powerful labor unions to impotence and irrelevance.
It is time that our government put the interests of the millions who elected it ahead of the small group of employers who benefit from uncontrolled immigration. If it does not, the misery that corrupt foreign governments inflict on their own people will become a major determinant of wages and working conditions here in the United States.

586 words

James J. Treires in Newsweek. April 10, 1989

Vocabulary

l. 3:	to claw	–	cf. the claw (dt. 'Klaue')
l. 13:	to extol	–	to praise highly
l. 24:	to condone	–	to excuse
l. 27:	sweatshop	–	a factory where workers work long hours for low wages under bad conditions
l. 38:	work force	–	here: labour market
l. 43:	to inflict sth. on sb.	–	to force sth. unpleasant on sb.

I. Language

1. Vocabulary (ohne Wörterbuch zu bearbeiten)

   In the following (items a-g) you are to deal with the underlined words/expressions within the given context.

   a) 1: "... but the same <u>heartwarming</u> story ..."
   Find a suitable substitute; keep to the sentence structure. (1 VP)

   b) 6: "... to their <u>adopted</u> country."
   Explain; you may change the sentence structure. (1 VP)

   c) 7–8: "Why should they be <u>denied</u> the same opportunities ..."
   Explain; you may change the sentence structure. (1 VP)

   d) 13: "... in a <u>large-circulation</u> weekly ..."
   Explain; you may change the sentence structure. (1 VP)

   e) 21: "... we are given the <u>distinct</u> impression ..."
   Find a suitable substitute; keep to the sentence structure. (1 VP)

   f) 21–22: "... citizens ... <u>deserve</u> no respect."
   Explain; you may change the sentence structure. (1 VP)

   g) 42: "... employers who <u>benefit</u> from ..."
   Find a suitable substitute; keep to the sentence structure. (1 VP)

   Find the corresponding **abstract** nouns (not the -ing-forms):

   h) 11: stupid
   17: to presume
   24: to praise
   26: decent (2 VP)

2. Grammar and Style (ohne Wörterbuch zu bearbeiten)

   a) 3–4: "After <u>scratching and clawing</u> their way to the United States, ..."
   Name the stylistic device used here and explain its function. (2 VP)

   b) 23: "The dark side of these upward-mobility tales is never discussed."
   Change the sentence into the active voice; begin with 'never'. (2 VP)

   c) 23–24: "<u>Using</u> child labor in the family business is not just condoned ..."
   36: "<u>Working</u> Americans who may want to limit ..."
   Name the -ing-forms and explain their grammatical functions. (2 VP)

II. Comprehension

Answer the following questions in complete sentences. Keep to the information given in the text, but do not quote.

1. In what respect is the story of the Vietnamese family typical of reports about immigrants that keep appearing in American media? (60–90 words) (3 VP)
2. What is the author's opinion about such stories, and what does he regard as the "dark side of these upward-mobility tales"? (80–120 words) (4 VP)
3. According to the author different groups of people hold different opinions about immigration. What groups are mentioned, what are their opinions about immigration, and what are the reasons for their attitudes? (60–90 words) (3 VP)

III. Comment (10 VP)

Choose one of the following topics: (200–300 words)

1. "The American dream that has lured tens of millions of all nations to our shores ... has not been a dream of merely material plenty .... It has been much more than that." (James Truslow Adams). – Explain and illustrate this statement.
2. A lot of Americans tend to see themselves as the "Chosen People". – Comment on this attitude, its roots and consequences.
3. Willy's father, Willy's brother Ben, Dave Singleman – three representatives of the American dream. – Describe the significance each of them has for Willy Loman.

IV. Translation (30 VP)

Death of a Salesman is the story of a man's life depicted in its final, tortured days. Having covered the New England territory by automobile for years, Willy Loman is now in his sixties, physically and mentally exhausted, and he can no longer meet the rigorous demands of his vocation. Despite the encouragement of his wife, Linda, he
5 knows that his life has not been successful, and the knowledge has brought him to the brink of self-destruction. Depressed by the emptiness of his old age, he is particularly anguished over the inability of his two sons to fulfill his aspirations for them.

Through a series of flashbacks, originating in Willy's fevered mind, the roots of his family's deterioration are gradually revealed. A man with an almost mystical belief in
10 his own concept of success, Willy has spent his life attempting to instill his values into his sons. He has preached his gospel of salesmanship – a brash personality, a ready smile, a fast joke, and a glittering appearance – as the key to fame and fortune; and fostering this philosophy in his boys, he has overlooked their weaknesses, thus unintentionally paving the way for their ruin.

194 words
Benjamin Nelson

Vocabulary

line 7:	to be anguished over sth.	–	to suffer from sth.
line 10:	to instill	–	to put into sb.'s mind
line 11:	brash	–	forsch, aufdringlich

Lösungsvorschlag

I. Language

1. Vocabulary

   a) moving, touching

   b) the country of their choice
   the country they have decided to live in
   the country they have chosen to move to
   the country they have chosen as their new home

   c) not be given, not have, not be granted

   d) a weekly paper which sells in great numbers
   a very popular weekly newspaper
   a very widely-read weekly paper

   e) clear, unequivocal, unmistakable, precise

   f) can claim no respect
   are not entitled to any respect
   cannot expect to be treated respectfully
   have no right to be treated with any respect

   g) take advantage from, profit from

   h) stupidity
   presumption, presumptuousness
   praise
   decency, decentness

2. Grammar and Style

   a) This is a metaphorical expression/a figurative expression/an image.
   The author wants to illustrate the difficulties, the efforts, and the struggles of the immigrants.

   b) Never do people/journalists discuss the dark side of these upward-mobility tales.

   c) Using is a gerund as a part of the subject of the sentence.
   Working is a present participle used as an adjective.

II. Comprehension

1. All Americans (except the Red Indians and the Eskimos) are immigrants or the children/offspring of immigrants. Therefore they like to read about successful new immigrants. The story of a poor Vietnamese, Korean, or Latin American family coming to the USA and realising their version of the American Dream (a better life, and material success by working hard and being proud of their independence from outside help), and in this process infusing new vigour into their adopted country, is a typical immigrant story Americans like to read about.

2. While not wanting to criticize the new immigrants the author stresses the "dark side" of such stories. Most immigrants are willing to work under conditions and for substandard pay which American workers do not accept, and in family businesses even the use of child labour is condoned or even praised. Apart from accepting these

bad working conditions as "normal", such a story then subtly transmits the message that American workers who insist on decent working conditions, decent pay, fringe benefits, health insurance etc are just lazy and not motivated enough to deserve a job. One can then hear people say: "If he (or she) really wanted a job, he could find one" – without taking into account what kind of jobs (e.g. in a sweatshop) are available.

3. Children of immigrants don't want to criticize newcomers. Their reasons:
   – why shouldn't they have the same chances their parents had.

   Those not directly affected by immigration are very enthusiastic. Their reasons:
   – they don't compete with them for jobs or housing
   – they have an abstract belief in the US as a melting pot and a land of opportunity
   – they are not directly affected by this new immigration.

   Working Amercans want to limit immigration because the immigrants' gains appear to be their losses.
   Their reasons:
   – the new immigrants' standards are lower
   – the labour unions which protect the working Americans have lost much power.

III. Comment

1. For those immigrants who primarily came for economic reasons, the aspect of material plenty, of a better life, of success probably was the most important aspect of the American Dream.

   Those fleeing political oppressions were more interested in the realisation of the ideas of the Enlightenment, of such thinkers as Locke, Rousseau and Montesquieu. The idea of a "government of the people, for the people, by the people" was something which for example had no chance of being realized in 19th century Germany. Therefore it can easily be understood that after the failed revolution of 1848 many German revolutionaries fled to the USA where those ideas had – to a certain extent – been realized. The best known of those probably is Carl Schurz who became a US Senator for Missouri and later Secretary of the Interior under President Hayes.

   The same applies to religious freedom. Europe realized this idea much later than the USA (although most New England colonies were pretty intolerant themselves as regards religion). Therefore the USA became a haven for religious groups which were oppressed and persecuted in other parts of the world.

   More generally speaking, the dream of a country where a completely new beginning is possible – because this country (or rather, half-continent) doesn't have to bear the burden of old traditions, structures, customs etc. – has a strong appeal, as in this country of opportunity a "new man" could develop. This "new man" could then really start with a clean slate and build up a new and better world.

   The above examples show that the American Dream has been more than just "a dream of merely material plenty."

2. The Old Testament calls the Jews the "chosen people", and describes the history and the relationship of the Jewish tribes and their God.

   As the Christians also see the Old Testament as a part of their holy book, it is quite natural that some of them should also claim to be God's "chosen people".
   This was especially the case with the Puritans (e. g. if you think of John Foxe's book 'The Book of Martyrs' and the Geneva Bible which provided a view of England as an

elect nation chosen by God to bring the power of the Antichrist – the pope – to an end). When Puritans emigrated to America, they took these ideas with them and they were convinced that they were building a "heavenly New Jerusalem", as a Virginia settler, Sir Thomas Doyle, put it in the early 1600s. The supremacy of the church over the state, or at least the very close connection of church and state in the early English colonies made this a popular idea; and even today some Americans think they are the "chosen people", and that America is "God's own country".

This attitude tempts some Americans to assume that they are something special and that their way of doing things is right for themselves and for everybody else. Thus a naive belief of a certain mission developed, which for example led to such a statement (a reason given for America's role in World War I) "... to make the world safe for democracy."

American involvement in Asia after World War II also led to grave misunderstandings and mistakes which inspired an American writer to write a book with the title 'The ugly American'. The Vietnam war led to some soul-searching and robbed America of its naiveté, causing many Americans to question their role as the "chosen people".

3. Willy's father seems to have been – as Ben tells it – a rugged, wild-hearted individual who could live on his abilities (e.g. making flutes) and wits and who travelled across America if the urge overcame him. He was independent; something Willy definitely is not but wants to be. He sees his father as a kind of model for the education of his boys; he thinks his father was "rugged, well-liked, and all-around". Willy doesn't see the irony that Biff is a bit like his father: travelling around and being irresponsible (Willy's father seems to have left his family as Ben went to Alaska to find him there).

Ben is a certain ideal for Willy. In the dream-sequences (Ben's appearances seem to have more of a dream quality than that of a real flash-back) Ben embodies everything Willy has aspired in his life; he is the man Willy was never able to be. Ben is the living reality of Willy's dream of material success; as a young man he walked into the jungle and came out a rich man, depending on nobody. On the one hand Ben always reminds Willy that he missed opportunities (perhaps he was too cowardly?), that he didn't escape the chains of a routine existence, that he didn't realize his dreams. On the other hand Ben is the man "who knew the answers", and Willy asks him for advice (about the education of his sons, even about his final suicide).

Dave Singleman is the one who convinced Willy that the career of a travelling salesman can be a satisfying realization of a man's dream of success. Singleman was a personality, well-liked and successful – all the things Willy is not (he himself says that people make fun of him – calling him a walrus – and that buyers just don't notice him and pass him by). But he showed Willy that the dream of success can be realized in a 'civilized' job, not only in romantic far-away places like Alaska or Africa.

IV. Translation

'Tod eines Handlungsreisenden' ist die Lebensgeschichte eines Menschen/die Geschichte eines Menschenlebens, dessen letzte qualvolle Tage dargestellt/ beschrieben werden. Nachdem Willy Loman jahrelang/viele Jahre lang das Gebiet/den Bezirk Neuengland mit dem Auto bereist hat, ist er jetzt über sechzig Jahre alt, körperlich und geistig erschöpft/am Ende; und (er) kann den harten/sehr großen Anforderungen seines Berufes nicht länger genügen/nicht mehr gerecht werden. Trotz der Ermutigung durch seine Frau Linda weiß er, daß sein Leben nicht erfolgreich war, und dieses Wissen/Erkenntnis hat ihn an den Rand der Selbstzerstörung gebracht. Bedrückt von der Leere seines Alters, leidet er besonders darunter, daß seine beiden Söhne unfähig sind, die Erwartungen, die er in sie gesetzt hat, zu erfüllen/realisieren.

Durch eine Reihe von Rückblenden, die ihren Ursprung in Willys fiebrig erregtem Gemüt/Seele haben, werden die Ursachen/Gründe für den Niedergang seiner Familie allmählich/nach und nach enthüllt. Als Mensch/Mann mit einem beinahe mystischen Glauben an sein eigenes Erfolgskonzept, hat Willy sein ganzes Leben lang versucht, seine Werte/Wertvorstellungen seinen Söhnen einzureden/nahezubringen. Er hat sein Evangelium der Verkaufstechnik – eine forsche Persönlichkeit, ein bereitwilliges Lächeln, ein rascher Scherz und eine blendende (äußere) Erscheinung – als den Schlüssel zu Ruhm und Reichtum gepredigt; und indem er diese Anschauung/Auffassung bei seinen Jungen förderte, übersah er ihre/deren Schwächen und bahnte so, ohne es zu wollen/ unabsichtlich den Weg zu ihrem Untergang/Niedergang/Ruin.

> **Leistungskurs Englisch (Baden-Württemberg): Abiturprüfung 1991**
> **Textaufgabe und Übersetzung**

Textaufgabe:

The outstanding quality of Arthur Miller's tragedy of the common man "Death of a Salesman" is its Americanism. This quality in the play is demonstrated by contrasting reactions of American and English reviewers. The English took the hero at face value and found little of interest in his person or his plight. For the literary critic Ivor Brown, for instance, there is almost nothing to be said for Loman who lies to himself as to others, has no creed or philosophy of life beyond that of making money by making buddies, and cannot be faithful to his helpful and long-suffering wife. Brooks Atkinson, on the other hand, thought Willy "a good man who represents the homely, decent, kindly virtues of a middle-class society". The Englishman treats Willy without regard for his American context, the New York reviewer sees him as the representative of a large segment of American society. When the literary critics measure the play against Greek and Elizabethan drama, they agree with the English evaluation; the hero seems inadequate. His lack of stature, his narrow view of reality, his obvious character defects diminish the scope of action and the possibilities of universal application. Against a large historical perspective and without the American context, the salesman is a "small man" who fails to cope with his environment.

Be that as it may, Miller's hero is not simply an induvidual who has determined on an objective and who strives desperately to attain it; he is also representative of an American type, the salesman, who has accepted an ideal shaped for him and pressed on him by forces in his culture. This ideal is the matrix from which Willy emerges and by which his destiny is determined. It is peculiarly American in origin and development – seed, flower and fruit. For Arthur Miller's salesman is a personification of the success myth, he is committed to its objectives and defined by its characteristics. "Death of a Salesman" deals with the rags-to-riches romance of the American dream.

Success is a requirement Americans make of life. Because it seems magical, and inexplicable, as it is to Willy, it can be considered the due of every free citizen, even those with no notable or measurable talents. The citizen may justly and perhaps even logically ask – if Edison and Goodrich can make it, why not me, why not Willy Loman?

The attitudes which the myth expresses have a long history in American culture. The success myth, as Max Weber has demonstrated, has roots in seventeenth-century bourgeois England; it came to this continent with the founding fathers and was later popularized by the efforts of Benjamin Franklin, its outstanding exemplar. The "island of opportunity" offered enough verification of the basic tenets of the doctrine to assure its triumph in the popular mind. Virgin land, undeveloped resources, the possibility of industrial progress, all allowed scope for enterprise and imagination. No man lacked an enterprise to turn his hand to. The successful man became the idol of the public; the road to success was pointed out from the pulpit, in the marketplace, by the family fireside. From Franklin through the nineteenth century and well into the twentieth, the success myth, and all the possible variations on it, did not lack prophets and interpreters. The success ideology developed a basic outline in the early Colonial period and its essential shape has not changed appreciably since.

569 words   *Thomas E. Porter (1969)*

Vocabulary:

line 4:	plight	serious and difficult condition
line 7:	buddy	(US coll.) friend
line 26:	to be the due of	rechtmäßig zustehen, gebühren
line 33:	tenet	principle
line 37:	pulpit	Kanzel

I. Language

1. Vocabulary (ohne Wörterbuch zu bearbeiten)
   In the following (items a–g) you are to deal with the underlined words/expressions within the given context.

   a) 9–10: "... treats Willy without <u>regard for</u> his American context, ..."
   Find a suitable substitute; keep to the sentence structure. (1 VP)

   b) 12–13: "...; the hero seems <u>inadequate</u>."
   Explain; you may change the sentence structure. (1 VP)

   c) 16: "... who <u>fails to cope</u> with his environment."
   Explain; you may change the sentence structure. (2 VP)

   d) 23: "..., he is <u>committed</u> to its objectives ..."
   Find a suitable substitute; keep to the sentence structure. (1 VP)

   e) 24: "... the <u>rags</u>-<u>to</u>-<u>riches</u> romance ..."
   Explain; you may change the sentence structure. (1 VP)

   f) 25: "... is a <u>requirement</u> Americans make of life."
   Explain; you may change the sentence structure. (1 VP)

   g) 34: "<u>Virgin</u> land, ..."
   Explain; you may change the sentence structure. (1 VP)

   h) Find the corresponding abstract nouns (not the -ing-forms):
   17: simply
   18: desperately
   21: peculiarly
   33: assure (2 VP)

2. Grammar and Style (ohne Wörterbuch zu bearbeiten)

   a) 5 "..., there is <u>almost</u> nothing..."
   9: "..., <u>kindly</u> virtues..."
   Classify each underlined word according to its word class in this context. (1 VP)

   b) 11–12: "When the literary critics measure the play against Greek and Elizabethan drama, they agree with the English evaluation;..."
   Rewrite the sentence using a participle construction. (1 VP)

   c) 28: "...– if Edison and Goodrich can make it, <u>why not me, why not Willy Loman?</u>"
   Name the two stylistic devices used here and explain their function. (2VP)

d) 35–36: "..., all allowed scope for enterprise and imagination. No man lacked an enterprise to turn his hand to."
Why is the article used before "enterprise" in the second sentence but not in the first? (1 VP)

II. Comprehension

Answer the following questions in complete sentences. Keep to the information given in the text, but do not quote.
1. In what way do the reactions of English and American reviewers differ from each other?
   (80–110 words) (4 VP)
2. Why does the author of the text see Willy Loman as a product of his country's culture?
   (60–90 words) (3 VP)
3. Why could the success myth become so influential in America?
   (70–100 words) (3 VP)

III. Comment

Choose <u>one</u> of the following topics: (200–300 words) (10 VP)
1. Characterize Biff and Happy and describe their relationship to their father.
2. The Requiem scene and its function in the play.
3. Melting pot and multi-cultural society: explain the two different concepts with reference to the United States.

IV. Translation

(30 VP)

We see from the beginning two <u>notions</u> of America's role in the world and reservations about each of them. We were to be an exemplary people, influencing others to imitate the <u>goodness</u> of the society we were creating. We were to be God's <u>avengers,</u> bringing order to those who <u>dared</u> rebel against God's <u>commandments.</u> Yet there were doubts in
5 both <u>respects</u>: whether we would really live up to our exemplary calling and whether we really were superior, in the eyes of God, to those we would control.

The vigor of America's religious self-understanding has been extraordinary throughout its <u>history</u>. We can still see in Ronald Reagan's second <u>inaugural</u> address the two elements: America as an example to the nations and America as bringer of order
10 through military might, and both as <u>ordained</u> by God. In the face of such an example many commentators suggest that it is time for America to abandon the <u>notion</u> of any <u>divine</u> mission and turn to a notion of national self-interest, the way most other nations in the world have done.

178 words   *Robert N. Bellah (1986)*

Vocabulary:
line 3:   avenger   a person taking revenge
line 10:   to ordain   to decide in advance, to command
line 12:   divine   göttlich

Lösungen

I. Language

1. Vocabulary

a) treats Willy without respecting/paying attention to/looking at/considering/taking into account/taking into consideration his American context

b) the hero seems to be too ordinary
the hero doesn't seem to fulfill the classical expectations of a hero
the hero doesn't seem to have the qualities of a hero
the hero seems to be imperfect

c) who cannot deal successfully with his environment
who is unable to live successfully in his society

d) he is devoted to/loyal to/dedicated to its objectives

e) the romance of somebody who started out very poor and ends up very rich
the dishwasher-to-millionaire romance
the success story of somebody who started poor and becomes rich

f) is something that Americans expect from life
is a demand Americans make of life
is something that Americans consider essential/vital
is something that Americans demand of life

g) unsettled/untouched/untilled land
land that has never been farmed/tilled/cultivated

h) simplicity, simplification, simpleness
despair, desperation
peculiarity
assurance

2. Grammar and Style

a) almost is an adverb
kindly is an adjective

b) (When) measuring the play against Greek and Elizabethan drama, the literary critics agree with the English evaluation

c) it is a rhetorical question; a question which requires no answer
it is a repetition of "why not"/it is an anaphoric use of "why not"

d) In the first sentence the word enterprise is used in an abstract (or general) sense, therefore no article is used
In the second sentence the word enterprise refers to something specific (an enterprise "to turn his hand to")

II. Comprehension

1. The English reviewers look at Willy as a person, an individuality, and do not consider his American context. They only see that he lies to himself and to others, has no creed or philosophy except to make money. Thus the hero of the play seems inadequate.

   The Americans naturally see him in his American context and see in him a representative of the decent and kindly virtues of a middle class American society.

The English and American critics agree when they measure "Death of a Salesman" against Greek and Elizabethan drama; Willy is inadequate and cannot compare with the heroes of classical drama.

2. As an American Willy has fully accepted the material aspect of the American dream. In his job as a travelling salesman success is the only acceptable aim he sees in life, and he thinks that success can be achieved by anybody who tries if he tries hard enough. He is committed to the myth of success and really believes in the American rags-to-riches romance.

3. One reason that the success myth could become so influential in the US is that it has a long history. The Puritan work ethics came from 17th century bourgeois England and was later greatly popularized. On the other hand this virgin country with its unlimited opportunities virtually invited hard working people to become successful. And the successful man became an idol of the public, and he was praised as a role model from the pulpit, in the market place, and in the family.

III. Comment

1. Biff is a young man in his early thirties who has not found himself yet. He dropped out of school after he flunked math. He was thrown off his tracks when he caught his father with another woman in a Boston hotel where he had travelled after his flunked math exam. This disappointment in his father whom he had idolized when he was a child made him roam the country, work in odd jobs after having lost his orientation.

   Now that he is home again he quarrels with his father all the time as, on the one hand, he wants his father to face reality and, on the other hand, he still doesn't know what to do with his life. In the course of the play he finds out that he does not want to join the rat-race in the city but live in the country and work with his hands, maybe as a carpenter. Then he can tell his father that he still loves him. His father is very happy and wants Biff to have some money, commits suicide so that Biff will get the money from his life insurance.

   Happy is Biff's younger brother, and in his childhood he idolized his father and his brother. But it seemed that his father preferred Biff, the older boy. Happy in a way follows in his father's footsteps as he deceives himself (and others) when he says what a great businessman he is while he only is the assistant of a buyer in a shop. He follows Willy's dream (which Biff calls the wrong dream) and always talks of one day being the number-one man. As he tries to live Willy's dream he cannot realize Willy's desperate situation, and although he says that he loves him, he treats him rather cruelly (e.g. when he leaves Willy in the restaurant to spend the evening with the two girls he picked up) and thoughtlessly.

2. Ironically, only Willy's wife Linda, his two sons – Biff and Happy – and his only friend (if he really was that) Charlie are present at his funeral. None of all the salesmen and buyers Willy thought would come have turned up (as they had done at Dave Singleman's burial). In this short scene, these four people show and state what relation they had with Willy, and where they now stand at the end of the play.

   Linda, the loyal and loving wife who tried do make life easy for Willy and always put her husband first (if you look at the scene where she says, "attention, attention must be paid...") shows that she had never really understood and known him. Her recurrent words "why did he do it?" and "I can't understand it" prove it. She is absolutely lost now that her husband is dead.

Charlie understands that as a salesman Willy had to have a dream as he was "riding on a smile and a shoeshine". But he does not see that you cannot really live if you have so shallow and trivial a dream as Willy had.

Happy has not really understood anything. He really believes in Willy's dream and thinks he can make it come true: "It's the only dream you can have – to come out number-one man. He fought it out there and this is where I'm gonna win it for him". Chances are that he will live an empty life just as Willy did.

Biff finally has found himself. He has realized that he cannot blame his father for his own aimlessness, and he cannot try to realize his father's dreams for him. Instead he must try to live his own individual life, and realize his own personal aims and ambitions. He can see that his father "had the wrong dreams; all,all wrong." It seems that Biff has undergone quite a development in the course of the play, he has learned to face himself with all his weaknesses.

3. The melting pot idea in America was – and for some people still is – that all the immigrants should give up their cultural and social peculiarities and their language and become members of a new race, the Americans. All their peculiarities are to be "melted down" and a new mixture or "alloy" will result. This idea was realized to a certain extent during the early times of the USA when almost all of the immigrants had a relatively homogeneous background (they came from Northern, Central or Western Europe, mostly were of Germanic stock and the majority were Protestants). The negroes as slaves were excluded from this concept – the US never considered a mixing of races with different colours of skin.

The idea of a multi-cultural society means that immigrants should of course adapt to their new country but that they need not give up their old cultural identity but that the various groups in the USA form a multi-facetted society. To describe this phenomenon some people talk about a "salad bowl" or a "vegetable soup". Those images are meant to express the fact that the various groups of immigrants give up some of their "flavour" to the greater American society but retain their individual identity.

Since immigrants from Eastern and Southern Europe came to the USA after the 1850s – and especially since newcomers from Asia and other continents came to America after World War II – this concept of a multi-cultural society has become more and more a reality in America. As President Kennedy put it, America is really "a nation of nations".

IV. Translation

Wir sehen/erkennen von Anfang an zwei Begriffe/Vorstellungen/Gedanken von/über Amerikas Rolle/Aufgabe in der Welt, und Vorbehalte/Einschränkungen gegenüber beiden. Wir sollten ein beispielhaftes/vorbildliches Volk sein und andere beeinflussen/dazu bringen, das Positive/Gute an der Gesellschaft, die wir schufen/aufbauten, zu übernehmen/nachzuahmen. Wir sollten Gottes Rächer sein und jene zur Ordnung rufen, die es wagten, gegen Gottes Gebote zu verstossen/aufzubegehren. Jedoch gab es Zweifel in beiderlei Hinsicht: Ob wir unserer vorbildhaften Berufung wirklich gerecht würden, und ob wir in den Augen Gottes wirklich jenen überlegen wären/besser wären als jene, die wir beherrschen/kontrollieren würden/über die wir Macht ausüben würden.

Die Kraft des religiösen Selbstverständnisses Amerikas ist während der ganzen amerikanischen Geschichte außerordentlich gewesen. Wir können in Ronald Reagans zweiter Amtsantrittsrede/Antrittsrede zur zweiten Amtsperiode (immer) noch die beiden Elemente feststellen/erkennen: Amerika als ein Beispiel für die Nationen/Völker, und Amerika als Ordnungshüter/-stifter durch/auf Grund Militärmacht, und beides als von Gott (verher)bestimmt. In Anbetracht/Angesichts eines solchen Beispiels meinen viele Kommentatoren, daß es für Amerika an der Zeit sei, die Idee jeglicher göttlichen Mission/Auftrags aufzugeben/von ... abzulassen und sich einem Konzept/einer Idee nationalen Eigeninteresses zuzuwenden, in der Weise/(so) wie es die meisten anderen Völker/Nationen auf/in der Welt (schon lange) getan haben.

> **Leistungskurs Englisch (Baden-Württemberg): Abiturprüfung 1992**
> **Textaufgabe und Übersetzung**

In the office of the World Controller for Western Europe lies a copy of "My Life and Work, by Our Ford". It is no coincidence that "Our Ford" is both the patron saint and prophet of Huxley's new world-state. "Fordism", he wrote in a contemporary essay, "demands that we should sacrifice the animal man (and along with the animal man large portions of the thinking, spiritual man) not indeed to God, but to the Machine. There is no place in the factory, or in that larger factory which is the modern industrialized world, for animals on the one hand, or for artists, mystics, or even, finally, individuals on the other. Of all the ascetic religions Fordism is that which demands the cruellest mutilations of the human psyche – demands the cruellest mutilations and offers the smallest spiritual returns". Fordism, the philisophy of applied science and industrialism, is the religion of <u>Brave New World</u>. By the double process of genetic manipulation and post-natal conditioning the World Controllers have succeeded in producing a race which loves its servitude, a race of standardized machine-minders for standardized machines who will never challenge their authority. The animal, thinking and spiritual man has been sacrificed in his entirety.

Huxley, comparing his novel with Orwell's <u>1984</u>, observes that in the latter a strict code of sexual morality is imposed. The society of Orwell's fable is permanently at war and therefore aims to keep its subjects in a constant state of tension. A puritanical approach to sex is therefore a major instrument of policy. The World-State, however, of <u>Brave New World</u> is one in which war has been eliminated and the first aim of its rulers is to keep their subjects from making trouble. Together with Soma, sexual licence, made practical by the abolition of the family, is one of the chief means of guaranteeing the inhabitants against any kind of destructive or creative emotional tension. The dreadful dangers of family life had first been pointed out by Our Ford or "Our Freud, as, for some inscrutable reason, he chose to call himself whenever he spoke of psychological matters". Once the world had been full of every kind of perversion from chastity to sadism; but the World Controllers had realized that an industrial civilization depended on self-indulgence. Chastity meant passion and neurasthenia, and passion and neurasthenia meant instability, which, in turn, meant a constant threat to civilization. Therefore life for the Brave New Worlders was made emotionally easy; in short, people were saved from having any emotions at all. No one was allowed to love anyone too much; there were no temptations to resist, and if something unpleasant were to happen, there was always Soma.

Soma and licensed promiscuity would probably have been sufficient in themselves to prevent the Brave New Worlders from taking any active interest in the realities of the social and political situation; circuses, however, are a traditional aid to dictators, and the Controllers of the World-State were no exception. Huxley's utopians were provided with a series of non-stop distractions guaranteed to prevent boredom and discourage idle speculation about the nature of things. Any frustrated religious instincts were provided for by the Ford's Day Solidarity Services, where, in a crude parody of the Holy Communion, dedicated Soma Tablets and the loving cup of ice-cream Soma were passed round. By these means the Controllers insured that the Brave New Worlders loved their servitude and never dreamt of revolution.

578 words   *Peter Bowering (1968)*

Vocabulary:

line 9:	mutilation	– injury, damage, deformation
line 21:	sexual licence	– uncontrolled sexual freedom
line 25:	inscrutable	– mysterious, difficult to understand
line 28:	self-indulgence	– Haltlosigkeit, Hemmungslosigkeit, Zügellosigkeit
line 28:	neurasthenia	– geringe nervliche Belastbarkeit, Nervenschwäche
line 38:	distraction	– Ablenkung, Zerstreuung

I. Language

1. Vocabulary (ohne Wörterbuch zu bearbeiten)

   In the following (items a-g) you are to deal with the underlined words/expressions within the given context.

   a) 2: "It is no coincidence that ..."
   Find a suitable substitute; keep to the sentence structure. (1 VP)

   b) 10: "... applied science ..."
   Explain, you may change the sentence structure. (1 VP)

   c) 13: "... a race of standardized machine-minders ..."
   Explain, you may change the sentence structure. (1 VP)

   d) 14: "... who will never challenge their authority."
   Find a suitable substitute; keep to the sentence structure. (1 VP)

   e) 15: "... has been sacrificed in his entirety."
   Explain, you may change the sentence structure. (1 VP)

   f) 16-17: "... a strict code of sexual morality is imposed."
   Explain, you may change the sentence structure. (2 VP)

   g) 29: "... which, in turn, meant ..."
   Explain, you may change the sentence structure. (1VP)

   Find the corresponding abstract nouns (not the -ing-forms):

   h) 16: comparing
   17: permanently
   25: chose
   39: idle (2 VP)

2. Grammar and Style (ohne Wörterbuch zu bearbeiten)

   a) 3-4: "Fordism" ... "demands that we should sacrifice the animal man" ..."
   Rewrite the sentence, replacing the verb "demand" by "want". (1 VP)

   b) 14: "The animal, thinking and spiritual man ..."
   21: "... to keep their subjects from making trouble."
   Define the underlined forms and explain their use. (2 VP)

   c) 31: "No one was allowed to love anyone too much ..."
   Transform into the active voice. (1 VP)

   d) 31-32: "... there were no temptations to resist ..."
   Rewrite the sentence, replacing the infinitive construction. (1 VP)

II. Comprehension

Answer the following questions in complete sentences. Keep to the information given in the text, but do not quote.

1. In what way does "Fordism" determine the nature of man?
   (90–120 words) (4 VP)
2. What is said about the importance of sexual licence and self-indulgence for the society in <u>Brave New World</u>?
   (60–90 words) (3 VP)
3. What are the Brave New Worlders additionally offered to prevent them from questioning their situation?
   (60–90 words) (3 VP)

III. Comment

Choose <u>one</u> of the following topics: (200–300 words) (10 VP)

1. Characterize John the Savage and comment on his function in the novel.
2. To what extent has Huxley's utopia come true today? Discuss some of the main aspects.
3. Why have the British had more difficulty than other member countries in finding their role within the European Community?

IV. Translation (30 VP)

The men and women returning from service in World War II faced a changed, and rapidly changing, world. The actual transition from the heroic tasks of war to the everyday activities of peace was, indeed, smoothly accomplished, with food rationing being retained for some years to ensure fair shares at fair prices so long as almost everything
5 was still in short supply. Perhaps the biggest immediate surprise to many people was that there was no return to the bad times that had followed earlier wars, a prospect which had caused some to dread, as a humorist put it, "peace breaking out". Instead, Britain moved on from the years of economic recovery to those of affluence, with high wages backed by extensive new social services, and with increased leisure made possi-
10 ble by the rapid advances of technology.

But in Britain as in many other countries the affluent society brought with it its own problems of increased crime – especially among the young – drug addiction, and violence. The affluent society had its counterpart in the permissive society, which opposed accepted standards in music, art, and literature, no less than in morals and discipline,
15 including self-discipline.

T. K. Derry, T. L. Jarman (1979) *193 words*

Vocabulary
line 7: to dread   – to fear
line 8: affluence – wealth, abundance
line 13: permissive – (often negative) allowing a great deal of, or too much, freedom in matters of morality, especially sexual morality

Lösungsvorschlag

I. Language

1. Vocabulary

   a) It is not (purely) by accident that
      It is not (just) by chance that
      It is not purely accidental that
      It is not pure chance that

   b) the opposite of pure science, meaning that it is used in (industrial) production
      science that is put to practical use
      science having an effect on (industrial) production

   c) people who have to look after machines
      people who supervise the running of machines
      people who are responsible for the running of machines
      people who operate machines
      people who control machines

   d) who will never question/object to/protest against/doubt their authority

   e) has totally/completely/wholly been sacrificed
      has been sacrificed in his totality/entity

   f) an austere/an uncompromising/a stern/a severe/a rigid code of sexual morality is forced on/upon people
      people have to/are forced to adhere to a ... code of sexual morality
      people have to live according to a ... code of sexual morality

   g) as a consequence/from a different point of view/consequently/as a result/therefore

   h) comparison
      permanence, permanency
      choice
      idleness

2. Grammar and Style

   a) Fordism ... wants us to sacrifice tha animal man

   b) present participle used as an adjective
      gerund after (a verb plus) preposition (to keep ... from)

   c) The system/Society/The World Controllers did not allow people/their subjects/the inhabitants of Brave New World to love anyone too much.

   d) there were no temptations that had to/were to be resisted
      there were no temptations that people would have to resist

II. Comprehension

1. Fordism is the philisophy (or religion) of applied science and industrial production, and man is made to conform to them. Applied science and industrialism need standardized people who operate machines. These people – in order to be standardized machine-minders – must lose their animal, thinking and spiritual qualities. This is achieved by genetic manipulation and forceful conditioning during childhood.
   Such a being is not a complete human being as he has been robbed of just those qualities which make him human: his creativity and his artistic faculties, his thoughts, and even his individuality. He is a soulless automaton operating machines.

2. In the World-State of BNW war has been eliminated, and the most important aim of its rulers is stability – which can be achieved by eliminating tensions.

Sexual licence and self-indulgence help stabilize this society as they make deep emotions and serious attachments impossible and thus eliminate (destructive or creative) emotional tensions. Everybody loves everybody, but not so much that somebody might lose his balance (as the Savage did); and in case of an unpleasantness there was always Soma.

3. In addition to promiscuity and self-indulgence the people living in BNW were offered incessant distractions; circuses, as the text says. These distractions were an instrument to keep people busy and happy and to keep them from asking questions and prevent idle speculation. If any religious instincts still needed to be satisfied, the Solidarity Services (a crude parody of the Holy Communion) provided a perverted answer.

Thus the New Worlders were kept satisfied and never thought of challenging the existing order of society.

III. Comment

1. John the Savage is the son of two New Worlders, but he grew up on a Savage Reservation. John grew up among the Indians on the Reservation and absorbed some of their customs and beliefs (e.g. the Penitente Cult). Another great influence on his character and view of the world is the plays of Shakespeare – which he read and whose values he accepted wholesale and without questioning (this plays quite a role in John's relationship with Lenina). And he heard about Brave New World from his mother (who tried to teach him some BNW values) and is very eager to get to know more about it – and therefore he accompanies Bernard and Lenina back to Brave New World.

John's character is influenced by all his experiences and he is a strange mixture of naiveté and philosopher. He seems to be a strong character but he cannot bear the tension between the conflicting values he faces. This leads to violence and finally to John's suicide.

John's function in the novel is to give the author a possibility to look at Brave New World "from the outside", so to speak, and to discuss this utopia's strengths and weaknesses. No proper New Worlder can ask pertinent questions about the system of Brave New World because he is "imprisoned" in the system by his bottling, sleep-teaching, and conditioning.

You need somebody from outside of a system to discuss the merits of this system – and this is what takes places in the scene with Mustapha Mond who explains the system of Brave New World to him (chapters XVI and XVII). Thus you could say that in a way John is the most important character in Brave New World.

2. If you look at the scientific aspect it can be said that biology has taken great strides in the direction of Brave New World. Although the "Bokanovsky Process" cannot be duplicated (yet?), biologists can produce absolutely identical organisms by cloning. And gene-manipulation can alter the genetic material of living organisms. Thus the scientific basis does exist if a society should want to develop towards something like Brave New World.

Although nothing like Soma has been invented yet, drugs do play quite a role in our society. Alcohol is an accepted and legal drug, as are, for example, some pep pills, tranquilizers, and sleeping pills – all of which are widely abused. A wide range of illegal drugs – from marihuana to heroin and cocaine and others – are also rife in our society and cause serious problems. As most of these drugs are used to escape what is perceived to be the unpleasantness of reality, these drugs in a way play the same role as Soma does in Brave New World. But using drugs is frowned upon in our society and escaping reality by taking drugs is not an accepted standard of behaviour.

Our affluent and permissive society seems to be very much interested in providing distractions for everybody. The leisure industry is one of the fastest growing sectors of industry.

There is one great difference between our world and Brave New World, though. We have the possibility of a conscious choice as we are not manipulated biologically, and have the possibility to decide what sort of life we want to lead. And as the events of the last few years have shown, people do not want to be managed by totalitarian systems but have a yearning for the freedom to decide their own future.

3. Britain's ambivalent attitude towards Europe after World War II can be seen if you consider Churchill's call for "political action directed towards European union" in 1946 – and his 1951 refusal to join with any federation of Europe. Then Macmillan tried to join the EEC in 1961, as did Wilson in 1967 – and in both instances De Gaulle vetoed the attempt. Only after three years of negotiation was the Heath government finally successful in 1973 and joined the EEC. (The following Labour government decided to stay in after the electorate decided 2:1 in a referendum in favour of Europe in 1975).

Some of the difficulties can be explained by Britain's history. Traditionally, Britain tried not to get involved in European affairs. In the past, she tried to achieve a balance of power in Europe (with no nation strong enough to endanger Britain's position in world politics) without any direct involvement or long-term pacts. Thus it is a completely new idea to become an active part of Europe after such a long time of relative isolation from Europe. In the course of centuries, Parliament in Westminster has become the absolute sovereign in the English political system. What Parliament decides becomes the law of the land (there is no institution like the US Supreme Court in Britain). The European Community demands that some decisions be transferred to European institutions (the Commission, the Council of Ministers, and the European Parliament), and this is something very few politicians in Britain can stomach.

Until the time after World War II Britain looked much more towards her Empire and Commonwealth than towards Europe.. Although the ties with the Commonwealth are now more sentimental and have lost most of their economic importance, the British still have a tendency to feel very close to the English-speaking world. But economic realities dictate that Britain form a closer relationship with Europe.

The special Atlantic relationship with the USA (although it is more wishful thinking than a viable reality nowadays) is another reason for Britain's reluctance to join Europe.

IV. Translation

Die Männer und Frauen, die vom Einsatz im 2. Weltkrieg zurückkamen/-kehrten, waren mit einer veränderten und sich rasch verändernden Welt konfrontiert/sahen sich ... gegenüber. Der eigentliche Übergang von den heroischen/heldenhaften Aufgaben des Krieges zu den alltäglichen Tätigkeiten im Frieden ging tatsächlich/wirklich reibungslos vonstatten/wurde ... vollzogen, wobei die Rationierung/Bewirtschaftung von Lebensmitteln (noch) für einige Jahre beibehalten wurde, um eine gerechte Verteilung zu gerechten Preisen zu gewährleisten/sicherzustellen, solange fast alles noch knapp war. Für viele Leute war es vielleicht die größte unmittelbare Überraschung, daß es keine Rückkehr/Rückfall in die schlechten Zeiten gab, die auf frühere Kriege gefolgt waren; eine

Aussicht, die einige/manche Leute hatte befürchten lassen, daß, wie es ein Humorist ausdrückte/formulierte, "der Frieden ausbrechen" würde. Stattdessen schritt Großbritannien weiter von den Jahren der wirtschaftlichen Erholung zu jenen des Reichtums/ Wohlstands; mit hohen Löhnen, die durch umfassende neue Sozialleistungen unterstützt/ ergänzt wurden, und mit vermehrter/zusätzlicher Freizeit, die durch den raschen technischen Fortschritt möglich wurde.

Aber in Großbritannien wie in vielen anderen Ländern brachte die Wohlstandsgesellschaft ihre eigenen Probleme höherer Kriminalität – vor allem unter Jugendlichen –Drogenabhängigkeit und Gewalt(tätigkeit) mit sich. Die Wohlstandsgesellschaft hatte ihr Gegenbild/-stück in der tabufreien/allzu freizügigen Gesellschaft, die sich gegen die anerkannten/akzeptierten Normen in der Musik, Kunst und Literatur wandte/ablehnte, genauso wie gegen die der Moral und Disziplin, einschließlich der Selbstdisziplin.

> **Leistungskurs Englisch (Baden-Württemberg): Abiturprüfung 1993**
> **Textaufgabe und Übersetzung**

To say that God is everywhere in American life is as much a statement of fact as of faith. His name appears on every coin, on every dollar bill and in the vast majority of state constitutions. Schoolchildren pledge allegiance to one nation under Him. The President of the United States ends his speeches with a benediction: God bless America.

In a country born of a pilgrim's dream, a country that exalts freedom of worship as a sacred right, perhaps none of that is surprising. What *is* surprising is that for most of the ensuing 200 years, Americans have not stopped arguing about God. In the past decade alone, the U.S. Supreme Court has decided more religion cases than ever before, and each day brings a fresh crusade.

At issue is the meaning of the basic principle enshrined in the First Amendment of the U.S. Constitution: that Congress, and by later extension the states, "shall make no law respecting an establishment of religion, or prohibiting the free exercise thereof." The modern Supreme Court has taken that to mean that government cannot do anything that promotes either a particular faith or religion in general.

The fight at present is not so much over what people ought to believe; it is over what they can say, and where, and to whom. The battleground has spread from the courtroom to the schoolroom: In Decatur, Illinois, e. g., a primary-school teacher discovered the word 'God' in a textbook and ordered her class of seven-year-olds to strike it out, saying that it is against the law to mention God in a public school. She later apologized.

In the broadest terms, there are two main camps in this holy war. On one side are the "separationists", who argue that church and state must remain clearly apart and that government should not be in the business of endorsing one faith or another, or even of supporting all faiths in general. On the other side are the "accommodationists", who believe the "wall of separation" between church and state has grown too thick. By isolating God from public life, they argue, the courts have replaced freedom *of* religion with freedom *from* religion.

For the past 40 years or so, owing to a lengthy series of Supreme Court rulings, the tide has generally favored the separationists. But the debate has now arrived at a crossroads. Last month the Supreme Court heard arguments in a case that invites it to rewrite the canons of church-state law. The *Lee vs Weisman* case involves a Rhode Island rabbi whose prayer at a middle-school graduation was later ruled unconstitutional by a district court. The rabbi gave thanks to God for "the legacy of America, where diversity is celebrated and the rights of minorities are protected". The district court suggested that the invocation would have been fine if the rabbi had just left out all the reference to God. At the Supreme Court, the school board is arguing that so long as the prayer was not coercive, it did not violate the First Amendment.

The present Supreme Court may turn out to be the first accommodationist court in years. "The wall of separation between church and state is a metaphor based on bad history. It should be frankly and explicitly abandoned", Chief Justice William Rehnquist declared in 1985. Were a majority of Supreme Court Justices to agree with Rehnquist today, it could dramatically change the role that religion plays in America's marketplace of ideas – and ultimately, in every citizen's private life.

TIME (1991) *589 words*

Vocabulary:
line 9: crusade – Kreuzzug
line 22: to endorse – to give one's official approval or support to
line 30: canon – principle by which something is judged
line 34: invocation – a call upon God
line 36: coercive – compulsory

I. Language

1. Vocabulary (ohne Wörterbuch zu bearbeiten)

   In the following (items a-g) you are to deal with the underlined words/expressions within the given context.

   a) 10: "<u>At issue</u> is the meaning of ..."
   Explain; you may change the sentence structure. (1 VP)

   b) 10–11: "... in the First <u>Amendment</u> of the U.S. Constitution ..."
   Explain; you may change the sentence structure. (1 VP)

   c) 12: "... <u>prohibiting</u> the free exercise ..."
   Find a suitable substitute; keep to the sentence structure. (1 VP)

   d) 13–14: "... that <u>promotes</u> either a particular faith ..."
   Find a suitable substitute; keep to the sentence structure. (1 VP)

   e) 20: "<u>In the broadest terms</u>, there are ..."
   Find a suitable substitute; keep to the sentence structure. (1 VP)

   f) 28–29: "But the debate has now <u>arrived at a crossroads</u>."
   Explain; you may change the sentence structure. (1 VP)

   g) 32–33: "... where diversity is <u>celebrated</u> ..."
   Find a suitable substitute; keep to the sentence structure. (1 VP)

   Find the corresponding abstract nouns (not the -ing-forms):

   h) 2: vast
   5: born
   19: apologized
   21: remain (2 VP)

2. Grammar and Style (ohne Wörterbuch zu bearbeiten)

   a) 1–2: "To say that God is everywhere in American life is as much a statement of fact as of faith."
   Name the subject of the main clause. (1 VP)

   b) 4: "God bless America."
   Rewrite the sentence, using a modal auxiliary. (1 VP)

   c) 6: "... none of that ..."
   Which passage of the text does this phrase refer to? (1 VP)

   d) 6–7: "... for most of the ensuing 200 years, Americans have not stopped arguing about God."
   Classify the -ing forms. (1 VP)

e) 38: "The wall ... is a metaphor ..."
Find two more metaphors in the text. (1 VP)

f) 40: "Were a majority ... to agree ..."
Rewrite the sentence, replacing the underlined expression
by a different modal auxiliary. (1 VP)

II. Comprehension

Answer the following questions in complete sentences. Keep to the information given in the text, but do not quote.

1. In what ways does religion play an important role in American life
   and why is it at the same time a controversial issue?
   (80 – 120 words) (4 VP)

2. What are the two conflicting views in the new "holy war"?
   (40 – 60 words) (2 VP)

3. What is the issue in the *Lee vs Weisman* case and why does the author
   think the role of religion in America could change dramatically?
   (80 – 120 words) (4 VP)

III. Comment

Choose one of the following topics: (200 – 300 words) (10 VP)

1. Describe one landmark decision of the Supreme Court and its impact
   on American society.

2. One of the manners in which Americans worship is the so-called
   'electronic church'. Describe its main features and give your opinion
   on this American phenomenon.

3. "Brave New World" – paradise or nightmare?

IV. Translation (30 VP)

There is one question John does not ask Mustapha Mond in their long conversation, which contains the chief satiric elements of the entire novel. It is perhaps the one question the World Controller might have had some difficulty answering. What sense is there in complete happiness without a God to make it meaningful? If society is to be
5 stable for no other reason than that it may endure, if the products of the hatcheries and conditioning centres in the brave new world are to be happy simply because unhappiness is incompatible with stability, it seems that Mustapha must regard endurance as objectively valuable. But it is the senselessness of the World State that makes it an insane state, and insanity cannot be explained rationally. John does not ask the question
10 partly because it does not occur to him, partly because he wants to sleep with Lenina and so sees a great deal of sense in continuing to live, but mostly because the view of the World State Huxley imposes on the reader is clearly not a view any of his characters can have.

Rudolf B. Schmerl   *185 words*

Vocabulary
line 5: to endure – to continue to exist
line 5: hatchery – Aufzuchtanstalt

Lösungsvorschlag

I. Language

1. Vocabulary

   a) The discussion is about the meaning of ...
   The problem / matter / subject / aspect / point (being) debated / discussed is ...
   What the argument is about is ...
   What they argue about is ...
   They argue about the meaning of ...

   b) ... in the first additional article of the US Constitution ...
   ... in the first addition to the US Constitution ...
   ... in the first new article that has been added to the US Constitution ...
   An amendment is an additional article to a constitution.

   c) ... not allowing / preventing / forbidding / not permitting / (restricting) the free exercise ...

   d) ... that encourages / supports / advances / favours / (aids) / (helps) / (fosters) either a particular faith ...

   e) In a general sense, there are ...
   Roughly speaking, there are ...
   Generally speaking, there are ...
   If you simplify, there are ...

   f) But the debate has now reached a critical / crucial / decisive stage.
   But the debate has now come to a decisive point.
   But the debate has now come to a point where alternate decisions are possible.
   But the debate has now come to a point where a new course might be decided upon.

   g) ... where diversity is praised / cherished / extolled / lauded / applauded / glorified / acclaimed / worshipped / exalted ...

   h) vastness, (vastitude), (vastity)
   birth
   apology
   remainder, remains

2. Grammar and Style

   a) The subject of the main clause is: To say that God is everywhere in American life.

   b) May God bless America.
   God may bless America.

   c) This phrase refers to the first paragraph of the text.

   d) ensuing – present participle (used as an adjective)
   arguing – gerund (after certain verbs, e. g. to stop, to start)

- e) 9: crusade
  16: battleground
  20: two main camps
  20: holy war
  27: tide
  28–29: crossroads
  41–42: marketplace of ideas

- f) Should a majority ... agree ...
  If a majority ... should agree ...

II. Comprehension

1. God's name appears on coins and banknotes; He is mentioned in many state constitutions; the pledge of allegiance refers to God; and most presidential speeches end with the invocation that God may bless America. Thus a religious element (or at least the mentioning of God's name) pervades public life.
   It is a controversial subject inasmuch as the issue of religion has been hotly debated in the past 200 years; and there have been more Supreme Court decisions during the last 10 years than ever before. The problem is how narrowly the wording of the 1st Amendment should be interpreted.

2. The separationists insist on a very strict barrier between church and state, and therefore any involvement of the state in religious matters should be avoided (not even prayers at public schools are legal).
   The accommodationists believe that the wall between church and state has become too high and insurmountable. One of their arguments is that if you isolate God from public life, freedom of religion will be replaced by freedom from religion.

3. At a school graduation a rabbi thanked God for the legacy of America (the celebration of diversity and the protection of minorities). This prayer was ruled unconstitutional by a district court and will later be decided by the Supreme Court (the argument for the prayer being that as it was not coercive it was quite all right).
   For the last 40 years or so, the Supreme Court has been separationist. But in 1985 Chief Justice William Rehnquist used accommodationist arguments when arguing about the separation of church and state. Should the majority of the Supreme Court Justices follow his arguments in the above-mentioned case, this could dramatically change the situation.

III. Comment

1. *Anstatt eine "landmark decision" ausführlich darzustellen, werden drei verschiedene kurz vorgestellt.*

   Plessy versus Ferguson, 1896
   Homer Plessy, a negro, rode in a railroad car reserved for whites. He was convicted and appealed to the Supreme Court. The Supreme Court decided that his conviction was justified. It stated that providing "equal but separate" facilities for different races was constitutional. This "equal but separate" doctrine led to the segregation of the races in many areas of life in the South; it was the basis for the discrimination against negroes. This Supreme Court decision determined race relations for more than 50 years, especially in the South.

The only Southerner on the Supreme Court, Justice Harlan, did not agree with the majority and wrote a dissenting opinion, claiming "our constitution is color-blind".

Brown versus Board of Education of Topeka, 1954
Oliver Brown, a negro, tried to enroll his daughter Linda in a neighborhood elementary school. She was rejected, the school was segregated and accepted only white students.
Oliver Brown sued the Board of Education (one of the lawyers representing him, Thurgood Marshal, was later to become the first black Supreme Court judge) and the case was later accepted by the Supreme Court which unanimously ruled in his favor (overturning the doctrine of "equal but separate").
This decision was the end of legal segregation and a major victory for the civil rights movement. Of course, desegregation has been a long and bitter struggle which even today hasn't come to an end; but the above decision was the beginning of a new era of race relations in the USA.

United States versus The Washington Post, 1971, New York Times Company versus United States
The two newspapers had published a number of articles about America's involvement in the Vietnam war. Somebody in the Pentagon had 'leaked' some secret government documents on which these articles were based (hence the name "Pentagon Papers"). The government wanted to have these publications stopped.
The Supreme Court decided that just because the papers were classified 'secret' by the government did not justify such a step. The press is to serve the interest of governed, not the government. "The government's power to censor the press was abolished so that the press would remain forever free to censure the government."
This decision (and some others, for example about the Watergate tapes) strengthened the position of the press – and the media in general – in relation to the government. Thus it slowed the development towards what some people call the 'imperial presidency' and encourages an in-depth coverage of political affairs which is very important in a democratic society.

2. The "electronic church" tries to make most of its medium, television; and by adapting to television it has become something typical for our times.
TV, being the "look and forget" medium, does not offer televangelists a chance for a sermon in the normal format. Instead of the "electronic church" tries to give an endless stream of easy answers to difficult questions. TV preachers must say what they want to put across to their audience quite simply and quickly – and it must be entertaining or else viewers may choose a different program. TV is no medium for subtle differentiation, everything must be unambiguous; so the preacher must make his audience feel secure and certain of his message. TV is not efficient as a medium of changing people's minds, so their beliefs and attitudes must be bolstered and reinforced – it is no good trying to challenge the viewers' convictions. A positive approach to life as well as the feeling that it is alright to look out for yourself makes religious TV programs quite effective (also in monetary terms; if a televangelist follows the above guidelines, his audience will send him quite a substantial sum for his religious enterprise). The "electronic church" uses all sorts of shows which are successful on commercial TV.
I am of the opinion that having a religious program on TV is quite all right as some people do not want to or cannot go to church but want to take part in some religious service – even if only indirectly. But that rather refers to the broadcasting of a 'normal' religious service on TV.

I don't think that the "electronic church" as it developed in the United States is an appropriate way of worship as it seems to have degenerated into purely a spectacle. These spectacles seem to put more emphasis on the requirements of TV than on religious principles and seem to be more interested in the viewers' contributions than in providing spiritual help.

3. The answer to these alternatives depends on your view of life, and of man and his place in society. But I think that the overwhelming majority of people would call Brave New World a nightmare.

In this society you are manipulated from fertilization to death – there is no chance whatsoever of individual development. Any individual ideas or plans are regarded as deviations from normal, and you are punished for them (sent to a rehabilitation centre or into exile to some isolated place – depending on how "badly" you are affected)! If you think of the French Revolution and its ideals – freedom, equality and brotherhood – and how the different societies of our world try to secure a maximum of freedom in the framework of an open and democratic society you can see that the society of Brave New World is opposed to all those endeavours, and therefore can only be regarded as a nightmare for modern man.

In really terribly depressing times of war, economic depression or anarchy people may be tempted to view Brave New World as a sort of paradise where you have stability, your material needs are provided for and you do not have to face hunger, war or social upheaval.

IV. Translation

Es gibt eine Frage, die John Mustapha Mond in ihrem/deren langen Gespräch/Unterhaltung, das die hauptsächlichen/wichtigsten satirischen Elemente des ganzen Romans enthält, nicht stellt. Es ist vielleicht die eine Frage, die dem Weltaufsichtsrat/Weltkontrollrat (eventuell) (etwas) Schwierigkeiten bei der Beantwortung hätte machen können/gemacht hätte/. die der Weltkontrollrat wohl nur mit einiger Mühe hätte beantworten können. Welchen Sinn hat/liegt in vollkommenes Glück, ohne einen Gott, ihm Bedeutung zu verleihen/wenn nicht ein Gott es mit Bedeutung erfüllt/wenn es keinen Gott gibt, um ihm Bedeutung /Hintergrund/Sinn zu geben. Wenn die Gesellschaft aus keinem anderen Grunde/nur überdauern soll/möge/stabil sein soll, als daß/damit sie weiterbestehen soll/möge; wenn die Produkte/Erzeugnisse/Geschöpfe der Aufzuchtanstalten und Konditionierungszentren in der schönen neuen Welt einfach deshalb/nur glücklich sein sollen, weil Unglücklichsein unvereinbar ist mit Stabilität; scheint es, daß Mustapha das Überdauern/Weiterbestehen (der Gesellschaft) als objektiv wertvoll betrachten/halten/ einschätzen muß. Aber gerade die Sinnlosigkeit des Weltstaates macht ihn zu einem absurden Staat/Wahnsinnsstaat – und Absurdität/Wahnsinn kann nicht vernünftig/rational erklärt werden. John stellt die Frage nicht, teils/teilweise weil sie ihm nicht einfällt/er nicht darauf kommt,teils weil er mit Lenina schlafen möchte/will und daher viel Sinn im Weiterleben sieht/das Weiterleben für sehr sinnvoll hält, aber vor allem/hauptsächlich weil die Sicht des Weltstaates, die Huxley dem Leser aufzwingt,/-drängt/-nötigt offenkundig eine Sichtweise ist, die keine seiner (Roman) Gestalten/Charaktere haben kann.

> **Leistungskurs Englisch (Baden-Württemberg): Abiturprüfung 1994**
> **Textaufgabe und Übersetzung**

In Chapter 16 of <u>Brave New World</u> Huxley puts into the mouth of the Controller an explanation of exactly what has happened in the process of constructing utopia. Instability has been removed, chance and fluctuation have been removed, and the implications are formidable. "You can't make tragedies without social instability," the Controller says.
5 Tragedy, worry, suffering have all gone. All the components of life's daily difficulties have been removed. But so have all the major influences that characterize human life. Where would poetry and painting be without love and death? It is not a simplistic equation – suffering equals the production of great art –, but a question of the value of experience, and the value of life without experience. Even the happiness that the Controller
10 claims as the great achievement can have no intensity. To imagine human nature flourishing in this bland and sterile context is impossible.

Unlike the other characters, the Controller is aware of what has been lost. Happiness in the past, he argues, has been no more than 'overcompensation for misery'. Hygienic happiness has replaced picturesque squalor, and picturesque happiness. The implication is
15 that this is the only way of getting rid of the squalor. Shakespeare has to be sacrificed for the good of mankind.

But mankind has to be sacrificed, too. In order to maintain stability, intelligence and imagination must be conditioned and controlled. The Deltas and Epsilons are necessary, not only to provide a section of the population that will contentedly perform the neces-
20 sary menial tasks, but to balance the Alphas. Without Alphas, Epsilons would be meaningless, and vice versa. A society composed entirely of Alphas – "separate and unrelated individuals of good heredity and conditioned so as to be capable, within limits, of making a free choice and assuming responsibilities" – would be disastrous. The Controller has to make this point. The Alphas are the privileged, aware of themselves as privileged
25 but not regarded as such by the others, who retain all that can be allowed of human nature. When they get together in an independent situation, the 'Cyprus experiment' is the result: "Within six years they were having a first class civil war," the Controller explains. In other words, human nature is quarrelsome, competitive, aggressive, selfish, and the brave new world has removed the possibility for people to show themselves at
30 their worst.

The heights have been removed from human existence, but so have the depths. Huxley presents the dilemma with the utmost clarity, and if his characters lack the substance we look for in fiction, they demonstrate unequivocally the nature of a society without fiction. Mustapha Mond, the Controller, is himself a character worth pausing over, for he is
35 the man of intelligence and understanding who has to be the exception that proves the rule. Neither Bernard nor his friend Helmholtz, superlatively Alpha plus though he be, would be capable of interpreting the brave new world for the benefit of the Savage in the way the Controller can. Bernard is not aware of the full implications of his introduction of the Savage to civilization, for either party. Mond was given the choice, at an earlier
40 stage in his career, between rebellion – and exile – and responsibility, and chose the latter with a certain regretful lingering over what the former might have contained. He is the high priest of rationalism on the terms demanded by the society he serves. But he is an instrument, and he has to recognize the limitations of his power. Without his acceptance of subservience to an Idea greater than human, or at least greater than his
45 own concept of himself, his means of power would vanish.

604 words *Jenni Calder (1976)*

Vocabulary:

line 10/11:	flourishing	– growing in a healthy manner
line 11:	bland	– here: dull, uninteresting
line 33:	unequivocally	– clear, unmistakably
line 41:	lingering	– über etwas verweilen
line 44:	subservience	– Unterordnung

I. Language

1. Vocabulary (ohne Wörterbuch zu bearbeiten)

In the following (items a – i) you are to deal with the underlined words/expressions within the given context.

a) 9 – 10: "... the Controller claims as the great <u>achievement</u> ..."
Find a suitable substitute; keep to the sentence structure. (1 VP)

b) 13 – 14: "Hygienic happiness has replaced picturesque <u>squalor</u>, ..."
Find a suitable substitute; keep to the sentence structure. (1 VP)

c) 19: "... not only to <u>provide</u> a section of the population ..."
Explain; you may change the sentence structure. (1 VP)

d) 28: "... human nature is <u>quarrelsome</u>, competitive ..."
Explain; you may change the sentence structure. (1 VP)

e) 32: "... with the <u>utmost</u> clarity, ..."
Explain; you may change the sentence structure. (1 VP)

f) 37: "... capable of interpreting the brave new world <u>for the benefit</u> of the Savage ..."
Explain; you may change the sentence structure. (1 VP)

g) 39: "... to civilization, <u>for either party</u>."
Find a suitable substitute; keep to the sentence structure. (1 VP)

h) 45: "... his means of power would <u>vanish</u>."
Find a suitable substitute; keep to the sentence structure. (1 VP)

Find the corresponding abstract nouns (not the -ing-forms):

i) 3: remove
17: maintain
23: assume
35: prove (2 VP)

2. Grammar (ohne Wörterbuch zu bearbeiten)

a) 9: "Even the happiness that the Controller ..."
12 – 13: "Happiness in the past, he argues, ..."
Why is the definite article used in the first example (l. 9) but omitted in the second? (1 VP)

b) 36 – 37: "Neither Bernard nor his friend Helmholtz, superlatively Alpha Plus though he <u>be</u>, would <u>be</u> ..."
Explain the difference between the two verb forms. (2 VP)

c) 42: "... on the terms <u>demanded</u> by the society ..."
Explain the underlined grammatical form and rewrite the sentence using a subordinate clause. (2 VP)

II. Comprehension

Answer the following questions in complete sentences. Keep to the information given in the text, but do not quote.

1. How is human nature affected by the "bland and sterile context" of the brave new world?
   (90 – 120 words) (4 VP)
2. How are the Alphas and Epsilons characterized and why would "Epsilons be meaningless without Alphas and vice versa"?
   (60 – 80 words) (2 VP)
3. How does the author characterize Mustapha Mond and his role in the system of <u>Brave New World</u>?
   (90 – 120 words) (4 VP)

III. Comment

Choose <u>one</u> of the following topics: (200 – 300 words) (10 VP)

1. In <u>Brave New World Revisited</u>, Aldous Huxley states the existence of "man's almost infinite appetite for distractions." Discuss the view in the context of <u>Brave New World</u> and today's social reality.
2. To what extent is Lenina a representative character of <u>Brave New World</u>?
3. America expects Europe to play a more active military role in international affairs. Discuss this problem.

IV. Translation

Historians and statesmen <u>are apt to see</u> the first eighty years of the present century as a period of British decline: Britain has lost her place as one of the world's Great Powers, she <u>ceased</u> to rule a mighty empire, and she was pushed out of her position of economic pre-eminence. The ordinary people, however, might be forgiven for doubting whether
5 any of this mattered. Their standard of living did not just improve; it was transformed out of all recognition. Of all history's revolutions none has been more materially significant than the sudden blossoming of mass prosperity in the first twenty-five years after 1945. There is no single explanation for this transformation, nor was it a solely British phenomenon – all the advanced industrial nations experienced the same change. Its main
10 causes were relatively full employment, rising wages, often <u>boosted by</u> a trade union movement which was more powerful than ever before, technical improvements, which brought luxury articles within the grasp of wage-earners, and the provision by the government of a range of services <u>cushioning the people against sickness and poverty</u>. But not everyone enjoyed this prosperity. The plight of the aged and homeless was and is a
15 reproach to what was called the 'affluent society'.

W. Robson (1983) *203 words*

Vocabulary:

line 1:	to be apt to do sth.	– to have a tendency to do sth.
line 13:	to cushion sb. against sth.	– to protect sb. from sth. harmful
line 14:	the plight	– die Not

Lösungsvorschlag

I. **Language**

1. Vocabulary

   a) success / accomplishment / attainment

   b) dirt / misery / poverty

   c) to supply a section of the population
      to make a section of the population available
      they are supposed to provide society with ...

   d) argumentative; likes to fight / argue / have a row

   e) with complete clarity
      with the utmost clarity
      with perfect clarity

   f) in order to help the Savage understand it
      so that the Savage can understand it
      in order to guide the Savage
      to make the Savage understand it

   g) for both of them
      for both sides
      for this party as well as for that one

   h) would disappear (into thin air)
      would fade away
      would be destroyed
      would cease to exist
      would be annihilated

   i) removal / remove / Remove / remover
      maintenance
      assumption
      proof

2. Grammar and Style

   a) In the first sentence the abstract noun 'happiness' is more closely defined by the following relative clause and 'happiness' is, therefore, meant in a more specific sense. In the second example the abstract noun is used in a more general sense.

   b) In the first case ("... though he be ..."), 'be' is a subjunctive. In the second case ("would be ..."), 'be' is part of a conditional, in the infinitive form.

   c) 'Demanded' is a past participle used to shorten a relative clause.
      ... on the terms that are demanded by the society he serves.

II. Comprehension

1. The "sterile context" of the brave new world has led human nature into a mental desert from which there is no escape. Whatever was worth living for, has been deliberately abolished – namely those features that used to stand for happiness and health as well as those that rather revealed the negative aspects of life. Sorrow, misery, pain and instability no longer exist, a development that is accompanied by a complete deprivation of great works of art and the real experiences of life. Since an obvious interrelationship between art and life cannot be denied, and life has been reduced to sheer practicalities, art is not possible anymore. Even one of the pillars of the society, the happiness of the brave new world, has become merely make-believe, without any real substance.

2. Due to their intelligence and readiness to take on responsibility, they can act within conditioned limits, according to their own free will. This also helps them to be aware of their unique position, unlike the less intelligent Epsilons who are completely left in the dark when it comes to their place in society. They are solely needed to do the unskilled work and thus guarantee continuous balance and stability, the effects of society mainly based on Alpha-intelligence being shown in the Cyprus experiment.

3. Mustapha Mond's intelligence and access to otherwise hidden information have provided him with the utmost awareness of what the brave new world happiness and stability really mean. He is the only character in the novel able to grasp and interpret the meaning of the Savage's sudden appearance in the brave new world. He knows exactly what the consequences both on a personal and a wider social level could be. Having had the choice between revolt (and being sent to an island) or becoming one of the Controllers, he chose the latter in order to serve something that was well beyond his own self and his notion of human society.

III. Comment

1. In his famous novel *Brave New World*, Aldous Huxley created a futuristic society in which daily distractions have taken on a completely new dimension, inasmuchas life is not dominated by work anymore, but by an increasingly indomitable thirst for fast entertainment.

   Having proved in earlier writings that he had a good eye for both psychological and social issues, Huxley this time hinted at what he expected society to look like towards the end of the twentieth century.

   The new society according to Huxley has reduced the human being to a more or less machine-like creature whose obvious lack of emotions and interpersonal relations in a "perfect" society deprived of real feelings lets him turn to other activities that can provide the satisfaction he is otherwise forbidden. Emotionless sex (mostly performed in perfunctory "one-night stands"), all sorts of futuristic sports designed to make people spend both money and surplus energy, cold and pragmatic conversations in similarly cold surroundings revolving around the all-time question (who goes to bed with whom?), form the basic ingredients meant to stabilize a society that just cannot afford to have thinking, sensitive people.

   To what extent does this society now come close to today's social reality? Nowadays work has certainly lost its overpowering significance in the forming of one's average day, having rather turned into a means for financing an ever-increasing need for extremely costly leisure-time activities that are supposed to fill a void in our lives. This need can hardly be explained in a rational way. But it is right here that our society and the one in the brave new world are on common ground. Both societies have reached high standards of living where (at least in Europe) squalor and dirt have been reduced and where the average life expectancy is very high. People have everything and most people can even make their wildest dreams come true. This certainly explains why people in highly industrialized, wealthy societies always go for nicer, higher, better, bigger instead of sometimes settling for second best. Dissatisfaction, suppressed needs or plain satiation will finally lead (or have already led) to lighter forms of entertainment such as half-witted gameshows or more violent forms such as, for example, science fiction films like "<u>Rollerball</u>" or "<u>The Running Man</u>", where the boredom and emptiness of everyday life can only be compensated by bloodsports eventually leading to the death of competitors.

2. As has often been said before, Huxley mainly uses type characters in his novel in order to illustrate a preeminent superficiality and perfunctoriness of a world completely devoid of feeling, compassion and real love. A world that is smoothly run by a small élite towering over a select pre-conditioned class of intelligent Alphas can only generate a sterile and bland environment. In this context, Lenina Crowne, one of the main protagonists in the novel, represents a perfect example of a Brave New Worlder, to such an extent that one has to ask oneself whether Huxley had more in mind for her than just producing yet another type-cast character, fitting well into the social context of his utopian nightmare.

At first sight, Lenina is a well-conditioned, pretty and fairly successful product of the brave new world. Her idea of a fulfilled sex-life has been limited to a neutral state between lavish hunger and the bare necessities in a world where keeping up appearances characterizes the struggle for uniformity.

When she first meets John the Savage, the intruder from an unknown, outside world that is not hers, the reader cannot help feeling that here is a chance for her to escape from the coldness of utopia, to be rescued from the artificiality she was thrown into, even more so since John tries to cast Lenina into a Shakespearean role-model with all the necessary ingredients. This attempt to lift Lenina into the ranks of thinking and emotive people must fail because as soon as she has to face situations or characters that do not fit into her one-dimensional view of life, her conditioning starts to crack and she resorts to soma.

This is where Lenina's real function in the novel is clearly outlined. She could have been used as a sole link between two incompatible worlds but this was not what the author had in mind. His presenting her as a well-adjusted puppet in a sterile world helped him to render the contrast between the worlds more blatant and striking. By opposing John's seriousness and Lenina's inadequacy and ridiculousness, Huxley reveals the many shortcomings of a world where feelings and love cannot exist.

3. The relationship between America and Europe has always been one of hidden hostility, the roots of which often being interpreted as "mere family differences" or even plain "anti-Americanism" on the one hand, Europhobia on the other. Using these expressions to define a relationship that is vital for the Atlantic Alliance can be called straight cynicism but there must be a kernel of truth, whose importance has been overrated over the years by extremist groups who cannot accept that multifarious differences between equal partners must necessarily lead to opposing viewpoints and heated debates about the respective military roles.

On the one hand America has always criticized Europe for not readily accepting the deployment of nuclear weapons on its territory, an attitude that has certainly induced the USA to withdraw more and more from Europe, and at the same time challenging the European countries to take a more active part in international affairs. This readiness has been all the more increased by a striking reticence on the part of the Europeans to support the American forces in joint actions against terrorism or war-faring countries (such as Irak in 1991).

On the other hand, in favour of this reticence, it is clear that America has certainly been involved in world-wide atrocities and that Europe especially has witnessed a growing fear of a nuclear catastrophe, a fear made worse after the Chernobyl disaster.

American expectations may be justified against the background of a world being more and more divided into small but explosive danger zones where even a 'super power' cannot carry the load all alone but rightly calls for a joint effort characterized by an equal share of responsibility and by continuous consultation and consideration.

IV. Translation

Historiker und Staatsmänner neigen dazu, die ersten achtzig Jahre dieses Jahrhunderts als einen Zeitabschnitt anzusehen, der im Zeichen des britischen Niedergangs steht/ stand/der vom Niedergang Großbritanniens gekennzeichnet ist/war: Großbritannien/es hat seine Stellung/seinen Rang als eine der Großmächte der Welt/als eine der Weltmächte/verloren (auch: es verlor), seine Herrschaft über ein mächtiges Weltreich ging zu Ende/neigte sich dem Ende zu, und es wurde aus seiner wirtschaftlichen Vormachtstellung verdrängt

Den einfachen/gewöhnlichen Leuten jedoch mag man es nachsehen/verzeihen, wenn/daß sie bezweifeln/bezweifelten, daß irgendetwas davon von Bedeutung war. Ihr Lebensstandard verbesserte sich nicht bloß, er veränderte sich in unvorstellbarem Maße/bis fast zur Unkenntlichkeit. Von allen Revolutionen der Geschichte war keine materiell bedeutsamer/ist keine ... bedeutsamer gewesen als das plötzliche Aufblühen des Wohlstands für die (breite) Masse in den (ersten) 25 Jahren nach 1945.

Es gibt nicht nur eine Erklärung/keine Einzelerklärung/Man kann diesen Wandel nicht so einfach erklären/mit einer einzigen Erklärung abtun/für diesen Wandel, auch handelte es sich nicht um eine ausschließlich britische Erscheinung/auch war es kein allein britisches Phänomen – alle hochentwickelten/weiterentwickelten Industrienationen erlebten/ durchliefen die gleiche Veränderung. Ihre Hauptursachen waren weitgehende/ relative Vollbeschäftigung, steigende Löhne, oft in die Höhe getrieben/oft nach oben schnellen gelassen von einer Gewerkschaftsbewegung, die mächtiger war als je zuvor, technische Verbesserungen, die Luxusartikel für Lohnempfänger/Arbeitnehmer erschwinglich machten, und die Bereitstellung/die Einrichtung einer Reihe von staatlichen Sozialleistungen/Leistungen, die die Menschen im Falle von/bei Krankheit und Armut (absichern) absicherten. Aber nicht jeder kam in den Genuß/durfte an diesem Genuß teilhaben/dieses Wohlstands. Die Not der Alten und Obdachlosen war und ist noch immer ein Vorwurf an eine Gesellschaft, die sich "Wohlstandsgesellschaft" nennt.

Leistungskurs Englisch (Baden-Württemberg): Abiturprüfung 1995
Textaufgabe und Übersetzung

There is an unusual concern with automobiles in The Great Gatsby. Fitzgerald's use of cars suggests an essential relevance to the society he treats and contributes to an impression of externalization, of lives without internal direction, of casual accidents and wrecks as representing almost a norm. There is logic, therefore, that the tragedies of the novel should be precipitated by the auto accident in the valley of ashes and that Myrtle Wilson should die as brutally and impersonally as she does, struck down and left to die on the highway, like a dog.

The impression of restless movements and casual wrecks comments on the society in the novel, but that society is revealed most deeply in Fitzgerald's depiction of his characters. His characterizations are an important dimension of the novel's art. It is through the eyes of Nick Carraway, the narrator, that the other characters are observed, and as a marginal participant they are also measured by him. He is in particular a character double of Gatsby, having in his own life many parallels with Gatsby's experience. Both grew up in the Midwest, where they have their "winter dreams" before coming East to settle on Long Island, and deal – in different ways – in "bonds". They are neighbors who live in adjoining houses, one vast and overshadowing, the other small and sensible; and they both come into contact with the Buchanans' set at East Egg and have an affair with a young woman of that set during the same summer. By the end of that summer Carraway's illusions are shattered, along with Gatsby's greater ones. Sane and moderate, Carraway is a continuing reminder of Gatsby's aberrancy, but in his modest stature – his inhibitions and lack of boldness – he is also a reminder of Gatsby's heroic size.

At the same time, in his normative voice, he acts as a critic of the Buchanans – from the moment they appear, until he repudiates them formally at the end. At the opening, Carraway remembers the words of his father: "Whenever you feel like criticizing any one ... just remember that all people in this world haven't had the advantages you've had." The question of advantages and "fundamental decencies", of background and class, is relevant to the novel, but as East Egg reveals, social advantages and fundamental decencies do not mean the same thing. The Buchanans express, in a refracted and concentrated way, at least one aspect of the very rich; and they are in particular closely identified with the leisured, polo-playing rich class of Long Island, a class that held a peculiar fascination for Fitzgerald, in its special attitudes and reactions to life, and upon which he has commented astringently in The Great Gatsby.

In the opening chapter Fitzgerald indicates not only that the Buchanans and Jordan Baker are wealthy, but also that they have been moulded by the social and economic class to which they belong. Buchanan is not complicated; he is seen in the clear outline of a few characteristics – his arrogance and intimidating physical strength. The relation of his arrogance to his social background is implied in the opening scene when Carraway remarks: "Wedging his tense arm imperatively under mine, Tom Buchanan compelled me from the room as though he were moving a checker to another square." That Buchanan regards other people as figures to be moved about at his will is a comment upon his assumptions of class.

566 words *Robert E. Long (1979)*

Vocabulary

line 5: to precipitate — to hasten, to cause sth. to happen sooner
line 20: aberrancy — unusual or even abnormal behaviour
line 23: to repudiate — to reject
line 32: astringent — harsh, severe
line 36: to intimidate — einschüchtern

I. Language

1. Vocabulary (ohne Wörterbuch zu bearbeiten)

In the following (items a – g) you are to deal with the underlined words/expressions within the given context.

a) 1 – 2: "Fitzgerald's use of cars suggests an <u>essential relevance</u> to the society he treats ..."
Explain; you may change the sentence structure. (2 VP)

b) 15 – 16: "... who live in <u>adjoining</u> houses ..."
Explain; you may change the sentence structure. (1 VP)

c) 18 – 19: "... Carraway's illusions are <u>shattered</u> ..."
Find a suitable substitute; keep to the sentence structure. (1 VP)

d) 20 – 21: "... his inhibitions and <u>lack of boldness</u> ..."
Explain; you may change the sentence structure. (2 VP)

e) 30: "... with the <u>leisured</u>, polo playing rich class ..."
Explain; you may change the sentence structure. (1 VP)

f) 34 – 35: "... they have been <u>moulded</u> by the social and economic class ..."
Find a suitable substitute; keep to the sentence structure. (1 VP)

g) 38 – 39: "Tom Buchanan <u>compelled</u> me <u>from</u> the room ..."
Explain; you may change the sentence structure. (1 VP)

Find the corresponding abstract nouns (not the -ing forms):
h) 9: reveal
19: sane
25: remember
37: imply (2 VP)

2. Grammar (ohne Wörterbuch zu bearbeiten)

a) 10 – 12: "<u>It is</u> through the eyes of Nick Carraway, the narrator, <u>that</u> the other characters are observed ..."
What is the function of this construction?
Rewrite the sentence without using it. (2 VP)

b) 12 – 13: "He is in particular a character double of Gatsby, having in his own life many parallels with Gatsby's experience."
Rewrite the sentence by replacing the -ing form. (1 VP)

c) 34 – 35: "... the social and economic class to which they belong."
Rewrite the sentence, omitting the relative pronoun. (1 VP)

II. Comprehension

Answer the following questions in complete sentences. Keep to the information given in the text, but do not quote.

1. What is the symbolic function of cars in <u>The Great Gatsby</u>?
   (50 – 80 words) (2 VP)

2. The author of this text compares Carraway and Gatsby. What are his conclusions?
   (80 – 120 words) (4 VP)

3. What are Fitzgerald's intentions in using Carraway as a critic of the Buchanans?
   (70 – 100 words) (4 VP)

III. Comment

Choose <u>one</u> of the following topics: (200 – 300 words) (10 VP)

1. "Daisy is a banal, cowardly woman without any feelings."
   Comment on this statement.

2. <u>The Great Gatsby</u> was written in the 1920s. Is it still relevant in our time? Give your reasons.

3. "Europe needs America as a balancing force against the uncertainties contained in the post-cold-war era."
   Comment on this statement.

IV. Translation (30 VP)

In the United States the political debate about immigration has always been marked by vigorous calls for restriction. The most ardent advocates of this policy are often children of immigrants who wear their second-generation patriotism outwardly and aggressively. This position forgets that it was the labor and efforts of immigrants – often the parents
5   and grandparents of today's restrictionists – that made much of the prosperity of our nation possible. Even the fiercest xenophobes have had a hard time arguing that turn-of-the-century groups such as Italian and Polish peasants or the much attacked Chinese and Japanese had a long-term negative effect on the country. Instead, these now successful and settled groups are presented as examples, but exception is taken to the newcomers.
10 There is irony in the spectacle of Americans who bear clear marks of their immigrant origins being among the most vocal adversaries of continuing immigration. Consequences of heeding their advice would be serious, however. Although regulation and control of the inflow from abroad are always necessary, suppressing it would deprive the nation of what has been so far one of its main sources of energy, innovativeness, and
15 growth.

(191 words)   Portes/Rumbaut (1990)

Vocabulary

line 6:	xenophobe	– someone who hates or fears foreigners
line 9:	to take exception to sth./s.o.	– Anstoß nehmen an etw/jdn.
line 11:	vocal	– here: expressing oneself freely and noisily
line 12:	to heed	– here: to consider seriously

Lösungsvorschlag

I. Language

1. Vocabulary

a) ... is of great/enormous importance/significance to the society he treats/deals with ...
... characterizes very well/perfectly the society he treats/deals with ...
... is very significant/very important for the society he treats/deals with ...

b) ... houses that are next to each other/one another ...
... neighbouring houses ...

c) ... are destroyed/are crushed/are ruined/are wiped out

d) ... missing courage ...
Carraway cannot be called a hero.
Carraway has no courage/does not have enough courage/is not very courageous.
Carraway is not much of a hero.

e) ... people who do not have to make a living/who do not have to work for a living ...
... people who can spend most of their time on spare-time activities ...
... a class with a lot of spare time ...

f) ... they have been formed/shaped/influenced/ "conditioned" by ...

g) ... made me leave the room (by force)/urged me to leave/forced me to leave ...

h) revelation
sanity
remembrance, memory
implication

2. Grammar

a) The other characters are observed through the eyes of Nick Carraway (Nick Carraway's eyes).
This construction is mainly used to put emphasis on one particular part of the sentence or idea the author wants to highlight.

b) He is in particular a character double of Gatsby, who has in his own life many parallels with Gatsby's experience.
He is in particular a character double of Gatsby as he has in his own life .../due to the fact that he has ...
He is in particular a character double of Gatsby as his own life parallels Gatsby's experience in many ways/due to the fact that his own life ...

c) ... the social and economic class they belong to.

II. Comprehension

1. Long has attributed two symbolic aspects to the treatment of cars in this novel. There is on the one hand Myrtle Wilson's tragic death in a car accident, giving cars some sort of sinister, death-carrying meaning. On the other hand, cars represent the inhuman, careless and unscrupulous East Egg society: just like cars they are constantly on the move and their way of life becomes faster and faster. In addition to this, only material values count in their aimless search for pleasure.

2. The similarities between Gatsby and Carraway are rather superficial ones: both coming from the Midwest they want to settle on Long Island in order to make it in the world of finance and economy. They both succumb to the shallow attractiveness of money and glamour and fall for two young women from the East Egg set. By the end of a long, tumultuous summer, they have both lost the dreams they came to the East for. Here the similarities end because as can be seen in the difference between their houses, they each stand for a different set of values: Carraway represents the sober, rational Mid-westerner and cannot match the romantic idealism of Gatsby whose detachment from reality forms a stark contrast to Carraway's down-to-earth attitude.

3. As already mentioned, Carraway stands in stark contrast to the rich classes from East Egg to which the Buchanans belong. The Buchanans are rolling in money and can concentrate on the nice things life has got to offer and which money can buy: sport, fantastic properties and expensive cars make their world go round. Although Carraway is attracted by this wealth and carefree life, he is rational and realistic enough to see through the surface of this world and can thus be used as the main critic of the emptiness of the society Fitzgerald depicts.

III. Comment

1. *"Daisy is a banal, cowardly woman without any feelings." Comment on this statement.*

   There are quite a few examples in this novel which may justify one to call the main female protagonist Daisy Buchanan a banal woman and a coward. Although it appears to be rather obvious that she is, and has been, in love with Gatsby for many years, she has never had the 'guts' to openly live this relationship and do what her heart tells her to do. Does this reticence to embark on an insecure journey into the future with somebody who is more or less an eternal dreamer make her a banal coward?

   In my opinion the answer can only be "no" because there is certainly more to her than meets the reader's eye. She has certainly withdrawn into a submissive, deferential role, a role rather suitable for women in the 1920s, indulging in her enormous wealth, making herself out to be something like a fragile fairy-tale princess who can haunt any man's dreams.

   She has, however, merely taken on this one-dimensional character, thus hiding behind an emotionless passivity and marked stupidity which do not sound right and give reason to examine her character more carefully.

   The first noticeable incongruity in her character is her surprising choice of husband. After having gone through a romantic love affair, she has now opted for a life with a narrow-minded brute of a husband who gives her financial security but deceives her and has occasional fits of unpremeditated violence.

She seems to have been shaped by him into the mindless puppet on a string whose only function is a representative one. At times, however, she does show a deeper insight into the state of things, for example when she says that it is better for women to grow up stupid and unsuspecting, thus demonstrating that she is only acting out a theatrical role.

One can hardly call her a banal woman because she clearly chooses her own way of life and is not prepared to part with her cosy situation, not even for the love of her life.

2. *The Great Gatsby was written in the 1920s. Is it still relevant in our time? Give your reasons.*

It has often been said that Fitzgerald's most successsful novel *The Great Gatsby* is all about the American Dream, its promises as well as its shortcomings, hence its timelessness. This is certainly true, at least to some extent, because the most important ideas and concepts that made up the overall notion of "The Dream" still have a major impact on today's society, be it the strong American belief in the rags-to-riches theory or the notion of America being the land of unlimited opportunities.

However, cataloguing this novel solely as "yet another one about the same old topic" would be unfair to the author's initial intention as in my opinion Fitzgerald was certainly striving for a work of art that could be easily read throughout this century. For that, he had to deal with other topical issues, issues which were beginning to take shape at the time when the novel was written, were becoming more and more relevant as time was going on.

There is on the one hand a society that increasingly gives in to cheap and easy entertainment in an environment that has lost any sense of direction in a fast-moving, materialistic world. The values that used to be of predominant importance such as love, sympathy, empathy or just plain concern for your next-door neighbour have been replaced by hurried sex, fast cars and commercial business: it is clear that here only the most ruthless can survive. On the other hand, there is the deep love Gatsby feels for Daisy, a stark contrast to the downfall of virtues this society otherwise conveys, a love that is as relevant today as it was seventy years ago since it is used as a counterpoint to the all-devouring modernity that has been growing on us and may well get the better of us soon.

3. *"Europe needs America as a balancing force against the uncertainties contained in the post-cold-war era." Comment on this statement.*

Throughout the twentieth century, the relationship between Europe and America has constantly been challenged, put to the test and redefined.

Celebrated as Europe's saviour at the end of World War II, room was given to an increasing US influence in Europe which went necessarily hand in hand with its evergrowing stature as the world policeman and the only world power capable of preventing the Eastern bloc from taking the Western countries by storm.

With the inevitable breakdown of communism and the consequences this entailed, America had to rethink her position and, having gone through times of economic crises itself, crises which she is still going through, she now expects more from her European partners than most of them were, and still are, prepared to give. As a result, their relationship, hardly the most harmonious at the best of times, has been more than once conflictual and has led to slogans such as "Europhobia" or "anti-Americanism", thus putting in a nutshell what the relationship was really like.

Bearing this in mind, one may think that now, with communism's power having diminished, Europe could well do without the towering presence of its alliance partner. Giving in to this assumption may well lead to disaster because the post Cold War era has proved until now to be at least as unpredictable as the long phase of cold war when the enemy was clearly defined and everybody knew what was what. Now, the world map has again been altered into a lot of danger zones, turning our planet into a timebomb that may explode any time.

This leads to the conclusion that all parties involved should be aware of the fact that only a thorough and well-balanced cooperation will secure peace in the world and any individual effort will probably add to the uncertainties the new world order conveys.

IV. Translation

In den Vereinigten Staaten ist/war die politische Debatte/Auseinandersetzung über/mit Fragen der Einwanderung schon immer durch heftige/nachhaltige Rufe nach Beschränkungen gekennzeichnet/gewesen. Die glühendsten Verfechter/Anhänger dieser Politik sind oft (selbst) Kinder von Einwanderern, die sich ihren Patriotismus der zweiten Generation offen und aggressiv ans Revers heften/die ihren Patriotismus als Vertreter der zweiten Generation offen und aggressiv zur Schau stellen/die offen und aggressiv mit ihrem Patriotismus der zweiten Generation umgehen. Diese Position/Dieser Standpunkt /Diese Haltung läßt jedoch außer acht/bedenkt jedoch nicht, daß der Schufterei/ Mühe und Anstrengungen/Bemühungen der Einwanderer – oft der Eltern und Großeltern derer, die (sich) heute/jetzt für Beschränkungen stark machen/einsetzen/eintreten – zu verdanken ist/, daß es die Mühe und die Anstrengungen der Einwanderer – oft der Eltern und Großeltern derer, die heute für Beschränkungen sind – waren, die einen Großteil des Wohlstands unseres Landes möglich machten. Selbst die/den schärfsten/extremesten Fremdenhasser(n)/Ausländerfeinde(n) haben den Nachweis nicht erbringen können/ haben nicht nachweisen können,/ist der Nachweis nicht gelungen, daß Gruppen, die um die Jahrhundertwende kamen, wie (z. B.) die italienischen und polnischen Bauern oder die oft/häufig/stark angegriffenen/attackierten Chinesen und Japaner, sich auf lange Sicht negativ auf das Land auswirkten/auf lange Sicht eine negative Auswirkung auf das Land hatten. Stattdessen werden diese heute/jetzt erfolgreichen und integrierten/eingegliederten Gruppen als Vorbilder dargestellt/als gute Beispiele herangezogen, doch an den (jetzigen) Neuankömmlingen wird Anstoß genommen/während man an den jetzt ins Land kommenden Einwanderern Anstoß nimmt. Es liegt eine gewisse Ironie in der Tatsache, daß ausgerechnet Amerikaner, die selbst eindeutig als Nachkömmlinge früherer Einwanderer zu erkennen sind, bei den lautstärksten/vernehmbarsten Gegnern einer weiter anhaltenden/fortlaufenden Einwanderung zu erleben/zu bewundern sind. Es hätte jedoch schwerwiegende/verheerende Folgen, wenn man ihrem Rat folgen würde/wenn man ihren Rat ernstnehmen würde. Obwohl es immer nötig/notwendig ist, den Zustrom aus dem Ausland zu regeln und zu kontrollieren/unter Kontrolle zu halten, würde ein Unterdrücken/eine Blockierung dieses Zustromes die Nation/das Land einer seiner bislang/eine ihrer bislang/wichtigsten Quellen der Energie, Erneuerungskraft und Wachstum berauben/dem Land eine seiner wichtigsten Quellen nehmen, aus der es bisher (immer) seine Energie, seine Erneuerungskraft und sein Wachstumspotential gewonnen hat.

> **Leistungskurs Englisch (Baden-Württemberg): Abiturprüfung 1996**
> **Textaufgabe und Übersetzung**

Intervention Fatigue

No one should be surprised that US citizens are having an attack of intervention fatigue. However vast and dominating our international influence may be as an economic superpower, we are just not good at 19th-century-type military, colonialesque adventures. And given the way we are jerked around by politicians and press on what are called foreign-policy crises these days, it is a wonder the fatigue has not set in before. The trouble is that we may end up being as uncritical in our aversion to engagement overseas as we were in our former willingness to intervene practically everywhere. Right now we are faced with a dilemma. Without the Soviet Union and Hitler's hungry war machine before it, arguments for our involvement in foreign conflicts have to be improvised and then beaten, pushed and dragged to some semblance of national consensus. But such consensus gets ever more fragile. There are a number of obvious reasons why this is so.

First, we Americans are weak on geography and blissfully distant from most of the world's conflicts. Half the time we are being urged to leap into the affairs of a place we have only dimly ever even heard of, if we have heard of it at all. Second, we are regularly told, all of a sudden and seemingly out of nowhere, that the political fate of this place and its people is highly uncertain and of life-and-death concern to us. Then, as abruptly as it burst upon us, it will vanish from our politicians' consciousness and the news. It is the combination of this unfamiliarity and the suddenly proclaimed urgency of these places that, after a time, has begun to make skeptics of us all. Third, we expect infinite gratitude, not to mention moral perfection, from the side in the conflict with which we align ourselves. Big surprise: we get neither, only hurt feelings.

I think it is not wholly without justification that we expect our allies, clients and friends around the world to be model democrats and, above all, to love us. True, we act in our national interest and not out of sheer altruism and sometimes we have gotten the purpose and the moral values very wrong. But our history in this century has been marked by enormous, costly exertions for the sake of saving and helping others, including those who had started wars against us, devastated our allies and incurred an almost unimaginable toll in human life. In the case of World War II and the Cold War, the great power conflicts had a certain continuity to them; they arose, they persisted, they were there over time. We knew what they were and we knew what we feared.

Now it is as if we dart from place to place at an accelerated speed, proclaiming this guy a hero, that guy a monster and so forth and from time to time discovering that neither entirely fits the bill. People are sick of it and confused; they are inclining to a to-hell-with-the-whole-lot-of-them attitude that would be a great mistake. American security interests and humanitarian purposes are still very much alive and deserving respect, and it is possible to define them.

But they tend to get lost in the razzle-dazzle of instantly proclaimed and instantly called-off foreign crises. If the administration does not finally want to be overwhelmed in its foreign policy by a tide of hostile public opinion, it really needs to know how to make an honest, compelling case for those interventions it deems necessary.

601 words   *Meg Greenfield in* NEWSWEEK *(1993)*

I. Language

1. Vocabulary (ohne Wörterbuch zu bearbeiten)

In the following (items a–e) you are to deal with the underlined words/expressions within the given context.

a) 6: "... our <u>aversion</u> to engagement overseas ..."
Explain; you may change the sentence structure. (1 VP)

b) 10/11: "But such <u>consensus gets</u> ever <u>more fragile</u>."
Explain; you may change the sentence structure. (2 VP)

c) 20/21: "... with which we <u>align ourselves</u>."
Explain; you may change the sentence structure. (1 VP)

d) 27: "... <u>devastated</u> our allies ..."
Find a suitable substitute; keep to the sentence structure. (1 VP)

e) 39/40: "... how to make an honest, <u>compelling case</u> for those interventions ..."
Explain; you may change the sentence structure. (2 VP)

Find the corresponding <u>abstract nouns</u> (not the -ing forms):

f) 17: abruptly
29: certain
33: to incline
40: necessary (2 VP)

2. Grammar and Style (ohne Wörterbuch zu bearbeiten)

a) 13: "Half the time <u>we are being urged</u> to leap ..."
Put into the active voice. (1 VP)

b) 19/20: "... we expect infinite <u>gratitude</u> ..."
Rewrite the sentence using the adjective "grateful". (2 VP)

c) 21: "... we get <u>neither</u>, only hurt feelings."
What does "neither" refer to? (1 VP)

d) Find four informal or colloquial expressions in the text. What effect is created by the frequent use of colloquialisms? (2 VP)

II. Comprehension

Answer the following questions in complete sentences. Keep to the information given in the text, but do not quote.

1. What is the Americans' attitude towards political involvement abroad, and what dilemma are they faced with?
(60–100 words) (3 VP)

2. What explanations does the author give for the present attitude of the American public?
(60–100 words) (3 VP)

3. What is the author's view of America's foreign policy in the past, and how does she judge the situation today?
(80–120 words) (4 VP)

III. Comment

Choose *one* of the following topics: (200–300 words) (10 VP)

1. As the only remaining world power the US has the responsibility to act as the "world police".
Discuss this view.

2. Many Euroskeptics demand that Britain should pull out of the European Union and manage her own affairs.
Do you agree?

3. Compare the two main characters in F. Scott Fitzgerald's novel: Jay Gatsby and Tom Buchanan.

IV. Translation (30 VP)

Unfortunately Gatsby never recognizes the grandeur or the immaturity of his romantic vision. He never completely sees through the ultimate limitations of his aspirations. In any view of the world man is always subject to time and change. But when an individual like Gatsby strives on earth for an ideal world of youth and beauty that is beyond time,
5 he is both overwhelmed and damned. Fitzgerald, unlike Gatsby, knew that man was always engaged in a struggle with time and decay, that one could never arrest the passage of youth, sustain an idealized moment of love forever or repeat the past. Failing to realize the destructiveness of time, Gatsby tries to live in a world where past, present and future are all one. The inevitable result of his effort is unutterable depression and failure.
10 Gatsby also suffers from a form of moral myopia. He does not recognize the speciousness of the world of the very rich where he searched for fulfilment. He fails to see that the Buchanans, representative of a class with its origins and ways of life nourished by wealth, are mean, selfish and spiritually poor, yet extremely powerful.

Thomas J. Stavola, 1979 *192 words*

Lösungsvorschlag

I. Language

1. Vocabulary

a) ... our dislike to engage ourselves ...
 ... our unwillingness to engage ourselves ...
 ... we are unwilling/reluctant to engage ourselves ...
 ... an engagement overseas is definitely against our liking ...

b) ... there is less and less agreement ...
 ... people are not in full agreement any more ...
 ... the agreement they once had is not that stable any more ...

c) ... which we support ...
 ... whose side we take ...
 ... which we back ...
 ... which we are friends with ...

d) destroyed/ruined/harmed

e) ... to provide people with arguments which may convince them of the urgency/necessity of those interventions ...
 ... to make people see/understand the necessity of those interventions ...
 ... to argue in a convincing manner in order to make people see reason and accept those interventions ...

f) abruptness
 certainty
 inclination/incline
 necessity

2. Grammar and Style

a) They are urging us.
 People are urging us.

b) We expect them to be infinitely grateful.

c) Neither refers both to "infinite gratitude" and to "moral perfection".

d) "We are just not good at ..."
 "this guy ..., that guy ..."
 "People are sick of it"
 "a to-hell-with-the-whole-lot-of-them attitude"
 "the razzle-dazzle"

 The colloquial forms give the text a more personal and humourous touch and add a hint of irony that ought to demonstrate the author's rather critical attitude towards America's interventionist past. They also make the text more interesting and easier to grasp, thus provoking a reaction from the reader who can put himself into the author's frame of mind.

II. Comprehension

1. After their country having been the policeman of the world for quite some time, the American citizens now seem to be in favour of a form of moderate isolationism. This is mainly due to the fact that their traditional enemies such as Nazi Germany and what was known as the Eastern bloc no longer figure as a major threat and although their status as a leading power remains intact, the wish to interfere overseas has gone. In addition to this, recent US administrations have been faced with the dilemma of not being able to succeed in getting across their main objectives or hasty policy changes, which has led to a common disagreement concerning foreign affairs.

2. The present attitude of the American public can be traced back to various issues in which the people were asked to support one side without even knowing why or where their new "partner" was geographically situated. Some of the issues are made out to be of paramount importance, but they then disappear as quickly as they emerged. A last point is that American citizens are never fully pleased with what becomes of these issues, owing to most of their partners lacking the necessary gratitude and even the most basic democratic principles.

3. Whenever the Americans had to intervene in world affairs, the general opinion was that it happened for humanitarian reasons and was for a just cause. This has become part of American heritage and has shaped the American frame of mind for more than a century. Be it the fight against the Nazis or the American counterbalance against Communism, public approval has always been guaranteed. This approval has turned into anger, discontent and finally indifference due to the fact that most actions are characterized by sheer activism and unreflected turnabouts. This could prove to be a dead end for American foreign policy, matters being made worse by the fact that the Americans <u>have</u> always <u>been</u> willing to support intervention, if and when they are made to see the point of it all.

III. Comment

1. *As the only remaining world power the US has the responsibility to act as the "world police". Discuss this view.*

   Recent American history has been characterized by several interventionist activities which have on the one hand provoked some harsh criticism and on the other general approval, especially from her European partners. With the breakdown of communism and the end of the very successful era of American containment policies, America has to redefine its international role, even more so since the voices at home demanding a concentration on interior problems have multiplied no end. The fact that the USSR as the eternal threat and world power always to be taken into consideration is no more has certainly not facilitated the American task of guaranteeing world freedom, supporting countries in need and sorting out its manifold domestic problems. Quite to the contrary, with the splitting up of the former Eastern bloc into a variety of prospective danger zones, America has to do more than its share to keep world order and relies more than ever before on the help of other developed countries to quench simmering conflicts. These countries do not always come up to American expectations: be it for reasons that are purely constitutional (as in Germany) or because of an inherent anti-Americanism (as in France), America cannot always be sure of the necessary support.

Can we really expect them to always step in when need be, can we as an ever-growing European community of mostly wealthy states cede most responsibilities to the Americans who have to take care of conflicts happening in countries they have never even heard of? The answer clearly must be "no" because the world cannot rely on the economic and military power of one country, even if the country in question is the only remaining super power and the most advanced force in modern technologies. In the same way as the Europeans have come to the conclusion that a united Europe is the only way to safeguard their future, the rest of the world will have to get its act together and either give the USA its full support or make sure that inter-European conflicts can be solved by a European institution alone.

2. *Many Euroskeptics demand that Britain should pull out of the European Union and manage her own affairs. Do you agree?*

If we have a closer look at Britain's history, it becomes quite obvious that her rather ambivalent attitude towards Europe took shape long before the idea of a European community came to the fore. On the one hand, there has always been a strong isolationist and insular tendency in order not to get mixed up too strongly in European affairs and on the other hand, there used to be an ardent opposition against her integration at various points in history which was mainly instigated by France under *De Gaulle*. If we then take into account the undeniable fact that the British strictly believe in self-sufficiency and therefore cling to the decisions of Parliament, it is at least understandable that they do not want to be dictated to by a far-away, ominous institution in Brussels which does not seem to have done the country any good so far anyway. This rather narrow-minded view has recently been spurred by Britain's apparent unwillingness to sort out her problem with the mad-cow disease. Not only did the whole issue widen the gap between the two sides, but it also fanned the flames of the fires of those people who have always tried to keep the Union at arm's length.

The question now is whether a highly industrialized country that ought to be one of the pillars of the European Community should be driven to self-imposed isolation and thus a self-imposed setback by a group of people that has well and truly forgotten to jump on the band-wagon. Not so long ago when the social chapter of the Maastricht Treaty was not accepted (thus disallowing the British workers the rights other, less economically-favoured countries such as Portugal have long since accepted), it was revealed to what extent the anti-European attitude of some groups has relegated Britain to – to one of the lower ranks in the European hierarchy. If Britain does not want to be left out in the preparations for the technological and economic requirements for the coming years, she will have to reconsider her position and try to adapt to an institution that is able to get along with, but ought not to do without, one of its most complicated partners.

3. *Compare the two main characters in F. Scott Fitzgerald's novel: Jay Gatsby and Tom Buchanan.*

Fitzgerald's novel *The Great Gatsby* has been called a man's book, which is true, inasmuch as the most important protagonists are male and the women in the novel do not seem to develop a *character* of their own. Nevertheless, if we have a closer look at the quality of the author's characterization, we can easily see that he has given a lot of importance to the female because whatever the male characters do, whatever character trait they reveal and wherever they get their motivation from, it has always directly or indirectly to do with their relationship or would-be relationship with Daisy Buchanan.

It is quite unnecessary to enumerate all the differences between Gatsby and Tom, since there are so many, from their background to their different approaches to everyday life. If one wants to get to the centre of these two protagonists, one has to compare them with regard to their relationship with Daisy and their way of handling a love affair. Here it becomes more than obvious that they cannot be more different and that Fitzgerald used the two characters in question as a means of demonstrating his personal opinion about the situation of America in the twenties. Thus Gatsby and Tom are heightened to quite a different level that goes beyond the significance of a mere character, i. e. they both acquire a symbolic function that ties in with Fitzgerald's ideas about the American Dream, its consequences for American society, its shortcomings and final failure. Hence it can be suggested that Gatsby stands for the old romantic qualities such as perseverance, a strong belief in loyalty and truthfulness, qualities with which he tries to win back Daisy, whereas Tom personifies (in his relationship with Daisy) the inflexible, narrow-minded American who takes everything (especially her) for granted and thus leads to the downfall of the old values. The fact that Tom's approach finally carries the day only puts emphasis on the fact that the author was convinced that even then, the American Dream was doomed.

IV. Translation

Unglücklicherweise erkennt Gatsby nie die Größe/Großartigkeit und/oder die Unreife/fehlende Reife seiner romantischen Sichtweise./Die Größe oder doch eher die fehlende Reife seiner romantischen Sichtweise bleiben Gatsby leider verborgen.

Er durchschaut nie vollständig, daß seinem Streben letztlich doch Grenzen gesetzt sind./Er erkennt niemals ganz, daß sein Streben irgendwann an seine Grenzen stoßen wird.

In jedem Weltbild/Wie immer man es auch betrachtet/Aus welchem Blickwinkel man es auch betrachtet, ist der Mensch immer/stets der Zeit und dem Wandel unterworfen/unterliegt der Mensch immer dem Einfluß von Zeit und Veränderung.

Aber sobald ein Individuum/jemand wie Gatsby auf der Erde/auf Erden nach einer idealen Welt von Jugend und Schönheit strebt/eine Idealwelt bestehend aus Jugend und Schönheit erstrebt/anstrebt, die jenseits der Zeit liegt/die außerhalb der Zeit liegt, so ist er sowohl überwältigt als auch verdammt/überwältigt und zugleich zum Scheitern verurteilt.

Anders als Gatsby wußte Fitzgerald, daß der Mensch schon immer in einen Kampf mit der Zeit und dem Verfall verstrickt war/gewesen ist/sich schon immer mit der Zeit und dem Verfall bekämpft hat, daß es niemals möglich/machbar ist, das Vorübergehen der Jugend aufzuhalten/daß man dem Vorbeiziehen der Jugend nie Einhalt gebieten kann/dem Vorüberziehen der Jugend Einhalt zu gebieten, einen idealisierten Moment/Augenblick der Liebe für immer festzuhalten/immer weiter und bis in die Ewigkeit hinauszuzögern oder die Vergangenheit zu wiederholen/oder die Gegenwart wieder aufleben zu lassen.

Unfähig, die zerstörerische Kraft der Zeit zu erkennen/Da es Gatsby nicht gelingt, die zerstörerische Kraft/das zerstörerische Potential der Kraft zu erkennen, versucht Gatsby/er, in einer Welt zu leben, in der Vergangenheit, Gegenwart und Zukunft eins sind/zu einer Einheit verschmelzen.

Das unvermeidliche Ergebnis seiner Bemühungen ist unaussprechliche Niedergeschlagenheit und Versagen/Das zwangsläufige Ergebnis seines Bemühens ist eine tiefe Depression und ein Scheitern, deren Ausmaß nicht in Worte gefaßt werden kann.

Gatsby leidet auch an einer Art moralischer Kurzsichtigkeit./Was seine Moral angeht, so leidet diese an einer gewissen Form der Kurzsichtigkeit.

Er durchschaut (eben) nicht den trügerischen Schein der Welt der Superreichen/sehr Reichen, wo er versuchte, seine Erfüllung zu finden/wo er nach Erfüllung suchte. Die Einsicht bleibt ihm verwehrt, daß die Buchanans als Vertreter einer Klasse, deren Ursprung und Lebensweise vom Reichtum genährt werden, zwar gemein, egoistisch und geistig arm sind, aber trotzdem eine Machtposition innehaben/zwar gemein, selbstsüchtig und geistig arm, aber dennoch extrem mächtig sind.

> **Leistungskurs Englisch (Baden-Württemberg): Abiturprüfung 1997**
> **Textaufgabe und Übersetzung**

But above the gray land and the spasms of bleak dust which drift endlessly over it, you perceive, after a moment, the eyes of Doctor T. J. Eckleburg. The eyes of Doctor T. J. Eckleburg are blue and gigantic – their retinas are one yard high. They look out of no face, but instead, from a pair of enormous yellow spectacles which pass over a non-
5 existent nose. Evidently some wild wag of an oculist set them there to fatten his practice in the borough of Queens, and then sank down himself into eternal blindness, or forgot them and moved away. But his eyes, dimmed a little by many paintless days under sun and rain, brood on over the solemn dumping ground. [...]
   The only building in sight was a small block of yellow brick sitting on the edge of the
10 waste land, a sort of compact Main Street ministering to it, and contiguous to absolutely nothing. One of the three shops it contained was for rent and another was an all-night restaurant, approached by a trail of ashes; the third was a garage – *Repairs. George B. Wilson. Cars bought and sold.* – and I followed Tom inside.
   The interior was unprosperous and bare; the only car visible was the dust-covered wreck
15 of a Ford which crouched in a dim corner. It had occurred to me that this shadow of a garage must be a blind, and that sumptuous and romantic apartments were concealed overhead, when the proprietor himself appeared in the door of an office, wiping his hands on a piece of waste. He was a blond, spiritless man, anaemic, and faintly handsome. When he saw us a damp gleam of hope sprang into his light blue eyes.
20 "Hello, Wilson, old man," said Tom, slapping him jovially on the shoulder. "How's business?"
   "I can't complain," answered Wilson unconvincingly. "When are you going to sell me that car?"
   "Next week; I've got my man working on it now."
25 "Works pretty slow, don't he?"
   "No, he doesn't," said Tom coldly. "And if you feel that way about it, maybe I'd better sell it somewhere else after all."
   "I don't mean that," explained Wilson quickly. "I just meant –"
   His voice faded off and Tom glanced impatiently around the garage. Then I heard foot-
30 steps on a stairs, and in a moment the thickish figure of a woman blocked out the light from the office door. She was in the middle thirties, and faintly stout, but she carried her surplus flesh sensuously as some women can. Her face, above a spotted dress of dark blue crêpe-de-chine, contained no facet or gleam of beauty, but there was an immediately perceptible vitality about her as if the nerves of her body were continually smoul-
35 dering. She smiled slowly and, walking through her husband as if he were a ghost, shook hands with Tom, looking him flush in the eye. Then she wet her lips, and without turning around spoke to her husband in a soft, coarse voice:
   "Get some chairs, why don't you, so somebody can sit down."
   "Oh, sure," agreed Wilson hurriedly, and went toward the little office mingling immedi-
40 ately with the cement color of the walls. A white ashen dust veiled his dark suit and his pale hair as it veiled everything in the vicinity – except his wife, who moved close to Tom.
   "I want to see you," said Tom intently. "Get on the next train."
   "All right."
45 "I'll meet you by the news-stand on the lower level."

She nodded and moved away from him just as George Wilson emerged with two chairs from his office door.

We waited for her down the road and out of sight. It was a few days before the Fourth of July, and a gray, scrawny Italian child was setting torpedoes in a row along the railroad track.

"Terrible place, isn't it," said Tom, exchanging a frown with Doctor Eckleburg.

"It does her good to get away."

"Doesn't her husband object?"

"Wilson? He thinks she goes to see her sister in New York. He's so dumb he doesn't know he's alive."

So Tom Buchanan and his girl and I went up together to New York – or not quite together, for Mrs. Wilson sat discreetly in another car. Tom deferred that much to the sensibilities of those East Eggers who might be on the train.

She had changed her dress to a brown figured muslin, which stretched tight over her rather wide hips as Tom helped her to the platform in New York. At the news-stand she bought a copy of *Town Tattle* and a moving-picture magazine and in the station drugstore some cold cream and a small flask of perfume. Upstairs, in the solemn echoing drive she let four taxicabs drive away before she selected a new one, lavender-colored with gray upholstery, and in this we slid out from the mass of the station into the glowing sunshine.

827 words   F. Scott Fitzgerald, THE GREAT GATSBY, Chapter II

Vocabulary

line 1:	spasm	–	sudden movement
	bleak	–	depressing
line 5:	wag	–	person fond of making jokes
	oculist	–	eye doctor
line 10:	to minister	–	to serve
	contiguous	–	touching, neighbouring
line 16:	blind	–	hier: Attrappe
	sumptuous	–	rich and luxurious
line 18:	anaemic	–	pale, without enough blood
line 32:	sensuously	–	sexually attractive
line 33:	crêpe-de-chine	–	soft silk cloth
lines 34/35:	to smoulder	–	to burn slowly
line 36:	flush	–	directly
line 49:	scrawny	–	thin
	torpedo	–	hier: Feuerwerkskörper
line 57:	to defer to	–	to show respect for
line 59:	muslin	–	thin fine cotton cloth
line 61:	Town Tattle	–	scandal magazine of the Twenties

I. Language (ohne Wörterbuch zu bearbeiten)

Answer questions 1–6 dealing with the underlined words/phrases or structures within the given context. Follow the instructions added to each item.

1. 11/12: "... another was an all-night restaurant, <u>approached</u> by a trail of ashes;"
   Explain; you may change the sentence structure. (1 VP)

2. 13: "Cars bought and sold."
   What other phrase could Wilson use to advertise his business? (1 VP)

3. 20–23: "How's business?"
   "<u>I can't complain</u>", answered Wilson ... "<u>When are you going to sell me that car</u>?"
   Imagine Tom is talking to Myrtle later in her apartment in New York about this conversation. Write down in reported speech what he would say. (2 VP)

4. 25: "Works pretty slow, <u>don't he</u>?"
   What is unusual about the question tag? What does it tell you about the speaker? (2 VP)

5. 28: "<u>I just meant</u> –"
   Explain the function of this elliptic (incomplete) sentence in the given situation. (2 VP)

6. 46/47: "... just as George Wilson <u>emerged</u> with two chairs <u>from</u> his office door."
   Find a suitable substitute; keep to the sentence structure. (1 VP)

7. Find the corresponding <u>abstract nouns</u> (not the -ing forms):
   2: to perceive
   15: to occur (1 VP)

II. Questions on the text

Answer the following questions in complete sentences. Keep to the information given in the text unless you are explicitly asked to go beyond it.

1. Explain the symbolic meaning of the eyes of Dr. T. J. Eckleburg in this passage and in the novel as a whole. (100–160 words) (5 VP)

2. In what way do the location and the interior of the garage reflect Wilson's situation? (80–120 words) (4 VP)

3. Analyse the way Tom talks to George and Myrtle Wilson. Show how his manner of speaking reflects his attitude towards these two characters. (40–60 words) (2 VP)

4. What do we learn about Myrtle Wilson's character and behaviour in this passage? (90–130 words) (4 VP)

III. Comment/Composition

Choose <u>one</u> of the following topics: (200–300 words) (10 VP)

1. Comment on Nick's role as a narrator and a character in the novel.

2. Which scene do you think is the climax of the novel: the scene in which Gatsby and Daisy meet again (Chapter V) or the showdown at the Plaza Hotel (Chapter VII)?
Give reasons for your choice.

3. "The American people think the USA is the envy of the world"
(Former US Vice President Dan Quayle).
What could have been his reasons for making this statement?
Do you think it is justified?

IV. Translation (25 VP)

Most societies, even liberal ones, do find it difficult to <u>accommoda</u>te newcomers when they come in large numbers over a short time, especially when economies are growing slowly or not at all. That is why it is <u>reasonable</u> to set limits on immigration, and also ask immigrants to <u>accommodate to</u> the laws, and partly to the cultures, of the countries they
5 come to. Yet, if societies are to hold together, all their citizens, <u>regardless</u> of colour or religion, need to share some common values and a sense of nationality.

The other side of this coin is that politicians should point out that immigration is the lifeblood of most nations. It brings enterprise, energy and variety to society and has for many centuries been the rule, not the exception. Few nations, least of all in Europe, are
10 ethnically pure. Most have benefitted hugely from immigrants.

Successful societies do not stand still; they need to be refreshed and revitalised. Similarly, all cultures, however admirable, need to adapt and develop. It is in the mixing of cultures, not in their <u>preservation</u> from change, that nations remain interesting and successful. The hope for humanity lies in fusion, not in fission.

The Economist, 1991   *196 words*

Vocabulary

line 8:   enterprise – Unternehmungsgeist
line 14: fission   – Spaltung, Teilung

Lösungsvorschlag

I. Language

1. A trail of ashes led up to an all-night restaurant.
   People could get to the restaurant on a trail of ashes.
   People could reach the restaurant on a trail of ashes.
   The restaurant could be reached via a trail of ashes.

2. We buy and sell cars.
   Second-hand cars.
   Used cars.
   Purchase and sale of cars.

3. I asked your husband how business was. He told me/He said he couldn't complain. He also wanted to know/Then he wanted to know when I was going to sell him that/my car.

4. You can't usually use this form in written English because it is grammatically incorrect. It is mainly used in slang/substandard/colloquial English and characterises Wilson as a member of the lower classes or as a rather uneducated person.

5. Wilson stops in mid-sentence because he is afraid of Tom and does not dare to contradict him; he does not want to risk annoying Tom who might then sell the car to somebody else. This lack of self-confidence on the part of Wilson is further emphasised by his generally submissive attitude.

6. ... appeared with two chairs at/turned up with two chairs at/put in an appearance with two chairs at.

7. perception
   occurrence

II. Questions on the text

1. The eyes of Doctor T. J. Eckleburg are only mentioned once in this novel, but their overpowering, unsettling presence can be felt throughout the passages set in the valley of ashes. With their disproportionate size, they seem to control the valley just like *'Big Brother'* was in control of George Orwell's futuristic society in *1984*.
   In this extract from the novel, however, this anonymous power ("they look out of no face ...", ll. 3/4) not only controls the valley and its people, but as an advertisement, it introduces the world of business with all its influences on the people.
   On a more ironic level and going beyond this extract, Dr. Eckleburg's eyes symbolise both the blindness and the distorted vision of some of the major characters in the novel. To some extent, all the characters are subject to some kind of blindness or blurred vision of reality, but the most outstanding example is certainly Gatsby himself who unendingly indulges in a romantic view of Daisy which finally leads to his downfall. The reality of the rich is restricted to their own enormously wealthy surroundings and makes them turn a blind eye to the problems of the other, less fortunate part of this society.

2. George Wilson is described as a ghost-like figure who has been working for years in order to make it but has now come to realise that life in the dreary valley of ashes has got the better of him. In fact, the man who is not even capable of standing his ground when encountering Tom, has taken on the typical features of the valley – desolation,

emptiness and isolation. Just like the area, he has lost touch with reality ("shadow of a garage", ll. 15/16). The interior of the building stands for failure, there is hardly anything for sale and the only noticeable thing in the garage is the wreck of a car, just like Wilson, who has become a wreck himself.

3. The character of a person is in particular given away by his/her manner of speaking as well as his/her language in general. This can be clearly seen in the passage where Tom makes full use of his origin and treats both the Wilsons in a domineering and condescending manner. He very obviously looks down on them and is in no way prepared to accept them as equals.

4. Myrtle's character has to be seen from two different angles. On the one hand, the woman and wife at home where she already discloses her sexual attractiveness, though she is no real beauty (l. 33). On the other hand, the mistress of a rich man who takes her out of her daily routine. These frequent trips to the luxury of the city seem to give her the strength and energy to cope with her otherwise desperate situation. As soon as she is with Tom, she casts her husband aside and plunges into the life of parties and little presents only her lover can give her. When she is with him, she tries to change into a society woman who wears a stylish dress and buys expensive perfume. The way she chooses the most extravagant taxi shows how easily she is able to overcome her poor background.

III. Comment/Composition

1. *Comment on Nick's role as a narrator and a character in the novel.*

    Although Gatsby is clearly the central figure of the novel, the narrator Nick Carraway takes on a key role in Fitzgerald's concept. This role is a very complex one and has to be examined thoroughly in order to understand not only the author's narrative technique, but even more the content of the novel and its structure.
    First of all, Nick is introduced as the narrator who wants to relate the events of one hot summer in New York and himself explains his suitability for the job. He is one of life's listeners, people trust him and confide in him. Being quite close to most of the main characters, he can pass on the most important bits of information in all their actuality and finds himself in the advantageous situation of being allowed to comment upon whatever goes on. This closeness is essential to his second role in Fitzgerald's novel, the one in which he does not feel at home in the same way as he does as narrator: Nick, the character who cannot easily detach himself from the events and who becomes more and more involved to the extent that he plans the action, helps to plot and organise, for example when he arranges Daisy and Gatsby's reunion.
    For the reader, this double role of being one of the protagonists can also be a problem, since we cannot be sure any more about the grade of his bias towards one or the other character. At the end of the novel, Nick very obviously takes sides and condemns the Buchanans and their friends as being responsible for what happened to Gatsby and his romantic dream.

2. *Which scene do you think is the climax of the novel: the scene in which Gatsby and Daisy meet again (Chapter V) or the showdown at the Plaza Hotel (Chapter VII)? Give reasons for your choice.*

    In a novel which does not put too much emphasis on action and action-packed scenes, the climax is not that easily pointed out. There are various scenes and events which are of vital importance to the plot and its development and there are situations which help to characterise a protagonist and his/her motives. However, the question remains which of the above-mentioned scenes can be qualified as a climax and what are the reasons for such a classification.

In more general terms it can be assumed that a novel has reached a climax when earlier events have been channelled into a situation of ultimate suspense and significance and when the outcome of such a situation is of paramount importance in, and highly influential on the remaining events of a novel. If we take this improvised definition into account and try to apply it to *The Great Gatsby*, we come to the conclusion that both chapter V and chapter VII qualify for such an estimation. Still, there is a marked difference between the two crucial scenes: inasmuch as Daisy and Gatsby's reunion triggers off a whole series of events finally leading to the catastrophe at the end, the showdown at the Plaza Hotel is only one of a fair number of climaxes or mere events which occur before the novel slows down a little prior to it eventually accelerating again with the deaths of Gatsby and Myrtle.

In the same way as these two scenes differ on a structural level (chapter V being at the origin of events, chapter VII being only one part of a series), they also differ in their content, thus forming a completely different sort of climax altogether. Chapter V witnesses the revitalisation of a love affair and allows both its protagonists to finally give vent to their suppressed feelings. If we take the romantic aspects in this novel as key elements of the author's intentions, then we have here to all intents and purposes the climax of *The Great Gatsby*. However, if this love-affair is only seen as one of many ingredients of the mixture that makes this novel, and if we turn our attention rather to the various character constellations within the novel, then the climax can surely be found in chapter VII. Both scenes are important for the novel, both scenes shape the further development of the plot, both culminate in a climax in their own right.

3. *"The American people think the USA is the envy of the world" (Former US Vice President Dan Quayle).*
What could have been his reasons for making this statement?
Do you think it is justified?

The statement by Dan Quayle concerning America's status in the world is quite an ambiguous one because it sounds as though he did not share this rather pompous self-evaluation or that he wants at least to cast a shadow of a doubt on it. This aforementioned ambiguity has to be borne in mind when discussing whether or not such a statement can be justified.

Ever since the early settlers set foot on American soil, this continent of unmeasurable proportions has fascinated whole generations, thus luring millions of hopefuls to its shores. Their motives for leaving their homeland varied, but they all shared one common aim, that is to make a new start in the land of unlimited opportunities and to join in the famous American success story. This myth has been kept alive for ages, added to by a very biased presentation of American values as invented by the American film industry. Certainly, there has never been a lack of clear signs that this myth (still) lives on: there have always been multifarious examples of people who made their mark or who realised their personal American dream. But, at the same time, whenever this myth was refreshed and adapted to ever-changing demands, there was a growing feeling that America's status as the envy of the world had long since been overshadowed by a development that ran counter to this prominent position. It cannot be denied that the once solid stronghold of democracy, political and religious freedom has lost some of its appeal. The widening gap between rich and poor, the existence of an underclass mainly consisting of blacks and coloured people, the lack of a social network to prevent people from being swallowed up by poverty and many other reasons for a constantly growing social unrest have harmed, if not almost destroyed, this idealised image of the USA. No matter what made Quayle make this statement, no matter how challenging or critical it was meant to be, it certainly shows how self-confident and condescending the people of this country still are. They still show the stamina that got them where they are now and recent events in politics and in the economy have revealed that America still assumes a leading role and many other countries are prepared to depend on her and to follow her example.

IV. Translation

Die meisten Gesellschaften, sogar die Liberalen, finden es wirklich schwierig,/Den meisten Gesellschaften, sogar den Liberalen, fällt es wirklich schwer, Neuankömmlinge/ Einwanderer aufzunehmen, wenn sie in großer Zahl/wenn viele von ihnen innerhalb kurzer Zeit/in einem begrenzten Zeitraum kommen, besonders/insbesondere wenn die (jeweilige) Wirtschaft (nur) langsam oder überhaupt nicht wächst/ wenn die (jeweilige) Wirtschaft (zu diesem Zeitpunkt) (nur) schleppend oder gar nicht vorankommt. Aus diesem Grunde ist es vernünftig/Deshalb ist es (auch) vernünftig, die Einwanderung zu begrenzen/der Einwanderung Grenzen zu setzen und Einwanderer auch aufzufordern/ und von Einwanderern auch zu fordern, sich den Gesetzen und zum Teil auch der Kultur (den Kulturen) der Länder, in die sie kommen, anzupassen.
Wenn Gesellschaften jedoch zusammenhalten sollen,/Sollen Gesellschaften jedoch/ allerdings zusammenhalten,müssen alle (ihre) Bürger ohne Rücksicht auf ihre Hautfarbe/ ungeachtet ihrer Hautfarbe oder Religion/Religionszugehörigkeit einige gemeinsame Werte und ein Nationalbewußtsein haben/teilen.
Die andere Seite dieser/der Medaille ist, dass Politiker darauf hinweisen sollten/darauf aufmerksam machen sollten/darauf verweisen sollten, dass (die) Einwanderung (durchaus) ein Lebenselixier/frisches Blut/eine Quelle der Erneuerung/lebensnotwendige Energie für die meisten Staaten/Nationen ist/bedeutet/darstellt.
Sie gibt/bringt/verschafft der Gesellschaft/einer Gesellschaft/der jeweiligen Gesellschaft Unternehmungsgeist, Energie und Vielfalt/verschiedene Einflüsse und ist seit vielen Jahrhunderten/ist über viele Jahrhunderte hinweg die Regel/die Regel gewesen, nicht die Ausnahme. (Nur) Wenige Nationen, am allerwenigsten die in Europa, sind ethnisch rein. Dabei haben die meisten außerordentlich/enorm von Einwanderern profitiert/Die meisten haben enorm von (diesen) Einwanderern/Neuankömmlingen profitiert/Dabei haben die meisten aus der Einwanderung Nutzen gezogen.
Erfolgreiche Gesellschaften stehen nicht still/In erfolgreichen Gesellschaften gibt es keinen Stillstand; sie müssen gestärkt/sie müssen neue Impulse bekommen und neu belebt werden/neue Anregungen erhalten. In diesem Sinne/In ähnlicher Weise müssen sich alle Kulturen, so bewundernswert sie auch sein mögen/ungeachtet der Bewunderung, die wir ihnen entgegenbringen mögen, anpassen und (weiter-/fort-)entwickeln. Nationen bleiben gerade dadurch interessant und erfolgreich, dass sich die/ihre Kulturen vermischen/miteinander verschmelzen und nicht dadurch, dass sie sich der Veränderung verschließen/sie sich vor Veränderung schützen./Gerade dadurch, dass sich die Kulturen vermischen und nicht dadurch, dass sich die Nationen vor Veränderung schützen, bleiben sie interessant und erfolgreich. Die Hoffnung für die Menschheit liegt in der Verschmelzung, nicht in der Spaltung. /Nicht Spaltung, sondern Verschmelzung heißt die Hoffnung für die Menschheit./Die Hoffnung für die Menscheit liegt (allein) im Miteinander, nicht im "Auseinander".

> **Leistungskurs Englisch (Baden-Württemberg): Abiturprüfung 1998**
> **Textaufgabe und Übersetzung**

A pause. Eliza hopeless and crushed. Higgins a little uneasy.

HIGGINS [*in his loftiest manner*] Why have you begun going on like this? May I ask whether you complain of your treatment here?

LIZA. No.

5 HIGGINS. Has anybody behaved badly to you? Colonel Pickering? Mrs Pearce? Any of the servants?

LIZA. No.

HIGGINS. I presume you dont pretend that *I* have treated you badly.

LIZA. No.

10 HIGGINS. I am glad to hear it. [*He moderates his tone*]. Perhaps youre tired after the strain of the day. Will you have a glass of champagne? [*He moves towards the door*].

LIZA. No. [*Recollecting her manners*] Thank you.

HIGGINS [*good-humored again*] This has been coming on you for some days. I suppose it was natural for you to be anxious about the garden party. But thats all over now. [*He
15 pats her kindly on the shoulder. She writhes*]. Theres nothing more to worry about.

LIZA. No. Nothing more for *you* to worry about. [*She suddenly rises and gets away from him by going to the piano bench, where she sits and hides her face*]. Oh God! I wish I was dead.

HIGGINS [*staring after her in sincere surprise*] Why? In heaven's name, why?
20 [*Reasonably, going to her*] Listen to me, Eliza. All this irritation is purely subjective.

LIZA. I dont understand. I'm too ignorant.

HIGGINS. It's only imagination. Low spirits and nothing else. Nobody's hurting you. Nothing's wrong. You go to bed like a good girl and sleep it off. Have a little cry and say your prayers: that will make you comfortable.

25 LIZA. I heard *your* prayers. "Thank God it's all over!"

HIGGINS [*impatiently*] Well, don't you thank God it's all over? Now you are free and can do what you like.

LIZA [*pulling herself together in desperation*] What am I fit for? What have you left me fit for? Where am I to go? What am I to do? Whats to become of me?

30 HIGGINS [*enlightened, but not at all impressed*] Oh, *thats* whats worrying you, is it? [*He thrusts his hands into his pockets, and walks about in his usual manner, rattling the contents of his pockets, as if condescending to a trivial subject out of pure kindness*]. I shouldnt bother about if I were you. I should imagine you wont have much difficulty in settling yourself somewhere or other, though I hadnt quite realized that you
35 were going away. [*She looks quickly at him: he does not look at her, but examines the dessert stand on the piano and decides that he will eat an apple*]. You might marry, you know. [*He bites a large piece out of the apple and munches it noisily*]. You see, Eliza, all men are not confirmed old bachelors like me and the Colonel. Most men are the marrying sort (poor devils!); and youre not bad-looking: it's quite a
40 pleasure to look at you sometimes – not now, of course, because youre crying and looking as ugly as the very devil; but when youre all right and quite yourself, youre what I should call attractive. That is, to the people in the marrying line, you under-

stand. You go to bed and have a good nice rest; and then get up and look at yourself in the glass; and you wont feel so cheap.

45 *Eliza looks at him, speechless, and does not stir. The look is quite lost on him: he eats his apple with a dreamy expression of happiness, as it is quite a good one.*

HIGGINS [*a genial afterthought occurring to him*] I daresay my mother could find some chap or other who would do very well.

LIZA. We were above that at the corner of Tottenham Court Road.

50 HIGGINS. [*waking up*] What do you mean?

LIZA. I sold flowers. I didnt sell myself. Now youve made a lady of me I'm not fit to sell anything else. I wish youd left me where you found me.

HIGGINS [*slinging the core of the apple decisively into the grate*] Tosh, Eliza. Dont you insult human relations by dragging all this cant about buying and selling into it. You
55 neednt marry the fellow if you dont like him.

LIZA. What else am I to do?

HIGGINS. Oh, lots of things. What about your old idea of a florist's shop? Pickering could set you up in one: he has lots of money. [*Chuckling*] He'll have to pay for all those togs you have been wearing today; and that, with the hire of the jewellery, will make
60 a big hole in two hundred pounds. Why, six months ago you would have thought it the millennium to have a flower shop of your own. Come! youll be all right. I must clear off to bed: I'm devilish sleepy. By the way, I came down for something: I forget what it was.

LIZA. Your slippers.

65 HIGGINS. Oh yes, of course. You shied them at me. [*He picks them up, and is going out when she rises, and speaks to him*].

LIZA. Before you go, sir –

HIGGINS [*dropping the slippers in his surprise at her calling him Sir*] Eh?

LIZA. Do my clothes belong to me or to Colonel Pickering?

861 words   G. B. Shaw, *Pygmalion, Act IV*

Vocabulary:
line 2: lofty – here: haughty, arrogant
line 15: to writhe – to twist the body with pain
line 47: genial – cheerful, friendly
line 53: grate – fireplace
line 53: tosh – (informal exclamation) rubbish
line 54: cant – hypocritical, insincere talk
line 59: togs – (informal) clothes

I. Language (ohne Wörterbuch zu bearbeiten)

Answer questions 1–7 dealing with the underlined words/phrases or structures within the given context. Follow the instructions added to each item.

1. 8: "I presume you dont pretend that <u>I</u> have treated you badly."
   Rewrite the sentence, emphasising 'I' in a different way. (1 VP)

2. 20: "All this <u>irritation</u> ..."
   Find a suitable substitute; keep to the sentence structure. (1 VP)

3. 28/29: "What am I fit for? What have you left me fit for?"
   Change into reported speech. Start as follows:
   Eliza asked ... (1 VP)

4. 38: "... all men are not <u>confirmed</u> old <u>bachelors</u> like me ..."
   Explain; you may change the sentence structure. (2 VP)

5. 47: "... a genial <u>afterthought occurring</u> to him."
   Explain; you may change the sentence structure. (2 VP)

6. 60/61: "... you would have thought it the millennium to have a flower shop of your own."
   Rewrite the sentence replacing the infinitive construction with an if-clause.
   What does millennium mean here? (2 VP)

7. Find the corresponding abstract nouns (not the -ing forms):
   8: to presume
   19: sincere (1 VP)

II. Questions on the text

Answer the following questions in complete sentences. Keep to the information given in the text unless you are explicitly asked to go beyond it.

1. Sum up how Higgins tries to calm Eliza down. What does this reveal about his attitude towards her?
   (120 – 180 words) (4 VP)

2. How does Higgins's and Eliza's manner of speaking characterize the roles they play in the first part of the text (ll. 1–24)?
   (60 – 80 words) (3 VP)

3. Describe the change in Eliza's behaviour in the second part of the text. Go beyond this excerpt and outline how the battle between the two continues until she leaves the house.
   (140 – 200 words) (5 VP)

4. Shaw called this play a "romance". What do you think this means and is this expression justified?
   (60 – 90 words) (3 VP)

III. Comment/Composition

Choose <u>one</u> of the following topics: (200–300 words) (10 VP)

1. Do you think "Educating Rita" is a modern version of Shaw's "Pygmalion"? Give arguments for and against.

2. Shaw once said, "If everyone in England learned to speak 'good' English, there would be much less friction in society."
   Discuss this statement; you may go beyond "Pygmalion" and "Educating Rita".

3. The American Dream – an idea of the past, a dream gone wrong, or a concept for the future? Discuss.

IV. Translation (25 VP)

In today's labour markets it is often assumed the main concern of employers is to recruit staff with the education needed for the increasingly skilled jobs available. But top academic qualifications are not the first consideration for companies, according to a recent study carried out in the US.

5   Much more important, it seems, is to make sure that recruits have "the right attitude". Most employers regard this as by far the most valuable asset when taking on new staff. Not far behind in their list of hiring priorities is that staff should have communication skills, followed by work experience. By contrast, the least important factor in recruitment was found to be teacher assessments and the reputation of the school from which the
10 employee graduated. It is believed that many employers have a deep hostility towards the academic community. This may explain, in part, why they are not interested in formal educational qualifications when hiring staff.

But other findings in the US study suggest that the overconcentration on "the right attitude" could be misplaced. The most important finding emphasises that raising the aver-
15 age educational level of workers in an establishment increases productivity noticeably. This suggests that companies which want to improve performance should concentrate on recruiting workers with high educational qualifications.

Financial Times, 1997   *210 words*

Vocabulary
line 6: asset   – Aktivposten, Plus
line 9: assessment – Einschätzung, Beurteilung

Lösungsvorschlag

I. Language

1. I am the one who has treated you badly.
   It is I/me who have/has treated you badly.
   The one/The person who has treated you badly is me.

2. anger/vexation/annoyance

3. Eliza asked what she was fit for. She wanted to know/She asked/She wanted to find out what he had left her fit for.

4. A confirmed bachelor is a man who is of the firm belief that it is better/to his advantage not to marry/not to get married. He has decided to always stay single/unmarried/remain unmarried.

5. After having given some thought to an idea or plan, he had another/a second/a new idea/plan that seemed even better than the first one. A new idea has come to his mind. A second plan has struck him/has come to him.

6. You would have thought it the millennium if you had had a flower shop of your own. A dream come true/paradise on earth/the best thing she could have got/utmost happiness/incomparable bliss/the best thing that can happen to the person in question

7. presumption; sincerity

II. Questions on the text

1. Eliza has evidently reached a critical point in her life. She does not know where to go and what to do but her "maker", Higgins, lacks the emotional involvement necessary to appreciate her dilemma. He makes her admit that no harm has been done to her and ignores the fact that he alone is the reason for her deplorable situation. His unlimited arrogance, his openly condescending attitude and self-centredness are best shown in his way of dealing with Eliza's obvious anger and depression. He not only suggests that she is simply having one of her habitual mood swings, but also disregards her desperate longing for love and recognition by telling her that both her private and financial future could be secured. Thus emphasis is put on the incompatibility of the two protagonists, namely the ambitious scientist and "confirmed bachelor" beyond reach of the naive and formerly cheerful girl who has been formed into a society girl deprived of both her roots and her future.

2. This first part of the excerpt can serve as a reminder of what the relationship between Higgins and Eliza used to be like before the girl had undergone her transformation. The reader/spectator seems to be about to witness an argument between a strict but rather self-righteous father and an angry and disappointed daughter. The girl, being rather uncommunicative and monosyllabic in her answers, is merely on the defensive, whereas Higgins's superiority is emphasized by his bossy and condescending approach.

3. In this part of the play, Eliza seems to become painfully aware of the fact that not only has her "education" left her with no prospects for the future, but even worse, the man who so violently effaced her past, still does not respect her or take her seriously and treats her like a child. In normal human fashion, her disappointment and despair turn into anger and make her want to hurt in return. This she does in a more subtle

way than could have been expected. The outward verbal abuse she was quite capable of as an ordinary flowergirl has now been changed to a very clever verbal attack which is the only weapon to fight back against Higgins's superior skills. Towards the end of this scene, she masterfully applies the sort of "linguistic meanness" that only the educated classes (according to the professor) are privy to. Being overly polite, calling him "Sir" to point out that they belong to different classes and hinting at the possibility that her expensive clothes might be needed again for more experiments, seem to hit Higgins at the core; but it is only when she gives back the ring he had bought her that he completely cracks up and is reduced to a swearing, screaming bundle of nerves. Eliza has beaten him on his own turf.

4. When going to the theatre was one of the basic means of entertainment, audiences were above all interested in having a good time, i. e. they wanted to have a good laugh or a good cry. Calling his play a romance was certainly a way of attracting larger audiences, since a romance promised a story of love, the problems two lovers had to deal with and often a real happy ending. Shaw's play cannot boast such an ending, the play is not about love, at least not in the strictest sense of 'romance', since the basic theme is a woman's fight for recognition and independence. It would certainly not be appropriate to call the play a romance.

III. Comment/Composition

1. *Do you think "Educating Rita" is a modern version of Shaw's "Pygmalion"? Give arguments for and against.*

   It is certainly possible to read the two plays as totally different descriptions of a woman struggling for independence. The difference in time and setting, the authors' approaches to the main themes and their stylistic differences make it possible to completely detach the two plays from each other. The settings the two heroines develop in are in many ways difficult to compare but still, if one takes into account what actually makes them want to change, what motives they have, what kind of urgent dream they both intend to hang on to, we easily see the common denominator from which arguments may be derived that establish "Rita" as a modern version of "Pygmalion". What are the points the two plays have in common?
   First of all we have to take a closer look at the characters. Both plays seem to have a similar cast: there is on the one hand young working-class Rita with her purely working-class environment tempted by a university professor and his upper middle class set of friends into a life that couldn't be more unlike the one she was leading before. On the other hand, we have the poor flower girl and her London street-life who is dragged out of her miserable surroundings by a rich professor and his scientific aspirations into a life that is also far removed from what she was used to. To these very obvious similarities can be added that both heroines have to give up the main makings of their former characters (one may be tempted to say the better ones) in order to assimilate into their new spheres of society. Moreover, not only do both have to deny their roots, but they also finally come to the conclusion that their metamorphoses have not necessarily been advantageous ones.
   There are certainly major differences in the way the authors/playwrights have gone about their paintings of the various characters, e. g. Frank and Higgins are different inasmuch as Frank becomes emotionally involved to a point where it is hard to believe the play does not take a turn towards a simple love story whereas Higgins remains as cold as a fish although he, too, loses his temper when verbally attacked by Eliza. These and many more points may speak against seeing the two plays as one of

a kind, but on the whole it has to be concluded that the basic ingredients and character constellations may well justify calling "Rita" a modern version of "Pygmalion".

2. *Shaw once said, "If everyone in England learned to speak 'good' English, there would be much less friction in society. "*
   Discuss this statement; you may go beyond "Pygmalion" and "Educating Rita".

   English society has always been called a class-ridden one, with all the defects such an attribute comprises. Be it exploitation of the lower classes, prejudices and injustice on all levels, Britain and its great class divide has often been referred to. This divide has even been applied to geographical differences leading to the so-called North-South divide where a geographical line was drawn between northern and southern England and the people living there. The south's previously overwhelming economic superiority was basically put down to the northerners' lack of intelligence and their inability to speak good English ("Is there intelligence north of Watford?" was an advert to be found all over London.) Later, in the 80s, the politics of the then leading lady Margaret Thatcher only added to the decline of the North and facilitated the birth of a new breed of well-spoken and successful young business people, the Yuppies.

   Taking this into account and bearing in mind that in both plays to be discussed the female protagonists manage to make their mark on society by just learning to speak properly and by imitating the manners of certain groups (the high society in "Pygmalion", the university circles in "Rita"), one might be inclined to agree with Shaw's statement about the interrelationship between a certain accepted code (RP) and the problems between the classes.

   This is, however, a bit far-fetched and gives too much credit to a code that is only spoken by a basic minority in Britain. At the same time, it must be stated that if we take Shaw's theory at face value, all speakers of one of the many varieties of English spoken all over Britain would be evaluated as second or third-class people. Good English may open some doors but reality proves that even people in higher positions throughout modern British society speak with seemingly strong or pronounced accents.

   Applied to Rita and Eliza it is safe to say that they already had the qualities that helped them to find access to "the other society", but only their capacity for assimilation languagewise gave them the means to make themselves heard and understood. This again could serve as an argument in favour of Shaw's theory, namely that only by being able to communicate with each other may the friction between the classes be erased.

3. *The American Dream – an idea of the past, a dream gone wrong, or a concept for the future? Discuss.*

   Throughout American history, the concept of the American Dream has taken on an overpowering mythical aspect that has gone far beyond its widespread misconception of "a dream of merely material plenty".

   There certainly were those immigrants who wanted to escape from economic misery, putting the little money they had left on this last hope of a better life in a country thousands of miles away. There were those, too, who were politically oppressed and not only tried to start anew in another country, but also wanted to put into action new ideas that had come up in Europe and later fell on fertile ground in a country where "anything goes". Finally, there were those seeking religious freedom and the possibility of fully living according to their respective beliefs.

   All these points are an integral part of the American Dream, but it has to be admitted that these are unfortunately ideas of the past which are nowadays, for various reasons, impossible to be carried out. Laws have been passed to curb immigration dramatically (at least concerning that to the traditional dreamlands such as America and Australia), very often making immigration altogether impossible due to very strange demands on the person willing to take that big step.

What has been maintained of the old concept of the American Dream is rather the grand idea of erasing one's past and starting all over again somewhere else where nobody has set foot before. This, however, is hardly possible in today's world where man has already explored (and mastered) the best part of formerly unknown terrain.

No, this concept has to be adapted to other areas of everyday life, the survival of mankind, the ever-changing demands of a world in transition, political and economic upheavals and modifications. The most obvious issue to benefit from such an adaptation would be the safeguarding of our environment, starting all over again, getting a second chance, doing things never done before to help an ailing Nature: this is where the American Dream and its values and ideas can still be usefully applied to.

IV. Translation

Auf dem heutigen Arbeitsmarkt wird oft angenommen/Die derzeitige Lage auf dem Arbeitsmarkt führt oft zu der Annahme, dass das Hauptinteresse der Arbeitgeber darin besteht/dass die Arbeitgeber hauptsächlich daran interessiert sind, die vorhandenen Arbeitsplätze, die eine immer höhere Qualifikation erfordern, mit Personal/Kräften zu besetzen, das eine entsprechende Ausbildung aufweist/die eine entsprechende Ausbildung aufweisen. Eine vor kurzem in den USA durchgeführte Studie hat allerdings aufgezeigt, dass Firmen nicht in erster Linie/nicht unbedingt die höchsten akademischen Grade berücksichtigt/dass Firmen nicht in erster Linie die höchsten akademischen Grade als wichtigstes Auswahlkriterium erachten.

Anscheinend ist es viel wichtiger, sich zu vergewissern/sicherzugehen, dass die neuen Arbeitskräfte/dass das neue Personal die richtige Einstellung haben/die richtige Einstellung hat./Es scheint (neuerdings) Priorität zu haben, die neuen Arbeitskräfte auf ihre richtige Einstellung hin zu überprüfen. Die meisten Arbeitgeber sehen darin das mit Abstand größte Plus, wenn sie neues Personal einstellen. Gleich danach steht auf ihrer Liste der Einstellungskriterien, dass die Mitarbeiter über eine (gewisse) Kommunikationsfähigkeit verfügen sollten. Arbeitserfahrung als weiteres Kriterium rangiert gleich dahinter. Im Gegensatz dazu ergab sich aus der Studie/fand man heraus, dass die Beurteilung durch die Lehrer (also Zensuren/Noten) und der Ruf der Schule, an der der Beschäftigte/Angestellte seinen Abschluss gemacht hat, die Kriterien/Gesichtspunkte sind, die für die Einstellung von Personal die geringste Bedeutung haben. Man geht davon aus/Man glaubt, dass viele Arbeitgeber Akademikern/Bewerbern mit Universitätsabschluss ausgesprochen feindselig gegenüberstehen/Man glaubt, dass viele Arbeitgeber gerade Akademikern besonders misstrauisch entgegentreten/begegnen. Dies mag zumindest ansatzweise als Erklärung dafür dienen, warum sie formale Bildungsabschlüsse nicht interessieren, wenn neues Personal eingestellt wird/Dies mag teilweise erklären, warum sie sich bei der Einstellung neuer Mitarbeiter nicht von rein formalen Bildungsabschlüssen in ihrer Entscheidung beeinflussen lassen.

Andere Ergebnisse/Resultate in der (erwähnten) amerikanischen Studie weisen allerdings darauf hin/deuten jedoch darauf hin, dass eine zu einseitige Ausrichtung auf die richtige Einstellung/dass die Überbetonung der richtigen Einstellung fehl am Platz sein könnte/in die falsche Richtung führen könnte. Das wichtigste Ergebnis macht deutlich/ stellt heraus/deutet darauf hin, dass ein Anheben des durchschnittlichen Bildungsstands der Arbeiter/Mitarbeiter in einem Unternehmen/in einer Firma die Produktivität erheblich/spürbar steigert/anwachsen lässt. Das legt nahe/Dies führt zu der Erkenntnis, dass Firmen/Unternehmen, die die Leistung verbessern wollen/die bessere Ergebnisse erzielen wollen, darauf Wert legen sollten/darauf achten sollten, dass Mitarbeiter mit hohen Bildungsabschlüssen eingestellt werden.

> **Leistungskurs Englisch (Baden-Württemberg): Abiturprüfung 1999**
> **Textaufgabe und Übersetzung**

President Clinton, who called race relations "America's constant curse" in his inaugural address, plans to do something about them. He has instructed his political staff to come up with something to help redeem the two monstrous defeats that US blacks, and the traditional liberal model of racial desegregation and racial equality, have suffered in the recent past.

The first blow arrived with an academic report that should have broken like a thunderclap. The report, from Harvard's graduate school of education, found that US public schools are now more segregated than at any time since the 1950s, when the de facto system of educational apartheid provoked the Supreme Court in 1954 to issue its landmark decision that set in train the civil rights movement.

More than two-thirds of black children, and three-quarters of Hispanics, are now in schools where minorities make up a majority of the student body. The drift of middle-class whites to private and religious schools is a minor factor. The main reason for the change is that the more conservative Supreme Court installed by Presidents Reagan and Bush has whittled away at the 1954 decision in Brown vs Board of Education, that racially segregated schools were against the Constitution. In a series of decisions, the new court has said that metropolitan school boards should not be required to bus children back and forth across cities to install a racial balance in schools that does not exist in the residence patterns. The result, the Harvard study said, was that: "In American race relations, the bridge from the 20th century may be leading back to the 19th."

The second blow to the old liberal tradition came from the US Appeals Court, which declared that California's Proposition 209, endorsed by 54 per cent of the state's voters in November '96, was constitutional. The proposition forbids the state government from considering race or sex when hiring staff, awarding state contracts or admitting students to state colleges.

This dismantles the old system of affirmative action – the attempt to increase the chances of blacks and other minorities securing jobs and higher education, thereby making the legal equality established by the civil rights movement a reality.

It was a process that began, in government, with the administration of President Nixon, not usually known for his liberal instincts. But then Nixon, and the America that elected him in 1968, had been through the wrenching experience of the wretched and unpopular war in Vietnam and something that began to smack of a civil war at home. The black riots that burned the hearts out of Watts in Los Angeles, Detroit and then Washington, and dozens of other cities in the years following the supposed triumphs of civil rights, demanded government response. Affirmative action for those who would respond to opportunity, and a welfare culture for those who would not, has been for almost 30 years the official remedy. The new Republican welfare bill that Clinton, a Democrat, signed into law and the success of Proposition 209, thus represent a counter-revolution in race relations. No wonder the president feels he must do something. But what? His remedy for the unpopularity among whites of affirmative action has just been a slogan: mend it, don't end it. Now he must do more. The White House will continue to fight Proposition 209 in the courts, probably going all the way to the Supreme Court, which will buy time. The White House is also proposing to expand college scholarships and grants, but these, too, could conflict with the demand for "an opportunity society that is colour blind".

45 The phrase comes from Ward Connerly, a successful black businessman, who led the fight for Proposition 209, on the principle that racial preferences are wrong and in the long run do no favours to black people. Connerly might be said to embody the social revolution that has transformed the lives of many blacks in the three decades since civil rights. There is now, thanks in part to affirmative action and the federal government's
50 equal opportunity programmes, a sizeable and growing black middle class. In this sense, "America's constant curse" is becoming a class problem, rather than a racial one.

698 words   GUARDIAN WEEKLY (1997)

Vocabulary:
line 1: curse	– s. th. that causes great trouble or harm
line 3: to redeem	– here: to compensate for s. th.
line 15: to whittle away at	– to make s. th. less effective
line 26: to dismantle	– to get rid of a system
line 31: wrenching	– extremely unpleasant
line 33: Watts	– a part of Los Angeles

I. Language

1. Vocabulary (ohne Wörterbuch zu bearbeiten)

   Answer questions a–f, dealing with the underlined words/phrases or structures within the given context. Follow the instructions added to each item.

   a) 2–3: "He has <u>instructed</u> his political staff to <u>come up with</u> something to help redeem ..."
   Find suitable substitutes; keep to the sentence structure. (2 VP)

   b) 9: "... system of <u>educational apartheid</u> ..."
   Explain; you may change the sentence structure. (1 VP)

   c) 9–10: "... provoked the Supreme Court in 1954 to issue its <u>landmark</u> decision ..."
   Explain; you may change the sentence structure. (1 VP)

   d) 19–20: "In American race relations, the bridge from the 20th century may be leading back to the 19th."
   What does this metaphor express? (2 VP)

   e) 47–48: "Connerly might be said to embody the social revolution ..."
   Rewrite the sentence without using a passive construction. (2 VP)

   Find the corresponding abstract nouns (not the -ing-forms):

   f) 17: to require
   24: to admit
   26: to increase
   47: to embody (2 VP)

II. Comprehension

Answer the following questions in complete sentences. Keep to the information given in the text, but do not quote.

1. What change concerning race relations was brought about by the Supreme Court decision in 1954?
(40 – 60 words) (2 VP)

2. What were the findings of the Harvard report and how does the author of this text explain them?
(80 – 120 words) (4 VP)

3. What were the ideas behind the "old system of affirmative action"? In what political situation was it created and what were its effects?
(100 – 150 words) (5 VP)

4. What are the aims behind Proposition 209 and why is it supported even by members of the black middle class?
(50 – 80 words) (2 VP)

5. What is President Clinton's attitude towards what he calls "America's constant curse"?
(40 – 70 words) (2 VP)

III. Comment

Choose one of the following topics: (200 – 300 words) (10 VP)

1. America has traditionally been called "the land of the free and the home of the brave. What is your opinion?

2. The European Union: hopes and fears in Britain.

3. Analyse Eliza's and Rita's motivations as students and their relationship to their teachers.

IV. Translation (25 VP)

If one puts aside momentarily all of the witty social criticism which Shaw's drama contains, it becomes a portrayal of life in which the will is the key to human motives. Essentially Liza Doolittle is transformed from a subhuman flower girl into a truly human being because she shakes off her fears, develops a will of her own and is able to meet Higgins
5 as an equal in the strife of wills.

At the beginning of the play, Liza's famous cockney outcry expresses both her bewilderment and fear in the face of pressures on her which she cannot resist and does not understand. Even after she has successfully passed the test at the garden party, she is still not fully human – as is indicated by her attempting to demand affection from Higgins in
10 return for fetching his slippers and making herself generally as indispensable as possible. Her final transformation takes place only when she asserts interests of her own which are not born of intimidation, knocking Higgins off his pedestal from which he has viewed her only as an object, awakening for the first time his anger and his genuine concern for her as a human being.

Norbert O'Donnell (1965) 197 words

Lösungsvorschlag

I. Language

1. Vocabulary

   a) He has told/asked/ordered ... to suggest, to propose, to find, to think of

   b) Schools or colleges in which racial segregation is still predominant; a system of schools or colleges only for blacks on the one hand and only for whites on the other.

   c) a decision of the utmost importance that will have a big influence on further developments and will set new standards.

   d) The bridge back to the 19th century stands for a certain stagnation in race relations, there has not been any progress. On the contrary, old patterns of segregation and racial hatred are very likely to be restored.

   e) People might say (that) Connerly embodies the social revolution ...
   One might say that Connerly embodies the social revolution ...

   f) requirement/requisition/request
   admission/admissibility/admittance
   increase/increment
   embodiment

II. Comprehension

1. Up to the year 1954, it had been the normal thing for children to go to racially segregated schools all over the USA. With the Supreme Court declaring the old system of segregated schools unconstitutional, times were bound to change. But it was only after the Brown vs. Board of Education decision that the civil rights movement got properly started and had a legal leg to stand on.

2. The findings of the report came as a surprise to most people. Among other things it was revealed that there is far more segregation in state schools today than in the years after the Supreme Court had declared the old system unconstitutional. Black children and children from other minority groups now form the majority at certain schools. This has led some members of the white middle class to send their children to private or church-run schools. The principal factor, however, is that in opposition to former, more liberal tendencies, the increasingly conservative Supreme Court has ruled on various occasions that school boards in the bigger cities do not have to bus children to balance out racial disproportions in state schools.

3. After having prepared the ground for racial equality with the increased impetus of the civil rights movement, affirmative action programmes were set up in the late 1960s to offer minorities a better start in life. They were supposed to raise their educational standards and consequently help them to compete for more highly qualified jobs. The general atmosphere in the U.S. was rather detrimental to the success of the programmes. They had just gone through the traumatic experience of the (lost) Vietnam war which had practically split the nation. Race riots had pushed the United States to

the verge of a bloody civil war and the highly esteemed achievements of the civil rights movement were jeopardized.
Affirmative action was set in motion in order to minimize the risk of racial imbalance. This could only work out in connection with other welfare programmes which should, over a period of time, have established a black middle class.

4. The idea behind proposition 209 is a society that rejects emphasis on the importance of race and/or colour (and also sex). Thus it is aimed at a system that gets rid of the programmes giving advantages to minorities in educational and professional matters. There are now even members of the black middle class who think that affirmative action actually runs counter to the black cause.

5. Being a member of the Democratic Party and closely linked to liberal ideas such as racial equality, Clinton has put his heart into fighting Proposition 209 with all his might. He even wants to extend the support for minorities by defending the old welfare programmes and by giving even more scholarships to members of the various minority groups.

III. Comment

1. This quotation certainly goes hand in hand with the old myth of the land of unlimited opportunities and the "rags to riches" fantasy. It is, however, a very ambivalent statement too because in the light of recent and historic events, the question may well be raised whether America can really come up to the expectations and ideas everybody seems to have.
As a traditional destination for immigrants, it is certainly true to say that it gave people a new lease on life, offered manifold opportunities to those who were really prepared to take risks and soon fulfilled the promise of "streets paved with gold".
Those first immigrants and the following generations had to leave their countries of origin for various, often rather violent, reasons. Be it for religious or economic purposes, America always offered a better perspective in the long run and for many newcomers a dream really came true.
Having fled an insecure home situation, being faced by a new continent where most parts had not yet been explored, a special breed of people was needed to first survive and then to try to tame the wilderness and turn America into what it represents today. America's history is one of courage and persistence, but these traits of character were mostly born out of despair and hopelessness. Those brave people certainly led their new country into the "American century" where the only superpower left plays the role of world policeman successfully. However, some people would probably rather talk about an act of safeguarding its hold on the world rather than an act of bravery. Thus it may well be adequate to cast a critical look at the American foreign policy of the outgoing 20th century.

2. Euroscepticism has always been an integral part of Britain's history, even before the European Union as we know it in its present form started to develop into the economic power it represents today. This rather reticent attitude towards things concerning Europe was very often fuelled from both sides. On the one hand, it has always been the policy not to get involved too much in foreign affairs while on the other hand, there have always been strongly anti-British tendencies trying to keep their influence on the European balance of power at a fairly low level.
Recent history has shown that the traditional British reservations concerning the Union have never really been unfounded (according to the British). The ban on British beef was received by the public as a treacherous act instigated by the European Union

in order to do serious harm to the British economy and by the same token it must be stated that many people today are still averse to the idea of being ruled by some bureaucrats in "far-away" Belgium. This, and many other more or less serious events have finally attributed to this still inherent feeling of having to be against Europe, having to hang on to the old system of insularity. Nevertheless, although some fears of the common people can be easily understood, it ought to be beyond discussion that Britain can only survive within the European Union as a driving factor and strong partner.

Fortunately there are many modern politicians who have grown up with this eternal conflict and have also tried to get to the very core of the problem. They know, and try to get it across to their voters, that another self-imposed isolationist attitude could set Britain back enormously.

3. The two female protagonists' motivations as "students" differ to a certain extent and at the same time influence their relationship to their teachers. Given their respective poor social backgrounds, one might argue that they are driven by the same burning desire to improve, get a better job and secure an otherwise dreary future. One would certainly think that this basic situation would make the two women two "nice students" to be easily moulded into whatever was needed. This, however, is completely wrong. Whereas Eliza, on the thin line between poverty and starvation, just wants to get out of the slum she has to live in and is at first not that keen on improving herself, Rita has her little plan already nicely worked out and has not got material improvement (to start off with) in mind. She wants to be able to talk about literature, to get what she was denied at a younger age, when her parents did not see it fit to give a young girl a good education. She has realized that she has already entered the dead-end-street of house-husband-children and is trying to escape before it is really too late. In a very similar way Eliza's life is already predestined and the prospects are not cheerful ones at all. She grasps her one and only chance to start all over again.

In these different sets of motivations can be found the keys to their different attitudes towards their teachers. On the one hand, Eliza is first of all submissive, scared and lacking the slightest hint of self-confidence whereas Rita, from the very beginning, has a certain way of opposing her tutor that is even close to making her the dominant character. This form of opposition verging on dominance is to be seen in Eliza's case only at the very end when she confronts her teacher in a battle of wills and inadvertently puts him back in place.

IV. Translation

Wenn man für einen Moment/für einen Augenblick die ganze/all die geistreiche/witzig gemachte Sozialkritik außer Acht lässt/ignoriert, die Shaws Stück enthält/die in Shaws Stück enthalten ist/zu finden ist, wird es zu einer Darstellung des Lebens, in welcher der Wille der Schlüssel zu den menschlichen Beweggründen ist/in welcher die menschlichen Beweggründe nur über den Willen zugänglich gemacht werden können. Eigentlich/Im Grunde wird Liza Doolitle von einem Blumenmädchen, das kein vollwertiger Mensch ist, zu einem richtigen/vollwertigen/akzeptablen menschlichen Wesen verwandelt, weil sie ihre Ängste los wird/abschüttelt/weil sie sich ihrer Ängste entledigt und (schließlich) in der Lage ist, Higgins im Willenskonflikt als ein ebenbürtiger Partner/Widersacher entgegenzutreten/und es schafft, Higgins als gleichstarker Widersacher zu zeigen, dass sie bereit ist, ihren Willen durchzusetzen. Am Anfang des Theaterstückes drückt Lizas berühmter Cockney-Aufschrei gleichermaßen ihre Verwirrung und ihre Angst aus im Bewusstsein/angesichts des Druckes, der auf ihr lastet, den sie nicht unter Kontrolle bekommt/mit dem sie nicht zurecht kommt und den sie (auch) nicht versteht/den sie (gedanklich) auch nicht verarbeiten kann. Selbst nachdem sie die Prüfung/den Test beim

Gartenfest erfolgreich bestanden hat, ist sie noch immer kein vollwertiger Mensch. Dies belegt ihr Versuch, Zuneigung von Higgins einzufordern als Gegenleistung dafür, dass sie seine Hausschuhe holt und sich überhaupt/im allgemeinen so unentbehrlich wie möglich macht.

Ihre endgültige Wandlung/Der Punkt/Der Moment wenn ihre endgültige Wandlung sichtbar wird, findet erst statt, als sie ihre eigenen Interessen geltend macht, die nicht von Einschüchterung bestimmt werden. Dabei stößt sie Higgins von seinem Sockel, von dem aus er sie bisher nur als Gegenstand betrachtet hat und erregt (gleichzeitig) zum ersten Mal seinen Zorn und sein echtes Interesse an ihr als Menschen.

> **Leistungskurs Englisch (Baden-Württemberg): Abiturprüfung 2000**
> **Textaufgabe und Übersetzung**

In Higgins's explosions of wrath, in his appalling tyranny of manner, we see an adult of exceptional power of speech behave with the emotional cruelty of a child. We ought to strongly disapprove of his intense, yet cheerful contempt for Eliza. But instead we enjoy the shocking manner with which he is allowed to disregard human decencies, and in our enjoyment is mingled a certain vicarious pleasure in the excessive egotism that in ordinary life we dare not allow ourselves.

In the clash between Higgins and Eliza, however, ego meets defiant ego. From the first moment there is something in Eliza which resists Higgins and which makes her finally his match. Despite the enormous superiority of class and money that Higgins uses unmercifully in the scene in Covent Garden, Eliza holds on firmly, comically, pathetically to her sense of her rights: "Aint no call to meddle with me, he aint", "He's no right to take away my character. My character is the same to me as any lady's". They are at cross-purposes from the beginning and remain so throughout much of the play. When Higgins resorts to "the most thrillingly low tones" in his best elocutionary style to impress Eliza, she is unimpressed: "I'm going away. He's off his chump, he is. I dont want no balmies teaching me". Yet the comedy of cross-purposes would not be so funny if it did not involve the feeling that Eliza is ultimately able to stand up to Higgins's bullying. This is not to deny that he can cause her real suffering, that his insensitivity amounts to cruelty at times. But Eliza was never the 'squashed cabbage leaf' that Higgins took her for; this is a special version of the Pygmalion legend in which the sculpture is alive from the start.

The relationship between Higgins and Eliza, and particularly its conclusion, has become *the* critical question of *Pygmalion*. From the moment that Max Beerbohm Tree evaded Shaw's clear directions and contrived to suggest a romantic ending by throwing flowers to Eliza just before the final curtain (on a purely theatrical level a nice touch, reversing the image at the end of Act I where Eliza threw her flowers at Higgins), the argument was on. Shaw was outraged, and wrote his polemic epilogue to show that Eliza actually married Freddy.

There remains a strong suspicion on the part of many readers and audiences that the refusal to allow Eliza to marry Higgins is a piece of Shavian paradox, a denial of the play's natural ending.

The final unresolved conflict between the two is the right ending for the play because it is the ultimate expression of the unique individuality of each. Higgins by temperament and situation has always bullied and domineered over Eliza; it has always been her instinct to defend herself and resist that bullying. The irony of the final situation is that his teaching has given her sufficient skill and self-confidence to resist him successfully, and this in turn inspires his respect: "By George, Eliza, I said I'd make a woman of you; and I have. I like you like this". But Eliza will not settle for less than love and that Higgins will not, cannot give her, because he cannot give himself to another person.

Some critics have argued that the scene represents the victory of one over the other, and in that victory an illustration of Shavian principle: for Eric Bentley 'Eliza turns the tables on Higgins' to show vitality prevailing over Higgins's purely rational approach. For Louis Crompton on the other hand, it is Higgins with his 'passion for improving the race' who is superior to Eliza with her 'ordinary human desire for the comforts and consolations of the domestic hearth'. But surely Shaw's intention is to maintain a comic balance between the two characters.

However, it is hard to do justice to the play merely in terms of comedy, to avoid making it seem to be just a delightful entertainment, a diversion from the more doctrinal Shaw. If comedy itself is to be regarded as more than a superficial and trivial genre, then the brilliant conception of the dramatic fable in *Pygmalion,* the fulness and richness of its comic characterisation deserve more than faint praise.

709 words   *Nicholas Grene, 1984*

Vocabulary:

line 1:	wrath	– extreme anger
line 5:	vicarious	– experienced by one person on behalf of the other
line 12/13:	to be at cross-purposes	– not to understand each other because each person has a different purpose in mind
line 16:	balmies	– here: madmen
line 24:	to contrive	– to manage to do something in spite of difficulties
line 41/42:	to turn the tables on	– den Spieß umdrehen
line 42:	to prevail	– sich durchsetzen
line 45:	domestic hearth	– home

Literary facts:

line 23:	Max Beerbaum Tree	– a famous director who staged Pygmalion with a happy ending in 1914. He also played the part of Higgins in the play's first successful run in London.
line 41:	Eric Bentley	– well-known literary critic
line 43:	Louis Crompton	– well-known literary critic

I. Language

1. Vocabulary (ohne Wörterbuch zu bearbeiten)

   Deal with the words/phrases or structures within the given context. Follow the instructions added to each item.

   a) 1: "... in his <u>appalling</u> tyranny of manner, ..."
   Find a suitable substitute for the underlined word; keep to the sentence structure. (1 VP)

   b) 4: "... the shocking manner with which he is allowed to <u>disregard</u> human decencies, ..."
   Find a suitable substitute for the underlined word; keep to the sentence structure. (1 VP)

   c) 17/18: "... Eliza is ultimately able to <u>stand up to</u> Higgins's bullying."
   Find a suitable substitute for the underlined word; keep to the sentence structure. (1 VP)

   d) 19: "... the '<u>squashed cabbage leaf</u>' ..."
   What attitude towards Eliza is suggested by this image? (1 VP)

   e) 24–25: "... throwing flowers <u>to</u> Eliza ..."
   26: "... threw her flowers <u>at</u> Higgins ..."
   What are the two attitudes contrasted here? (1 VP)

   f) 35–36: "... his teaching has given her sufficient skill and self-confidence ..."
   Change into the passive voice. (1 VP)

g) 38: "But Eliza will <u>not settle for less than</u> love …"
Explain the underlined phrase; you may change the sentence structure. (1 VP)

h) 50–51: "… the fulness and richness of its comic characterisation deserve <u>more than faint</u> praise."
Explain the underlined phrase; you may change the sentence structure. What rhetorical device is used here? (2 VP)

i) Find the corresponding abstract nouns (not the -ing-forms):
7: defiant
10: firmly (1 VP)

II. Comprehension

Answer the following questions in complete sentences. Keep to the information given in the text unless you are explicitly asked to go beyond it.

1. By what arguments and evidence does Nicholas Grene try to convince us that the quarrel between Higgins and Eliza is intense, and yet amusing? (130–160 words) (6 VP)

2. Why did Shaw write the epilogue, and what was the reaction of the public? (60–100 words) (3 VP)

3. Why, according to the author, is Shaw's ending the "right" one? (60–100 words) (3 VP)

4. What interpretations of the final scene have been suggested by other critics, and how does Nicholas Grene feel about them? (60–100 words) (3 VP)

III. Comment / Composition

Choose <u>one</u> of the following topics: (200–300 words) (10 VP)

1. Compare the two characters Higgins and Frank. What do they have in common and where do they differ?

2. What features of *Educating Rita* may have contributed to its success as a play?

3. In what ways has the 20th century been shaped by the US?

IV. Translation (25 VP)

In the heyday of the Empire, one aspect of the colonies concerned the British governing class very much. The territories overseas had to be administered, and this meant public offices – from governor down to customs officer.

Here was a new factor in the imperial drive. The British Empire was increasingly run
5 simply for the sake of those who ran it. In truth, not all were in the game merely for the high salaries they received. Many welcomed power and openings for achievement greater than they could have found in serving as rural magistrates or backbench Members of Parliament at home. Some had an intellectual curiosity to explore the history or languages of India. Whatever their motives, the administrators represented the ruling class.
10 The Empire, which provided them with jobs, became for them a mission, a sacred duty. They came to believe they were spreading the blessings of British civilization – and this belief was not without foundation. What had begun as a trading venture turned into a moral cause. The administrators began to consider the interests of those over whom they ruled. They drew the line only at one point: they would do anything for the subject peo-
15 ples except get off their backs.

S. W. Sears, 1973   202 words

Vocabulary:
line 1:   heyday   – Blütezeit
line 7:   magistrate – official who acts as a judge in the lowest courts
line 12: venture   – risky (business) activity
line 14: subject   – unterworfen

concern

Lösungsvorschlag

I. Language

1. Vocabulary

    a) shocking, terrifying, dreadful, terrible, awful

    b) ignore, neglect, not to pay attention to

    c) resist, oppose, defy, offer resistance to

    d) Higgins makes a condescending remark about her as a member of the lower classes. He does not respect her for what she is.

    e) On the one hand we witness a friendly gesture, flowers being offered to the girl. On the other hand the fact that Higgins is throwing flowers at Eliza expresses his anger at what the girl has been up to.

    f) She has been given sufficient skill and self-confidence (by his teaching).
    Sufficient skill and self-confidence have been given to her (by his teaching).

    g) The only thing Eliza will accept is true love. She will not put up with anything but love. She will put up with nothing except love.
    Only love will be acceptable to her. She will not be satisfied unless she gets the love she needs.

    h) ... deserve high/a lot of/full praise.
    The author uses here an understatement.

    i) defiance
    firmness

II. Comprehension

1. The quarrel between Higgins and Eliza draws its ambiguous quality basically from the male protagonist's thoroughly 'anti-social' behaviour towards Eliza as well as some other minor characters and in addition, the readers'/spectators' secret admiration of this outrageous conduct. Higgins is allowed to indulge freely in behaviour that runs counter to any social code existing at that time and the readers/spectators can enjoy some form of extravagant egotism they themselves are hardly likely to display in real life.
This conflict gains in intensity as the play slowly develops its plot because each character can boast enormous self-confidence and an even stronger belief in his or her own qualities.
Eliza never shows any sign of intimidation when confronted with Higgins and his wealth and social standing. Quite to the contrary, she even manages to put her foot down and put him in his place when necessary. His attempts at hurting her are often rebuked and the play is pure comedy at its best when Eliza counter-attacks and thus defeats his categorisation of her as a useless 'squashed cabbage leaf'.

2. Beerbohm Tree, one of the actors acting in Shaw's lifetime, once antagonised him and his concept of the play's final statement by throwing flowers to Eliza seconds before the curtain went down. Shaw was angered by this sheer act of romanticism to such an

extent that he announced Eliza's impending wedding with Freddy in his epilogue. Some may have taken this as a typical Shavian device but readers and theatregoers alike still hold with the idea of a happy ending as the more appropriate solution.

3. According to Grene only an open ending can do justice to the two protagonists' uniqueness. They will both stick to their principles when the opposing character is concerned.
Higgins will go on bullying Eliza and Eliza will try to put up a fight whenever this is possible. True to Shavian paradox, Higgins himself is responsible for Eliza's growing fighting spirit, and he finally admires her for it. Eliza, however, does not want his admiration. She wants to be loved. Love, however, is a feeling Higgins is neither willing nor able to offer.

4. There are critics who have suggested that one of the two main characters always gains the upper hand at the end of most of their countless arguments.
Bentley, e.g., claims that at certain points in the play the roles are completely reversed with Eliza getting the better of Higgins who is usually superior. These are the specific moments when Eliza's spontaneous, natural way disposes of Higgins's scientific approach.
If we believe another critic, Crompton, Higgins comes out unscathed after most arguments since his cause is a nobler one. Grene is not happy with either interpretation and yet again puts emphasis on the very ambiguous character of the play's ending.

III. Comment

1. The two plays "Pygmalion" by G. B. Shaw and "Educating Rita" by W. Russell are very much shaped by the highly intensive and amusing arguments between the various protagonists. These arguments are especially exciting because they start off as one-sided, male-oriented exercises in male superiority and dominance and develop into a well-balanced confrontation between equal partners. Both male characters have their important part in this development by taking their female counterparts onto an intellectual and behavioural level that may even help the female protagonists to outclass their male "challengers".
This seems to be the most blatant point Frank and Higgins have in common, namely the creation of two "new women" who are finally able to burn their bridges and lead a completely independent life (much to their creators' dismay).
But if we take another look at their behaviour throughout the two plays, we must bear in mind that apart from this basic "creative" bond they share, they really do not have much else in common.
From the very beginning their treatment of their protégés asking for private tuition could not have been more different. Whereas Higgins never shows the slightest respect for the "squashed cabbage leaf" out of London's gutter and only sees her as a useful element in a ludicrous bet with his friend and partner, Frank is well aware of his own shortcomings and makes it quite clear to Rita that he is certainly not the teacher who can help her to get to where she wishes to go. He is honest and does not look down on her social background. Quite to the contrary, he enjoys her liveliness and openness from which he benefits immeasurably.
Higgins is too set in his ways to even want to benefit slightly from Eliza. He has been brought up a snob and he will stay one for the rest of his life. He has never had to go through any disappointments the way Frank surely has. On a strictly private level, Frank has been a failure. This failure has been brought about by a professional cul-de-sac in which he has landed himself. He was deserted by his wife and his present girl

friend is having an affair with one of his colleagues. Thus he finds himself at a point in his life where only some fresh air from outside might give him some respite in his longing for self-destruction.

Higgins has no time for such things. His life is well ordered and there is no room for emotionally-involved relationships which might upset his orderly way of life. He does not want to love anybody and he would not recognise love if it dropped on his head. His self-absorption has led him into a similar dead end.

2. The success of a play can depend on many different factors. It may, at a certain time, correspond to a very specific social or cultural atmosphere and thus attract a wider audience's attention. Or it is set apart from the rest by a daring production using the latest technical gimmicks to make people come to the theatre in droves.

What about Russell's very successful and critically acclaimed play "Educating Rita"? Its success must have come as a big surprise to all people involved. Firstly it has no innovations to make it something special and secondly the action of the play is reduced to a vivid, but somehow lengthy dialogue between two completely different people who at first glance seem to be as incompatible as can be. Still, the play was and has been a real winner and even today has many features that win over hordes of contemporary students at schools or universities.

This success can be traced back to two different aspects. On the one hand there is its social relevancy as a clear statement about England's seemingly indestructible class-ridden society. On the other hand the reader/theatregoer finds himself confronted with language that has been taken straight from the streets and gives the whole play an air of authenticity that makes a nice change from the usual stifled "theatre-talk". Moreover, despite the fact that the play is structured around two characters who just sit and talk, laugh and argue together, this lack of exterior action has been replaced by some strong verbal action (and a little bit of slapstick) that not only cries out for closer inspection, but even today glues the theatregoer to his seat.

These, in my opinion, are the most important ingredients that have made this play so successful over the decades.

3. The question in what ways America has shaped the 20th century can be easily answered from various points of view.

Despite the fact that this world power has always found it difficult to get a good grip on its own home-grown problems, its global influence on all walks of life such as politics, social, cultural and technological questions cannot be denied.

America has been leading the former western world in its political and military fight against the big threats of the century, namely Nazism and Communism. By abandoning its self-chosen isolationist attitude, it has taken over control including the latest conflicts in Europe. Here, the Europeans were glad that there was a power which would assume responsibility and provide everything that was necessary to succeed.

This military leadership goes hand in hand with America's technological superiority. The U.S. led most major developments and is today at the forefront of any single project, be it on the technological or medical level.

But what about everyday life? In this respect most European countries have quietly undergone a very serious transformation into an Americanised society (despite France's weak efforts to save the French language). We are being americanised in all sectors of life, from the clothes we wear and the food we eat to what we watch and think. Hollywood and Mc Donald have taken over large parts of a European's cultural ideas and aspirations and there does not seem to be an end to it.

So the question is not really whether America has shaped the last century but rather it should be: will this century be the third American century?

IV. Translation

In der Blütezeit des britischen Empires/des Empires/des britischen Weltreichs beschäftigte ein Aspekt der Kolonien die herrschende Klasse Großbritanniens ganz besonders/hatten die Kolonien in einer Hinsicht/in einem Punkt eine sehr große Bedeutung für die herrschende Klasse in Großbritannien.

Die Gebiete in Übersee/Die überseeischen Gebiete mussten verwaltet werden und dies bedeutete öffentliche Ämter – vom Gouverneur bis hinunter zum Zollbeamten/und dies erforderte öffentliche Ämter, die vom Gouverneur bis hinunter zum Zollbeamten reichten.

Hier/Daraus ergab sich/entstand ein neuer Faktor im Streben nach Weltherrschaft/im Bestreben (der Briten), die Weltherrschaft zu erlangen. Das britische Empire/Das britische Weltreich wurde zunehmend/in zunehmendem Maße einfach für diejenigen regiert, die es regierten/einfach um deretwillen regiert, die es regierten.

In Wahrheit aber nahmen nicht alle nur wegen der hohen Gehälter, die sie bezogen/die sie erhielten, an diesem „Spiel" teil/waren nicht alle nur wegen ... beteiligt.

Viele begrüßten die Macht und die sich auftuenden/ergebenden Möglichkeiten etwas zu leisten/Viele begrüßten die Macht und die Aussicht auf Möglichkeiten etwas zu leisten, die (immerhin) größer waren als die, die sie vielleicht zu Hause als Richter auf dem Land oder als Hinterbänkler im Parlament vorgefunden hätten.

Einige hatten eine (gewisse) intellektuelle Neugierde/einen geistigen Wissensdrang, die Geschichte oder die Sprachen Indiens zu erforschen/zu erkunden/sich mit der Geschichte oder den Sprachen Indiens eingehender zu beschäftigen.

Was auch immer ihre Motive gewesen sein mögen, die Verwaltungsbeamten stellten (eben) die herrschende Klasse./Die Verwaltungsbeamten stellten, ganz gleich welche Motive sie hatten, die herrschende Klasse.

Das Empire/Weltreich, das sie mit Arbeitsstellen versorgte/das ihnen Arbeitsstellen verschaffte, wurde für sie zu einer Mission/Lebensaufgabe, (ja) zu einer heiligen Pflicht.

Sie kamen/gelangten zu der Überzeugung, dass sie die Errungenschaften/Segnungen der britischen Zivilisation verbreiteten und diese Überzeugung war nicht unbegründet/konnte durchaus belegt werden.

Was als gewagte/waghalsige Handelsunternehmung angefangen hatte, wurde zu einer Sache der Moral/wurde zu einer moralischen Angelegenheit.

Die Verwaltungsbeamten/Die Verwalter (des Empire) fingen an/begannen, die Interessen derer zu berücksichtigen, über die sie herrschten. Die Grenze zogen sie nur an einer Stelle/Dies ging nur bis zu einem gewissen Punkt: sie waren bereit, alles für die unterworfenen Völker zu tun, außer von ihnen abzulassen/nur von ihnen ablassen wollten sie nicht/nur ihr Land wollten sie ihnen nicht zurück geben.

Ihre Meinung ist uns wichtig!

Ihre Anregungen sind uns immer willkommen.
Bitte informieren Sie uns mit diesem Schein über Ihre Verbesserungsvorschläge!

Titel-Nr.	Seite	Fehler, Vorschlag

Damit lernen einfacher wird... **STARK**

10-VD8

Bitte ausfüllen und im frankierten Umschlag an uns einsenden. Für Fensterkuverts geeignet.

Zutreffendes bitte ankreuzen!

Die Absenderin / der Absender ist:

- ☐ Lehrer/in
- ☐ Fachbetreuer/in
  Fächer: _____
- ☐ Seminarlehrer/in
  Fächer: _____
- ☐ Regierungsfachberater/in
  Fächer: _____
- ☐ Oberstufenbetreuer/in
- ☐ Schulleiter/in
- ☐ Referendar/in, Termin 2. Staatsexamen: _____
- ☐ Leiter/in Lehrerbibliothek
- ☐ Leiter/in Schülerbibliothek
- ☐ Sekretariat
- ☐ Eltern
- ☒ Schüler/in, Klasse: 12
- ☐ Sonstiges: _____

Unterrichtsfächer: (Bei Lehrkräften!)

STARK Verlag
Postfach 1852
85318 Freising

Kennen Sie Ihre Kundennummer?
Bitte hier eintragen.

Absender (Bitte in Druckbuchstaben!)

Name/Vorname NINIC, Ana

Straße/Nr. Hausteinstr. 96A

PLZ/Ort 70180 Stuttgart

**Telefon privat
für Rückfragen** 0711-6483053

Geburtsjahr 82

E-Mail-Adresse aninica@web.de

Schule/Schulstempel (Bitte immer angeben!)

Hölderlingymnasium
Hölderlinstr. 27
70174 Stgt.

Abitur-Training für Schüler!

Den Ernstfall trainieren und souverän meistern mit maßgeschneiderter Abiturvorbereitung: konzentriertes Faktenwissen, Übungsaufgaben und schülergerechte Lösungen. Ideal zum selbstständigen Üben zu Hause. Da erfahren Schüler, worauf es wirklich ankommt, und erhalten Sicherheit für alle Prüfungen durch dauerhaften Lernerfolg.

Deutsch

Grundlagen, Arbeitstechniken und Methoden .... Best.-Nr. 944062
Aufsatz Oberstufe .... Best.-Nr. 84401
Abitur-Wissen
Textinterpretation Lyrik, Drama, Epik .. Best.-Nr. 944061
Abitur-Wissen
Deutsche Literaturgeschichte gk/LK .... Best.-Nr. 94405
Abitur-Wissen Deutsch
Prüfungswissen Oberstufe gk/LK .... Best.-Nr. 94400
Lexikon Autoren und Werke .... Best.-Nr. 944081

Religion/Ethik

Katholische Religion 1 – gk .... Best.-Nr. 84991
Katholische Religion 2 – gk .... Best.-Nr. 84992
Evangelische Religion 1 – gk .... Best.-Nr. 94971
Ethische Positionen
in historischer Entwicklung – gk .... Best.-Nr. 94951
Abitur-Wissen Ev. Religionslehre gk
Der Mensch zwischen Gott und Welt .... Best.-Nr. 94973
Abitur-Wissen Ev. Religionslehre gk –
Die Verantwortung des Christen .... Best.-Nr. 94974
Abitur-Wissen
Glaube und Naturwissenschaft .... Best.-Nr. 94977
Abitur-Wissen Jesus Christus .... Best.-Nr. 94978
Abitur-Wissen
Die Frage nach dem Menschen .... Best.-Nr. 94990
Abitur-Wissen Philosophische Ethik .... Best.-Nr. 94952
Abitur-Wissen
Freiheit und Determination .... Best.-Nr. 94954
Abitur-Wissen
Recht und Gerechtigkeit .... Best.-Nr. 94955
Abitur-Wissen
Religion u. Weltanschauungen .... Best.-Nr. 94956

Kunst

Grundwissen Malerei – LK .... Best.-Nr. 94961
Analyse und Interpretation – LK .... Best.-Nr. 94962

Sport

Sport Bewegungslehre – LK .... Best.-Nr. 94981
Sport Trainingslehre – LK .... Best.-Nr. 94982

Englisch

Englisch – Übersetzungsübung .... Best.-Nr. 82454
Englisch – Grammatikübung Oberstufe ... Best.-Nr. 82452
Englisch – Wortschatzübung Oberstufe .. Best.-Nr. 82451
Grundfertigkeiten des Schreibens .... Best.-Nr. 94466
Englisch – Textaufgaben zur Literatur .... Best.-Nr. 94462
Englisch – Grundlagen der Textarbeit ..... Best.-Nr. 94464
Englisch – Literaturgeschichte .... Best.-Nr. 94465
Englisch – Übertritt in die Oberstufe .... Best.-Nr. 82453
Abitur-Wissen Landeskunde GB .... Best.-Nr. 94461
Abitur-Wissen Landeskunde USA .... Best.-Nr. 94463

Französisch/Latein

Textaufgaben zur
Landeskunde Frankreich .... Best.-Nr. 94501
Französisch – Wortschatz .... Best.-Nr. 94503
Textaufgaben zur Literatur gk/LK .... Best.-Nr. 94502
Französisch – Literaturgeschichte .... Best.-Nr. 94506
Französisch – Textarbeit .... Best.-Nr. 94504
Wortschatzübung Oberstufe .... Best.-Nr. 94505
Interpretationshilfen 1 Lyrik .... Best.-Nr. 94507
Interpretationshilfen 2 Prosa .... Best.-Nr. 94508
Interpretationshilfen 3 Drama .... Best.-Nr. 94509
Lateinische Literaturgeschichte .... Best.-Nr. 94602
Latein Kurzgrammatik .... Best.-Nr. 94601
Latein Wortkunde .... Best.-Nr. 94603

Wirtschaft/Recht

Betriebswirtschaft – LK .... Best.-Nr. 94851
Volkswirtschaft – gk/LK .... Best.-Nr. 94881
Rechtslehre – gk .... Best.-Nr. 94882

Pädagogik/Psychologie

Grundwissen Pädagogik / FOS .... Best.Nr. 92480
Grundwissen Psychologie / FOS .... Best.-Nr. 92481

(Bitte blättern Sie um)

Abitur-Prüfungsaufgaben

Viele Jahrgänge der zentral gestellten Prüfungsaufgaben an Gymnasien in Baden-Württemberg, einschließlich des aktuellen Jahrgangs. Mit vollständigen Lösungen für die selbstständige Übung zu Hause!

Mathematik

Abiturprüfung Mathematik – LK ....Best.-Nr. 85000
Abiturprüfung Mathematik – gk ....Best.-Nr. 85100
Abiturprüfung Mathematik
Mündliche Prüfung – gk/LK ....Best.-Nr. 85101

Physik

Abiturprüfung Physik – LK ....Best.-Nr. 85300
Abiturprüfung Physik – gk ....Best.-Nr. 85320

Biologie/Chemie

Abiturprüfung Biologie – LK ....Best.-Nr. 85700
Abiturprüfung Biologie – gk ....Best.-Nr. 85710
Abiturprüfung Chemie – LK ....Best.-Nr. 85730

Geschichte

Abiturprüfung Geschichte – LK ....Best.-Nr. 85760
Abiturprüfung Geschichte – gk ....Best.-Nr. 85780

Gemeinschaftskunde

Abiturprüfung Gemeinschaftskunde LK ..Best.-Nr. 85800

Erdkunde

Abiturprüfung Erdkunde – LK ....Best.-Nr. 85900

Religion/Ethik

Abiturprüfung Religion ev. – gk ....Best.-Nr. 85970
Abiturprüfung Religion r.-k. – gk ....Best.-Nr. 85990
Abiturprüfung Ethik ....Best.-Nr. 85950

Deutsch

Abiturprüfung Deutsch – LK ....Best.-Nr. 85400
Abiturprüfung Deutsch – gk ....Best.-Nr. 85410
Abiturprüfung Deutsch
Mündliche Prüfung – gk/LK ....Best.-Nr. 85411

Englisch

Abiturprüfung Englisch – LK ....Best.-Nr. 85460
Abiturprüfung Englisch – gk ....Best.-Nr. 85470

Französisch

Abiturprüfung Französisch – LK ....Best.-Nr. 85500

Latein

Abiturprüfung Latein – LK ....Best.-Nr. 85600
Abiturprüfung Latein – gk ....Best.-Nr. 85630

Sport

Abiturprüfung Sport – LK ....Best.-Nr. 85980

Kunst

Abiturprüfung Kunst – LK ....Best.-Nr. 85960

Ratgeber für Schüler

Richtig Lernen – Tipps und
Lernstrategien für die Oberstufe ....Best.-Nr. 10483
Referate und Facharbeiten
für die Oberstufe ....Best.-Nr. 10484

Natürlich führen wir noch mehr Titel für alle Schularten. Wir informieren Sie gerne!

Telefon: 0 81 61/17 90   **Internet: www.stark-verlag.de**
Telefax: 0 81 61/179-51   **E-Mail: info@stark-verlag.de**

Bestellungen bitte direkt an:
STARK Verlagsgesellschaft
Postfach 1852 · 85318 Freising

Damit lernen einfacher wird...

STARK